DAY HIKES AROUND
San Luis Obispo

128 GREAT HIKES

Robert Stone
2nd EDITION

Day Hike Books, Inc.
RED LODGE, MONTANA

Published by Day Hike Books, Inc.
P.O. Box 865
Red Lodge, Montana 59068

Distributed by The Globe Pequot Press
246 Goose Lane
P.O. Box 480
Guilford, CT 06437-0480
800-243-0495 (direct order) · 800-820-2329 (fax order)
www.globe-pequot.com

Photographs by Robert Stone
Design by Paula Doherty

The author has made every attempt to provide accurate information in this book. However, trail routes and features may change—please use common sense and forethought, and be mindful of your own capabilities. Let this book guide you, but be aware that each hiker assumes responsibility for their own safety. The author and publisher do not assume any responsibility for loss, damage, or injury caused through the use of this book.

Cover photo: Bishop Peak, Hike 72
Back cover photo: San Simeon Point, Hike 15

ALSO BY ROBERT STONE

Day Hikes On the California Central Coast

Day Hikes On the California Southern Coast

Day Hikes Around Sonoma County

Day Hikes Around Napa Valley

Day Hikes Around Big Sur

Day Hikes Around Monterey and Carmel

Day Hikes In San Luis Obispo County, California

Day Hikes Around Santa Barbara

Day Hikes Around Ventura County

Day Hikes Around Los Angeles

Day Hikes Around Orange County

Day Hikes In Sedona, Arizona

Day Hikes In Yosemite National Park

Day Hikes In Sequoia & Kings Canyon Nat'l. Parks

Day Hikes In Yellowstone National Park

Day Hikes In Grand Teton National Park

Day Hikes In the Beartooth Mountains

Day Hikes Around Bozeman, Montana

Day Hikes Around Missoula, Montana

Day Hikes On Oahu

Day Hikes On Maui

Day Hikes On Kauai

Day Hikes In Hawaii

Table of Contents

THE HIKES

Big Sur Coast • Silver Peak Wilderness

San Simeon • Cambria • Cuyucos

Paso Robles to Atascadero

Morro Bay • Baywood Park • Los Osos

Avila Beach • Shell Beach • Pismo Beach
Grove Beach • Oceano

Nipomo to Point Arguello • Santa Maria • Lompoc

Carrizo Plain National Monument

Hiking San Luis Obispo County

San Luis Obispo County is located where the white sand beaches of Central California merge with the dramatic Big Sur coastline. The county's 84 miles of spectacular coastline includes wide, sandy beaches; windswept coastal dunes; rocky coves; jagged bluffs; grassy coastal terraces; protected bays and tidepools; wildlife sanctuaries; and a fertile, 1,400-acre estuary.

Heading inland from the Pacific Ocean are oak-studded hills, verdant farmland, pristine mountain lakes, and the Santa Lucia Range of the Los Padres National Forest. A chain of nine extinct volcanoes, 23 million years old, form a spine of peaks extending from the city of San Luis Obispo to the ocean at Morro Bay. San Luis Obispo rests in a beautiful valley amongst these volcanic morros and the rolling foothills of the Santa Lucia Mountain Range.

Day Hikes Around San Luis Obispo includes 128 day hikes throughout this central California coastal county. These trails take the hiker along the scalloped Pacific coastline to secluded coves and tidepools, to rocky promontories along the chain of volcanic morros, through wetland sanctuaries, and up cool interior valleys. Highlights include waterfalls, bluffs, sand dunes, lakes, rivers, swimming holes, canyons, extraordinary rock formations, and panoramic views. Many hikes are found in or near the college community; most are located in undeveloped tracts of land, state and county parks, and national forests which are home to an extensive network of hiking trails.

HIKES 1—28 explore the northern reaches of San Luis Obispo county, where the rugged Big Sur coast begins to evolve into sandy beaches and coastal terraces that wind around promontories. Because of the distance from the city of San Luis Obispo, these hikes are generally more remote or near small coastal towns. HIKES 29—39 are inland along the Santa Lucia Range, running parallel to the northern coastline.

HIKES 40—64 explore the beautiful Morro Bay–Montaña de Oro area. Morro Bay lies along the county's central coast, directly west of San Luis Obispo. A mix of fresh and salt water flow together in the estuary. It is among the earth's most productive habitats. Between the bay and Point Buchon is Montaña de Oro State Park, which encompasses 8,400 acres with 7 miles of coastline.

HIKES 65—91 are found within or near San Luis Obispo itself. The chain of morros and several natural reserves within the city contribute to many interesting trails.

HIKES 92—106 are a short drive west of San Luis Obispo around the Los Padres National Forest, Santa Margarita Lake, and Lopez Lake.

HIKES 107—125 continue southward down the coast, exploring headlands, beach coves, and huge sand dunes.

HIKES 126—128 are in the Carrizo Plain at the eastern end of the county along the San Andreas Fault. The massive basin has a unique geography and is rich with plant and animal life.

A quick glance at the hikes' summaries will allow you to choose a hike that is appropriate to your ability and desire. Each hike includes a map, driving and hiking directions, and an overview of distance/time/elevation. For further exploration, relevant maps are listed with each hike.

An overall map on the next page identifies the general locations of the hikes and major roads. Several area maps through the book provide additional details (underlined in the table of contents).

A few basic necessities will make your hike more enjoyable. Wear supportive, comfortable hiking shoes and layered clothing. Take along hats, sunscreen, sunglasses, drinking water, snacks, and appropriate outerwear. Ticks may be prolific and poison ivy flourishes in the canyons and shady areas. Avoid contact by using insect repellent and staying on the trails.

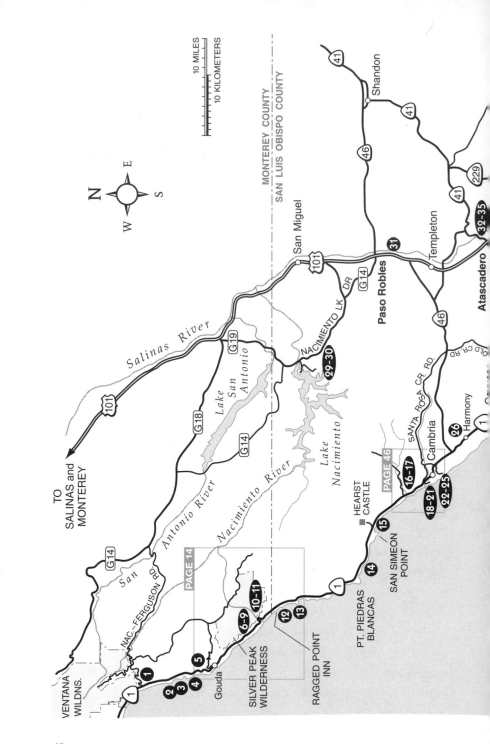

10 MILES

10 KILOMETERS

N

W E

S

MONTEREY COUNTY
SAN LUIS OBISPO COUNTY

Shandon

41

41

46

229

41

31

Templeton

32-35

San Miguel

101

G14

NACIMIENTO LK DR

Paso Robles

46

Atascadero

Salinas River

G19

NACIMIENTO

29-30

OLD CR RD

G18

Lake San Antonio

G14

SANTA ROSA CR. RD.

Harmony

1

26

Cambria

PAGE 46

16-17

101

San Antonio River

Nacimiento River

Lake Nacimiento

HEARST CASTLE

18-21

22-25

15

TO
SALINAS and
MONTEREY

G14

NAC.-FERGUSON RD.

San

PAGE 14

SAN SIMEON POINT

10-11

14

6-9

5

12

13

Gouda

SILVER PEAK WILDERNESS

RAGGED POINT INN

1

PT. PIEDRAS BLANCAS

1

2

3

4

VENTANA WILDNS.

1

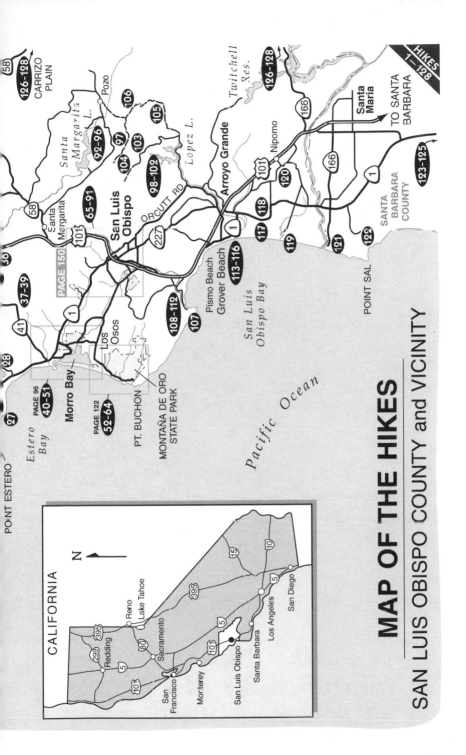

MAP OF THE HIKES
SAN LUIS OBISPO COUNTY and VICINITY

HIKES 1—128

CARRIZO PLAIN

126-128

58

Pozo

106

105

Santa Margarita L.

92-96

97

103

104

98-102

Lopez L.

65-91

San Luis Obispo

Santa Margarita

58

ORCUTT RD.

227

41

37-39

39

28

27

1

108-112

107

Los Osos

Morro Bay

PAGE 96

40-51

PAGE 122

52-64

PT. BUCHON

MONTAÑA DE ORO STATE PARK

PAGE 150

Twitchell Res.

126-128

166

Santa Maria

TO SANTA BARBARA

Arroyo Grande

Nipomo

101

166

120

1

123-125

118

117

119

121

124

SANTA BARBARA COUNTY

Pismo Beach
Grover Beach

113-116

113

San Luis Obispo Bay

POINT SAL

Pacific Ocean

Estero Bay

POINT ESTERO

CALIFORNIA

N

Reno
Lake Tahoe

395

Redding

299

5

80

Sacramento

395

15

10

5

San Diego

Los Angeles

5

101

San Francisco

Monterey

101

San Luis Obispo

Santa Barbara

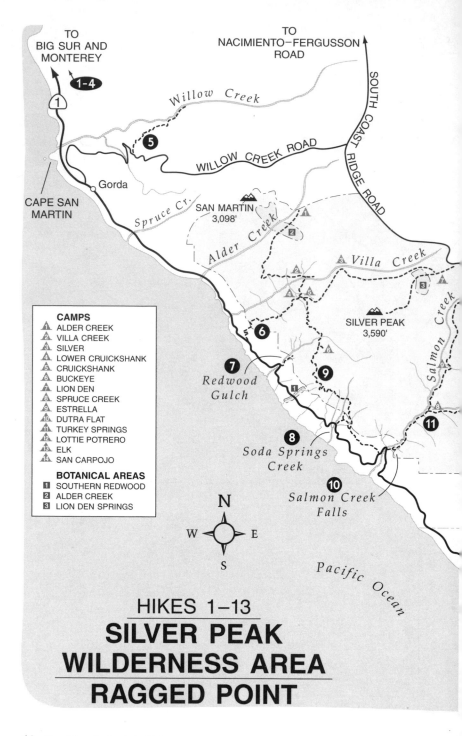

CAMPS

  ⛺ ALDER CREEK
  ⛺ VILLA CREEK
  ⛺ SILVER
  ⛺ LOWER CRUICKSHANK
  ⛺ CRUICKSHANK
  ⛺ BUCKEYE
  ⛺ LION DEN
  ⛺ SPRUCE CREEK
  ⛺ ESTRELLA
  ⛺ DUTRA FLAT
  ⛺ TURKEY SPRINGS
  ⛺ LOTTIE POTRERO
  ⛺ ELK
  ⛺ SAN CARPOJO

BOTANICAL AREAS

  1 SOUTHERN REDWOOD
  2 ALDER CREEK
  3 LION DEN SPRINGS

TO
BIG SUR AND
MONTEREY

TO
NACIMIENTO–FERGUSSON
ROAD

SOUTH COAST RIDGE ROAD

Willow Creek

WILLOW CREEK ROAD

Gorda

CAPE SAN MARTIN

Spruce Cr.

SAN MARTIN
3,098'

Alder Creek

Villa Creek

Salmon Creek

SILVER PEAK
3,590'

Redwood Gulch

Soda Springs Creek

Salmon Creek Falls

N
W E
S

Pacific Ocean

HIKES 1–13
SILVER PEAK
WILDERNESS AREA
RAGGED POINT

The rugged Silver Peak Wilderness, established in 1992, is located in the Santa Lucia Range of the Los Padres National Forest. This remote 14,500-acre wilderness at the southwestern corner of Monterey County is home to California's southernmost coastal redwoods. Three year-round creeks—Villa Creek, Salmon Creek, and San Carpoforo Creek—flow from the upper mountain reaches to the sea. A group of steep intersecting trails weave through this wilderness from the ocean to the mountain ridge, gaining nearly 3,600 feet within a couple of miles. The trails wind through open meadows, forest groves, lush stream-fed canyons, and ridgelines with sweeping coastal views.

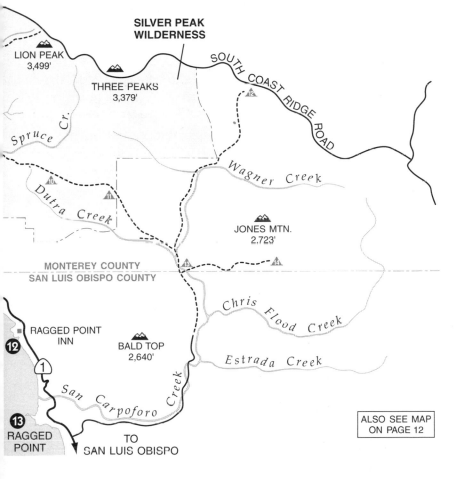

SILVER PEAK WILDERNESS

LION PEAK
3,499'

THREE PEAKS
3,379'

SOUTH COAST RIDGE ROAD

Spruce Cr.

Wagner Creek

Dutra Creek

JONES MTN.
2,723'

MONTEREY COUNTY
SAN LUIS OBISPO COUNTY

Chris Flood Creek

RAGGED POINT INN

BALD TOP
2,640'

Estrada Creek

San Carpoforo Creek

12

1

13
RAGGED POINT

TO
SAN LUIS OBISPO

ALSO SEE MAP
ON PAGE 12

Hike 1
Mill Creek Trail

Hiking distance: 3 miles round trip
Hiking time: 2 hours
Elevation gain: 600 feet
Maps: U.S.G.S. Cape San Martin
      Ventana Wilderness Map (Monterey County)

Summary of hike: The Mill Creek Trail follows the bucolic watershed up beautiful Mill Creek Canyon just south of the Ventana Wilderness. The trail meanders alongside Mill Creek through riparian vegetation under the dark shade of giant redwoods, maples, sycamores, and bay laurels. The hike ends at a campsite perched above the creek amidst a cluster of redwoods.

Driving directions: From Highway 1 at the Ragged Point Inn, located 23 miles north of Cambria, drive 20.2 miles north on Highway 1 to Nacimiento—Fergusson Road. The turnoff is 4.2 miles north of the Pacific Valley Ranger Station and 0.2 miles south of Kirk Creek Campground. Turn inland and wind up the paved mountain road 0.8 miles to the posted trail on the right at a distinct left horseshoe bend. Park in the pullout on the right by the trailhead.

Hiking directions: Climb 100 yards up the steep slope to a small saddle. Descend under a canopy of California bay laurel. The undulating path follows the north canyon wall high above Mill Creek. The creek can be heard but not yet seen, as towering redwoods carpet the canyon floor. Gradually drop down the hillside into a wet, lush forest of redwoods, maples, sycamores, bracken ferns, and moss-covered rocks at a half mile. Wind through the canyon, following the creek upstream. Rock hop over Lion Creek to a distinct but unmarked trail fork. Take the left fork and climb up a 15-foot slope. (The right fork ends 30 yards ahead.) Curve right, soon reaching a creek crossing. Rock hop over Mill Creek two consecutive times while passing waterfalls and pools. Scramble over a jumble of boulders at an old landslide, then follow a narrow ledge on the edge of the creek. The main trail curves to a plateau above the creek with a gorgeous campsite surrounded by a cluster of redwoods. This is our turn-around spot and a great place to explore the immediate surroundings. The trail continues up to the South Coast Ridge Road, but becomes indistinct just beyond camp.

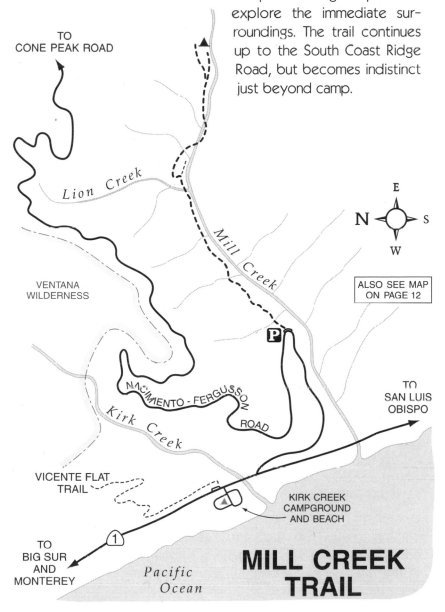

TO
CONE PEAK ROAD

Lion Creek

E
N ◇ S
W

VENTANA
WILDERNESS

Mill Creek

ALSO SEE MAP
ON PAGE 12

P

NACIMIENTO - FERGUSSON
ROAD

Kirk Creek

TO
SAN LUIS
OBISPO

VICENTE FLAT
TRAIL

KIRK CREEK
CAMPGROUND
AND BEACH

TO
BIG SUR
AND
MONTEREY

1

Pacific
Ocean

MILL CREEK TRAIL

Hike 2
Pacific Valley Flats

Hiking distance: 2 miles round trip
Hiking time: 1 hour
Elevation gain: 50 feet
Maps: U.S.G.S. Cape San Martin (Monterey County)
          Los Padres National Forest Northern Section Trail Map

Summary of hike: Pacific Valley is a flat, four-mile-long marine terrace along the southern Monterey County coastline. The wide expanse extends west from the steep slopes of the Santa Lucia Mountains to the serrated bluffs above the Pacific Ocean. This hike crosses the grassy coastal terrace to the eroded coastline a hundred feet above the ocean. There are dramatic views of Plaskett Rock, offshore rock formations with natural arches, and the scalloped coastal cliffs. Numerous access points lead to the grassland terrace.

Driving directions: From Highway 1 at the Ragged Point Inn, located 23 miles north of Cambria, drive 16 miles north on Highway 1 to the Pacific Valley Ranger Station on the right. The trailhead is across the highway from the ranger station. Park in the pullouts on either side of the road or in the parking lot at the station.

Hiking directions: The hike begins directly across the road from the ranger station. Step up and over the trail access ladder. Head west across the grassy expanse and past rock outcroppings on the left. Near the point is a rolling sand dune on the right with numerous trails and great overlooks. The main trail stays to the north of the dune, leading to the edge of the cliffs along the jagged coastline high above the pounding surf. At one mile, the trail ends at a fenceline above Prewitt Creek. The trails around the dunes connect with the bluff trail south to Sand Dollar Beach (Hike 3), then circle back to the first junction at the cliff's edge. Return along the same trail.

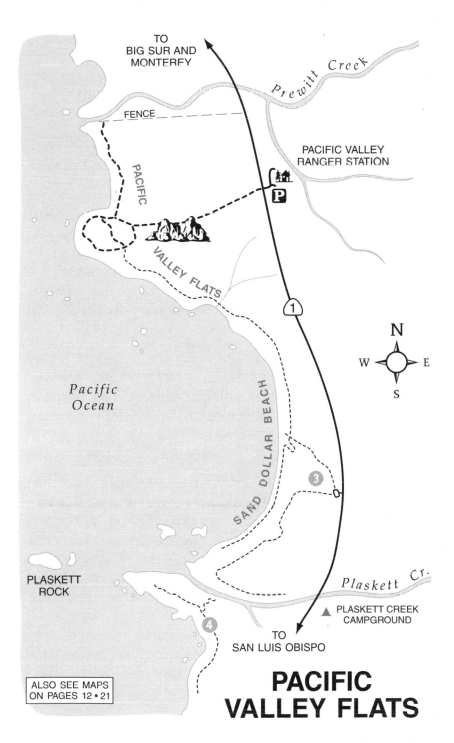

TO
BIG SUR AND
MONTEREY

Prewitt Creek

FENCE

PACIFIC VALLEY
RANGER STATION

PACIFIC

VALLEY FLATS

P

①

N
W → E
S

*Pacific
Ocean*

SAND DOLLAR BEACH

③

PLASKETT
ROCK

Plaskett Cr.

▲ PLASKETT CREEK
CAMPGROUND

④

TO
SAN LUIS OBISPO

ALSO SEE MAPS
ON PAGES 12 • 21

PACIFIC
VALLEY FLATS

Hike 3
Sand Dollar Beach

Hiking distance: 1.5 miles round trip
Hiking time: 1 hour
Elevation gain: 150 feet
Maps: U.S.G.S. Cape San Martin (Monterey County)
Los Padres National Forest Northern Section Trail Map

Summary of hike: Sand Dollar Beach is a protected horse-shoe-shaped sand and rock beach between two rocky head-lands jutting into the Pacific Ocean. The trail passes a picnic area lined with cypress trees to the steep eroded cliffs and a cliff-side overlook with interpretive signs. Plaskett Rock sits off the southern point. There are great coastal views of large offshore rock outcroppings. Cone Peak can be seen inland along the Santa Lucia Range.

Driving directions: From Highway 1 at the Ragged Point Inn, located 23 miles north of Cambria, drive 15 miles north on Highway 1 to the parking lot on the left (ocean) side, just north of Plaskett Creek Campground. Park in the lot (entrance fee) or park in the pullouts along the highway (free).

Hiking directions: The signed trailhead is at the north end of the parking lot. Walk up and over the stepladder, then descend through a shady picnic area. Cross the grasslands to a junction by a wooden fence. The right fork leads 30 yards to an overlook with an interpretive wildlife sign. Return to the junction and take the left fork down the switchbacks and a staircase to the shoreline. After exploring the crescent-shaped cove, return to the bluffs. An optional cliffside path heads one mile north to Pacific Valley (Hike 2).

From the Sand Dollar parking lot, a second trail leaves from the center of the lot to Plaskett Creek. Climb up and over the ladder, and cross the grassy coastal terrace to a cliffside over-look. The meandering path follows the grassy bluffs less than a half mile south to the deep ravine carved by Plaskett Creek.

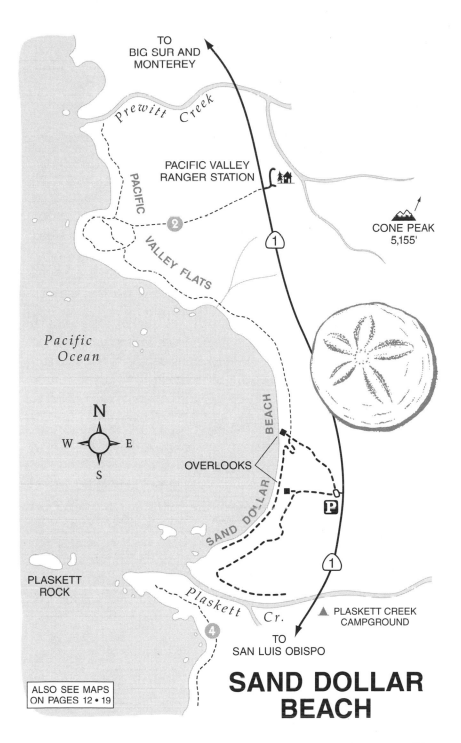

TO
BIG SUR AND
MONTEREY

Prewitt Creek

PACIFIC VALLEY
RANGER STATION

PACIFIC

②

VALLEY FLATS

CONE PEAK
5,155'

1

*Pacific
Ocean*

N
W ◈ E
S

BEACH

OVERLOOKS

SAND DOLLAR

P

PLASKETT
ROCK

Plaskett Cr.

④

▲ PLASKETT CREEK
CAMPGROUND

1

TO
SAN LUIS OBISPO

ALSO SEE MAPS
ON PAGES 12 • 19

SAND DOLLAR
BEACH

Hike 4
Jade Cove and Plaskett Rock

Hiking distance: 0.4 miles to 1.5 miles round trip
Hiking time: 30 to 60 minutes
Elevation gain: 150 feet
Maps: U.S.G.S. Cape San Martin (Monterey County)

Summary of hike: Jade Cove is a small rocky cove with smooth ocean-tumbled stones and nephrite jade. The isolated cove sits at the base of steep 100-foot serpentine cliffs eroded by the rough surf. The trail crosses the grassy marine terrace to the edge of the cliffs, where the coastal views are spectacular. Cape San Martin extends out to sea to the south. Plaskett Rock, a dramatic outcropping, sits offshore to the north.

Driving directions: From Highway 1 at the Ragged Point Inn, located 23 miles north of Cambria, drive 14.6 miles north on Highway 1 to the Jade Cove Beach trailhead sign. The sign is 3 miles north of Gorda and 0.4 miles south of Plaskett Creek Campground. There are pullouts on both sides of the highway.

Hiking directions: From the west (ocean) side of the highway, head over the access ladder. Continue down the steps, heading west across the wide, grassy terrace to the edge of the bluffs and a junction. To reach Jade Cove, zigzag down the steep, eroded cliffs. The descent is made easier with the help of switchbacks. Near the bottom, some boulder hopping is required to reach the shoreline. The path ends in Jade Cove amid the rounded stones. Return to the junction atop the bluffs.

To extend the hike, take the blufftop path to the north, skirting the edge of the cliffs a half mile to Plaskett Creek. A narrow path drops down the water-carved ravine to the creek. Another path follows the bluffs out on the headland that points toward Plaskett Rock. Return by retracing your path.

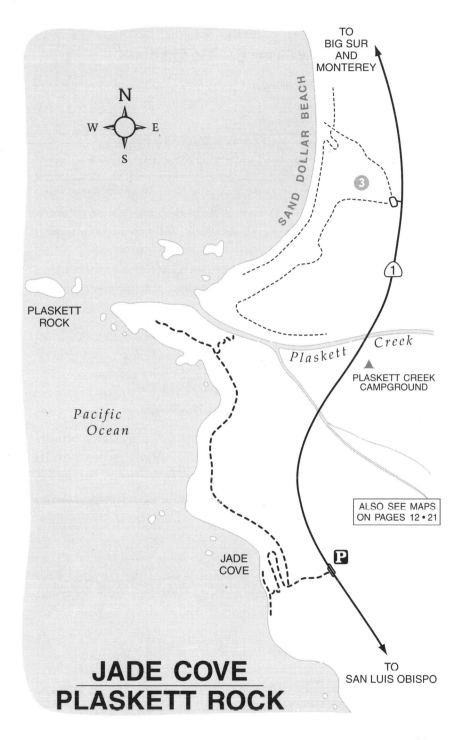

TO
BIG SUR
AND
MONTEREY

SAND DOLLAR BEACH

③

①

PLASKETT
ROCK

Plaskett Creek

▲
PLASKETT CREEK
CAMPGROUND

*Pacific
Ocean*

ALSO SEE MAPS
ON PAGES 12 • 21

JADE
COVE

Ⓟ

TO
SAN LUIS OBISPO

JADE COVE
PLASKETT ROCK

Hike 5
Willow Creek Trail

Hiking distance: 3.4 miles round trip
Hiking time: 2 hours
Elevation gain: 500 feet
Maps: U.S.G.S. Cape San Martin (Monterey County)
  Los Padres National Forest Northern Section Trail Map

Summary of hike: The Willow Creek Trail is a little gem tucked between the Ventana Wilderness and the Silver Peak Wilderness. The unmarked and seldom hiked trail (an old road) drops into an isolated stream-fed canyon under shady redwoods, oaks, and maples. At Willow Creek is an old, rickety "Indiana Jones" style suspension bridge that spans 80 yards across the gorge.

Driving directions: From Highway 1 at the Ragged Point Inn, located 23 miles north of Cambria, drive 12.5 miles north on Highway 1 to Willow Creek Road. The turnoff is 1 mile north of Gorda and 2.5 miles south of Plaskett Creek Campground. Turn inland and wind up the narrow, unpaved mountain road 2.4 miles to an unsigned road junction on the left. This road—the Willow Creek Trail—no longer accommodates vehicles. Park in the pullout on the right, 40 yards before the junction.

Hiking directions: Walk 60 yards up Willow Creek Road to the narrow, rutted road. Bear left and descend through the shade of pine and bay trees to an oak grove on a circular flat. Drop deeper into Willow Creek Canyon along the south canyon wall, passing a road on the left at 0.6 miles. The main road ends at 1 mile in a redwood grove, then continues as a footpath. Descend under the deep shade of the towering redwoods on the fern-lined path. Contour around a rocky, stream-fed gully, and traverse the lush hillside to an unmarked trail split. The left (lower) fork drops down to the creek at the dilapidated and unsafe suspension bridge spanning the gorge. To the left is a series of pools among a jumble of rocks. Back on the main trail, continue 0.15 miles to another unsigned trail fork. The left fork zigzags a short distance down to a campsite on a grassy flat perched 20 feet above Willow Creek. Back on the main trail, the right fork gradually descends to the creek, passing huge, mossy, fern-covered boulders and fallen redwoods. To the right are two small campsites surrounded by redwoods. Beyond the camp, the trail is overgrown and difficult to follow. Return by retracing your steps.

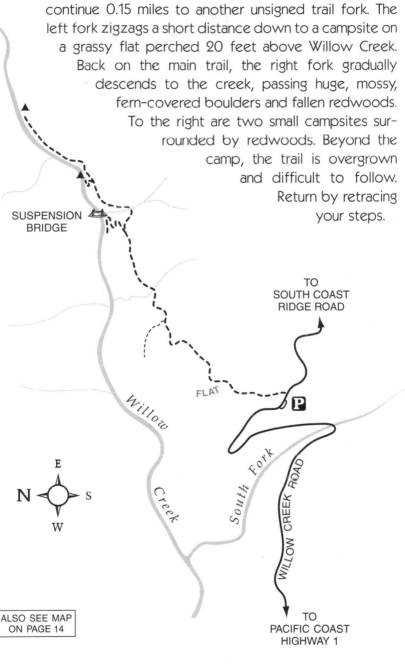

SUSPENSION
BRIDGE

TO
SOUTH COAST
RIDGE ROAD

P

FLAT

Willow

Creek

South Fork

WILLOW CREEK ROAD

E
N + S
W

ALSO SEE MAP
ON PAGE 14

TO
PACIFIC COAST
HIGHWAY 1

WILLOW CREEK TRAIL

Hike 6
Cruickshank Trail
to Upper Cruickshank Camp
SILVER PEAK WILDERNESS

Hiking distance: 5 miles round trip
Hiking time: 3 hours
Elevation gain: 1,200 feet
Maps: U.S.G.S. Villa Creek (Monterey County)
　　　　Los Padres National Forest Northern Section Trail Map

Summary of hike: The Cruickshank Trail in the Silver Peak Wilderness begins from Highway 1 and climbs the exposed oceanfront hillside to magnificent coastal vistas before dropping into Villa Creek Canyon. The lush canyon path winds through giant redwood groves to Lower and Upper Cruickshank Camps in an oak-shaded grassland.

Driving directions: From Highway 1 at the Ragged Point Inn, located 23 miles north of Cambria, drive 7.9 miles north on Highway 1 to the grassy parking pullout on the east (inland) side of the road by the signed Cruickshank trailhead.

Hiking directions: From the signed trailhead, climb switchbacks up the brushy mountain slope. Wind through the thick coastal scrub overlooking the ocean and offshore rocks. More switchbacks lead up the exposed south-facing slope to a ridge with sweeping coastal vistas at 900 feet. Descend a short distance into Villa Creek Canyon above the coastal redwoods carpeting the canyon floor. Traverse the south canyon slope through lush vegetation under oak and redwood groves. Pass the unexplained "Hjalmur's Loop" sign, and continue through the shade of the redwoods. Emerge from the forest to a picturesque view of the ocean, framed by the V-shaped canyon walls. Reenter the forest, passing a tall stand of narrow eucalyptus trees on the left. Cross a log plank over a seasonal stream to Lower Cruickshank Camp fifty yards ahead, a small camp with room for one tent. A quarter mile further is Upper

Cruickshank Camp in a large oak flat. This is our turn-around spot.

To extend the hike, two trails depart from the camp. To the left, the north Buckeye Trail crosses a stream by a giant redwood and descends 0.6 miles to Villa Creek Camp in a dense redwood grove at Villa Creek. To the right, the combined Cruickshank and Buckeye Trails cross through the camp to an oak-dotted grassland and a posted junction. The Buckeye Trail bears right and heads 3 miles south to Buckeye Camp (Hike 9). To the left, the Cruickshank Trail climbs 500 feet in 1 mile to Silver Camp and 1,500 feet in 3 miles to Lion Den Camp. (See map on page 14 for camp locations.)

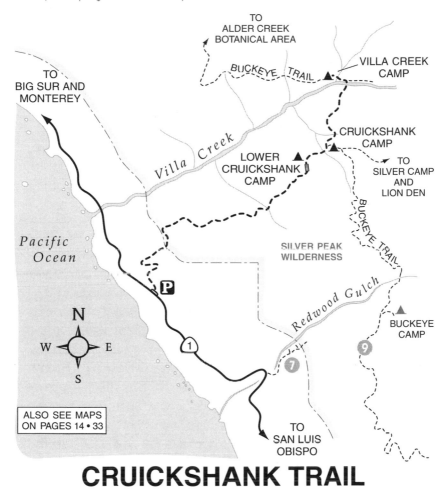

CRUICKSHANK TRAIL

Hike 7
Redwood Gulch
NATHANIEL OWINGS MEMORIAL REDWOOD GROVE

Hiking distance: 0.4 miles round trip
Hiking time: 30 minutes
Elevation gain: 200 feet
Maps: U.S.G.S. Villa Creek (Monterey County)
Los Padres National Forest Northern Section Trail Map

Summary of hike: Redwood Gulch is home to one of California's southernmost groves of coastal redwoods. The gulch is a narrow, eroded gorge with chutes of cascading water, small waterfalls, and a myriad of tub-size pools surrounded by huge boulders. This short trail begins at the creek bottom amidst the lush streamside vegetation and climbs through the dank, damp, atmospheric terrain beneath a magnificent stand of imposing redwoods.

Driving directions: From Highway 1 at the Ragged Point Inn, located 23 miles north of Cambria, drive 7 miles north on Highway 1 to the parking pullout on the east (inland) side of the road at the base of the horseshoe-shaped bend in the road.

Hiking directions: Walk up the wide path along the south side of the creek to the trail sign. Pass a rock fountain and descend to the streambed surrounded by towering redwoods. A short distance ahead is a waterfall cascading over a jumble of large boulders. At the base of the falls, the water disappears underground. The stream returns above ground west of the highway near the ocean. Continue along the south edge of the waterfall, climbing over fallen redwoods and boulders. Follow the steep path through a wet, dense forest with huge redwoods, boulders, and an understory of ferns. Several side paths on the left lead down to pools and smaller waterfalls. At just under a quarter mile is an old rock fire pit on a small flat. This is a good turn-around area. The undeveloped path continues up canyon, but it is a steep scramble and requires careful footing, especially on the descent.

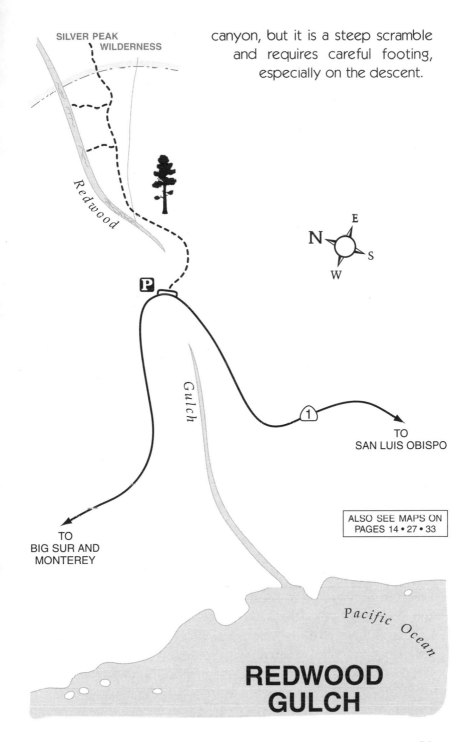

SILVER PEAK WILDERNESS

Redwood

P

Gulch

N E S W

1

TO SAN LUIS OBISPO

ALSO SEE MAPS ON PAGES 14 • 27 • 33

TO BIG SUR AND MONTEREY

Pacific Ocean

REDWOOD GULCH

Hike 8
Soda Springs and Lower Buckeye Trails
SILVER PEAK WILDERNESS AREA

Hiking distance: 3 miles round trip
Hiking time: 1.5 hours
Elevation gain: 750 feet
Maps: U.S.G.S. Burro Mountain (Monterey County)
Los Padres National Forest Northern Section Trail Map

Summary of hike: The Soda Springs Trail begins along Soda Springs Creek in the lush riparian vegetation of ferns, alders, and California bay laurel. The trail climbs the forested slope to an overlook with coastal views that extend south to the Point Piedras Blancas lighthouse and Point Buchon, beyond Morro Bay. The path descends to the Salmon Creek drainage, where there are magnificent views of Salmon Creek Falls.

Driving directions: From Highway 1 at the Ragged Point Inn, located 23 miles north of Cambria, drive 5.3 miles north on Highway 1 to the paved parking pullout on the east (inland) side of the road by the signed Soda Springs trailhead.

Hiking directions: At the trailhead, a left fork drops down to Soda Springs Creek by a waterfall and pool in a rock gorge. The Soda Springs Trail stays to the right and heads up the hill parallel to the creek to an unsigned junction. Bear right, away from the creek, and steadily gain elevation. Thread your way through verdant undergrowth on the shaded forest path. Cross a seasonal stream by a huge boulder, reaching a posted junction with the Buckeye Trail at a coastal overlook. The left fork continues to Buckeye Camp (Hike 9). This hike stays to the right on the lower portion of the Buckeye Trail. Cross through the stock gate, and traverse the hillside parallel to the coastline. The path levels out on a grassy plateau with sweeping oceanfront views. Descend from the ridge on the open slope with a great view of Salmon Creek Falls. Pass a water trough by an underground spring, and cross through two more trail gates. A few short switchbacks quickly descend the hill to the Buckeye Trailhead by the abandoned Salmon Creek Ranger Station. This is our turn-around spot. Return along the same route.

To extend the hike to Salmon Creek Falls, follow Highway 1 downhill (left) 0.1 mile to Salmon Creek, and follow the hiking directions for Hike 10.

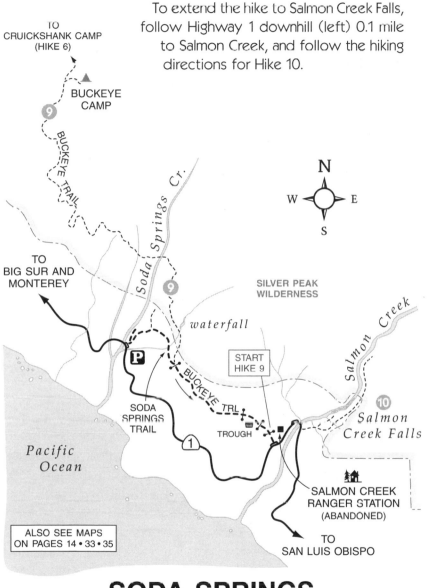

SODA SPRINGS
LOWER BUCKEYE TRAILS

Hike 9
Buckeye Trail to Buckeye Camp
SILVER PEAK WILDERNESS

Hiking distance: 7 miles round trip
Hiking time: 4 hours
Elevation gain: 1,600 feet
Maps: U.S.G.S. Burro Mountain and Villa Creek (Monterey Cty.)
Los Padres National Forest Northern Section Trail Map

Summary of hike: Buckeye Camp sits in a large meadow rimmed with oaks and pines in the mountainous interior of the Silver Peak Wilderness. The camp has a developed spring, picnic bench, and rock fire pit under a canopy of an immense bay tree with expansive overhanging branches. The trail begins from the abandoned Salmon Creek Ranger Station and climbs the exposed coastal slopes to views of Salmon Creek Falls and the Pacific. The path weaves in and out of several small canyons with shaded oak groves and passes an ephemeral 30-foot waterfall.

Driving directions: From Highway 1 at the Ragged Point Inn, located 23 miles north of Cambria, drive 3.8 miles north on Highway 1 to the paved parking area on the inland side of the road by the abandoned Salmon Creek Ranger Station.

Hiking directions: Walk through the trailhead gate at the north end of the parking area. Ascend the hillside on a few short switchbacks, passing through a second trail gate. Climb through the chaparral and grasslands, passing a trough and underground spring to a third gate. The path levels out on a grassy plateau that overlooks Salmon Creek Falls and the ocean. Traverse the hillside high above the ocean, and pass through a gate to a posted Y-fork at 1 mile. The Soda Springs Trail (Hike 8) bears left, returning to Highway 1 at Soda Springs Creek. Take the Buckeye Trail to the right. Cross a stream-fed gully with a seasonal waterfall off a sheer moss-covered rock wall. Climb out of the gully, following the contours of the mountains in and out of small oak-shaded canyons. Cross Soda Springs Creek at 2 miles to a grassy ridge a half mile ahead, where there are sweeping vistas from the coastline to the ridges and wooded canyons of the Santa Lucia Range. Follow the exposed ridge uphill to an elevated perch in an open pine grove above Redwood Gulch. Curve inland and descend into the rolling mountainous interior, reaching Buckeye Camp at 3.5 miles. Return along the same trail.

To extend the hike, the Buckeye Trail continues 2.5 miles to Upper Cruickshank Camp (Hike 6).

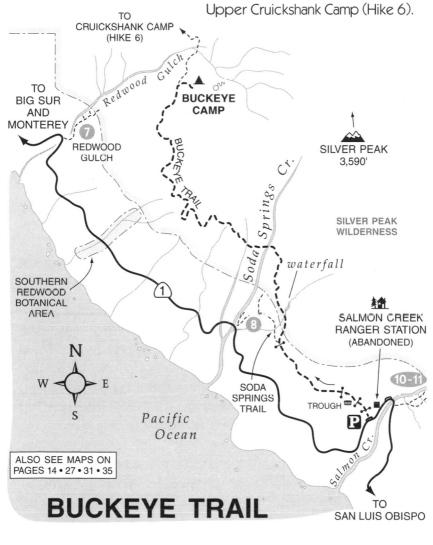

BUCKEYE TRAIL

Hike 10
Salmon Creek Falls
from Salmon Creek Trail
SILVER PEAK WILDERNESS AREA

Hiking distance: 0.6 miles round trip
Hiking time: 20 minutes
Elevation gain: 150 feet
Maps: U.S.G.S. Burro Mountain (Monterey County)

Summary of hike: The Salmon Creek Trail runs through the deep interior of the Silver Peak Wilderness in the Santa Lucia Mountains. The trail connects the coastline with the 3,000-foot South Coast Ridge Road. This short hike follows the first portion of the trail to the dynamic Salmon Creek Falls, where a tremendous volume of rushing water plunges from three chutes. The water drops more than 100 feet off the vertical rock face, crashing onto the rocks and pools below. A cool mist sprays over the mossy green streamside vegetation under a shady landscape of sycamores, maples, alders, and bay laurels.

Driving directions: From Highway 1 at the Ragged Point Inn, located 23 miles north of Cambria, drive 3.7 miles north on Highway 1 to the signed Salmon Creek trailhead at a sweeping horseshoe bend in the road. Park in the wide pullout on the right by the guardrail.

Hiking directions: Walk alongside the guardrail to the signed trailhead on the south side of Salmon Creek. Salmon Creek Falls can be seen from the guardrail. Take the Salmon Creek Trail up the gorge into the lush, verdant forest. Pass an old wooden gate, and cross a small tributary stream. Two hundred yards ahead is a signed junction. The right fork continues on the Salmon Creek Trail (Hike 11). Take the left fork towards the falls. Cross another small stream, then descend around huge boulders towards Salmon Creek at the base of the falls. Head towards the thunderous sound of the waterfall. Climb around the wet, mossy boulders to explore the various caves and overlooks.

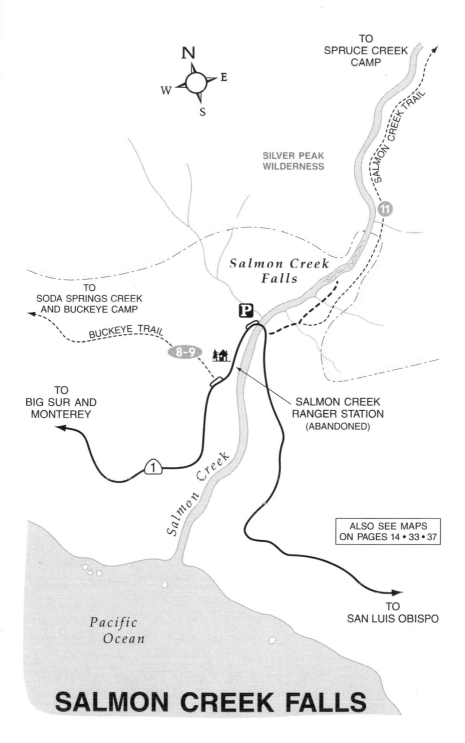

N
W   E
S

TO
SPRUCE CREEK
CAMP

SALMON CREEK TRAIL

SILVER PEAK
WILDERNESS

11

*Salmon Creek
Falls*

TO
SODA SPRINGS CREEK
AND BUCKEYE CAMP

P

BUCKEYE TRAIL

8-9

SALMON CREEK
RANGER STATION
(ABANDONED)

TO
BIG SUR AND
MONTEREY

1

Salmon Creek

ALSO SEE MAPS
ON PAGES 14 • 33 • 37

*Pacific
Ocean*

TO
SAN LUIS OBISPO

SALMON CREEK FALLS

Hike 11
Salmon Creek Trail
to Spruce Creek and Estrella Camps
SILVER PEAK WILDERNESS AREA

Hiking distance: 6.5 miles round trip
Hiking time: 3.5 hours
Elevation gain: 1,300 feet
Maps: U.S.G.S. Burro Mountain (Monterey County)
Los Padres National Forest Northern Section Trail Map

Summary of hike: The Salmon Creek Trail begins by Salmon Creek Falls (Hike 10) and follows the southeast wall of the V-shaped canyon through forests and open slopes. There are far reaching views up the canyon and down to the ocean. The trail, which cuts across the Silver Peak Wilderness, leads to Spruce Creek Camp and Estrella Camp. Estrella Camp sits in a large grassy meadow under the shade of oak, pine, and madrone trees. After crossing Spruce Creek, the cliffside path parallels Salmon Creek, overlooking endless cascades, small waterfalls, and pools.

Driving directions: Same as Hike 10.

Hiking directions: Head up the forested canyon on the south side of Salmon Creek to a junction at 200 yards. The left fork drops down a short distance to Salmon Creek Falls— Hike 10. Take the right fork, heading up the hillside to an over- look of Highway 1 and the Pacific. The path winds through the fir forest, steadily gaining elevation to a clearing high above Salmon Creek. The sweeping vistas extend up Salmon Creek canyon and down across the ocean. Follow the contours of the south canyon wall, with small dips and rises, to a posted junc- tion with the Spruce Creek Trail at 1.9 miles. Stay to the left and descend a quarter mile to Spruce Creek Camp on the banks of Spruce Creek. Cross Spruce Creek on a log bridge just above its confluence with Salmon Creek. Follow Salmon Creek upstream on the southeast canyon slope, overlooking a long series of cascades, pools, and waterfalls. Continually ascend the contour above the creek, crossing an old mudslide. The trail levels out on a grassy flat and enters the shady Estrella Camp at 1,500 feet. Descend 50 yards to the Estrella Fork of Salmon Creek, just beyond the camp. This is our turn-around area.

The trail continues past the creek, climbing 1,800 feet in 9.5 miles to the South Coast Ridge Road.

TO SOUTH COAST
RIDGE ROAD

Estrella Fork

▲ **ESTRELLA CAMP**

N
W · E
S

Spruce Creek

SILVER PEAK
WILDERNESS

▲ **SPRUCE CREEK CAMP**

SPRUCE CREEK
TRAIL TO
DUTRA FLAT

ALSO SEE MAPS
ON PAGES 14 • 35

Salmon Creek

⑩ *Salmon Creek Falls*

BUCKEYE TRAIL

🅿

8-9

TO
BIG SUR AND
MONTEREY

SALMON CREEK
RANGER STATION
(ABANDONED)

Pacific Ocean

① TO
SAN LUIS OBISPO

SALMON CREEK TRAIL

Hike 12
Nature and Cliffside Trails
RAGGED POINT INN

Hiking distance: 1 mile round trip
Hiking time: 30 minutes
Elevation gain: 300 feet
Maps: U.S.G.S. Burro Mountain

Summary of hike: The Ragged Point Inn is the last stop in San Luis Obispo County, just 1.5 miles south of Monterey County. The Ragged Point Cliffside Trail begins at the inn and cuts across the edge of a steep, rugged, north-facing cliff where the San Luis Obispo coast turns into the Big Sur coast. The trail ends at the black sand beach and rocky shore at the base of Black Swift Falls, a 300-foot tiered waterfall. Benches are perched on the cliff for great views of the sheer coastal mountains plunging into the sea. The Ragged Point Nature Trail follows the perimeter of the peninsula along the high blufftop terrace. There are several scenic vista points and an overlook.

Driving directions: From Cambria, drive 23 miles north on Highway 1 to the Ragged Point Inn and Restaurant on the left. Turn left and park in the paved lot.

Hiking directions: Take the gravel path west (between the snack bar and gift shop) towards the point. Fifty yards ahead is a signed junction at a grassy overlook. The Nature Trail continues straight ahead, circling the blufftop terrace through windswept pine and cypress trees. At the northwest point is a viewing platform. Waterfalls can be seen cascading off the cliffs on both sides of the promontory. Back at the junction, the Cliffside Trail descends down the steps over the cliff's edge past a bench and across a wooden bridge. Switchbacks cut across the edge of the steep cliff to the base of Black Swift Falls at the sandy beach. After enjoying the surroundings, head back up the steep path.

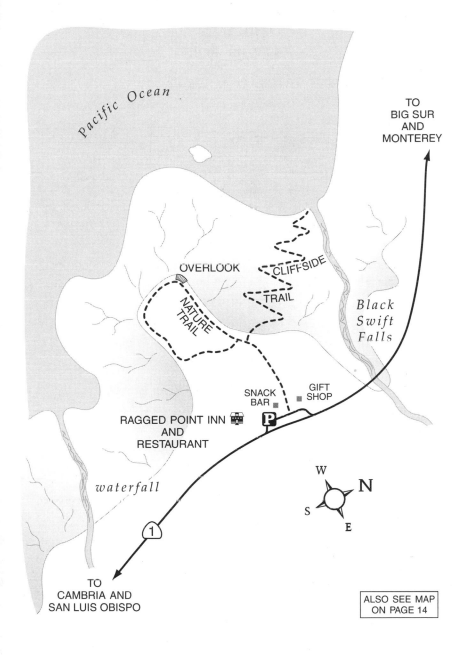

Pacific Ocean

TO
BIG SUR
AND
MONTEREY

OVERLOOK

CLIFFSIDE

NATURE TRAIL

TRAIL

Black Swift Falls

SNACK BAR

GIFT SHOP

RAGGED POINT INN
AND
RESTAURANT

P

waterfall

W N S E

1

TO
CAMBRIA AND
SAN LUIS OBISPO

ALSO SEE MAP
ON PAGE 14

NATURE and CLIFFSIDE TRAILS
RAGGED POINT INN

Hike 13
Ragged Point

Hiking distance: 0.8 miles round trip
Hiking time: 30 minutes
Elevation gain: 40 feet
Maps: U.S.G.S. Burro Mountain

Summary of hike: This hike crosses a marine terrace to Ragged Point, which is actually located 1.8 miles south of the Ragged Point Inn (Hike 12). From the point are overlooks of the scalloped coastline, a sandy beach cove, offshore rocks pounded by the surf, and Bald Top rising from the Santa Lucia Mountains. San Carpoforo Creek empties into the ocean north of Ragged Point. The well-defined trail crosses through Hearst Corporation ranchland to the headland. Although there are no public easements, the well-defined trails have been used by surfers, fishermen, and hikers for many years. Portions of the bluff top cliffs are unstable and caution is advised.

Driving directions: From Cambria, drive 21 miles north on Highway 1 to a large, unsigned dirt turnoff on the left at a right bend in the road. Turning left here is dangerous. Instead, continue 0.4 miles past the turnoff, and turn around after crossing the bridge over San Carpoforo Creek.

From the Ragged Point Inn and Restaurant, located 1.5 miles south of the Monterey County line, drive 1.8 miles south on Highway 1 to the wide turnout on the right, 0.4 miles south of the San Carpoforo Creek bridge.

Hiking directions: Cross over the fence and follow the wide path west. Walk through a scrub-brush meadow backed by the towering Santa Lucia Mountains. Enter a shady canopy of twisted pines on the soft pine needle path. Emerge from the forest to the edge of the 100-foot bluffs. From the north-facing cliffs of Ragged Point are views below of a crescent-shaped beach with magnificent rock outcroppings. Several paths weave along the bluffs to additional coastal views. A

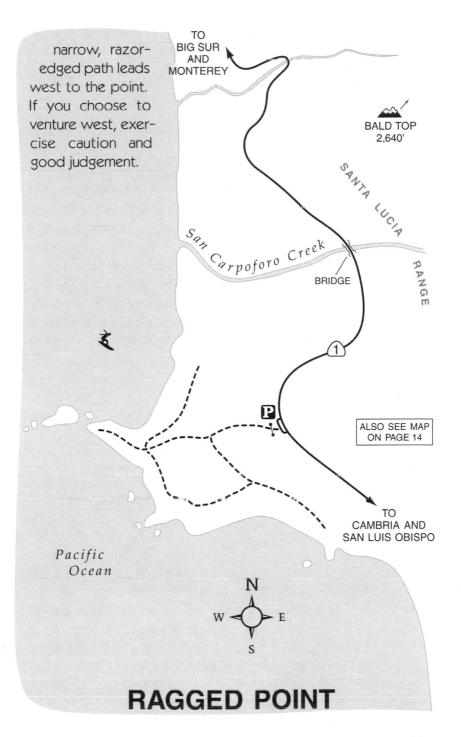

narrow, razor-edged path leads west to the point. If you choose to venture west, exercise caution and good judgement.

TO
BIG SUR
AND
MONTEREY

BALD TOP
2,640'

SANTA LUCIA RANGE

San Carpoforo Creek

BRIDGE

1

P

ALSO SEE MAP
ON PAGE 14

TO
CAMBRIA AND
SAN LUIS OBISPO

Pacific
Ocean

N
W E
S

RAGGED POINT

Hike 14
Piedras Blancas Bluffs

Hiking distance: 4.5 miles round trip
Hiking time: 2.5 hours
Elevation gain: 50 feet
Maps: U.S.G.S. Piedras Blancas

Summary of hike: Piedras Blancas, meaning *white rocks*, was named by Juan Cabrillo in 1572 for the offshore rocks covered by centuries of bird guano. Piedras Blancas Lighthouse, built in 1874, sits on windswept Point Piedras Blancas near the northern end of San Luis Obispo County. For a few months every winter and spring, thousands of elephant seals colonize the beaches and coves south of the lighthouse for breeding, birthing, and molting. This hike follows the Piedras Blancas Bluffs, a marine terrace backed by the western slopes of the Santa Lucia Mountains. The coastal trail overlooks the scalloped shoreline and rocky beaches past elephant seals, tidepools, outcroppings, natural arches, and the 74-foot lighthouse. The trail crosses through the private land of the Hearst Corporation. Although there are no public easements, the well-defined trails are frequently used by hikers, fisherman, and photographers.

Driving directions: From Cambria, drive 11.5 miles north on Highway 1 to the signed Vista Point parking lot on the left.

From the Ragged Point Inn and Restaurant, located 1.5 miles south of the Monterey County line, drive 10 miles south on Highway 1 to the signed parking lot.

Hiking directions: From the main (southern) parking lot and wildlife viewing area, head 0.2 miles southeast past the elephant seal interpretive displays. The bluff path extends 0.2 miles to the fenced overlook of the beach and coastline. Return to the opposite end of the parking lot and take the footpath along the edge of the cliffs, parallel to Highway 1. At a quarter mile the path reaches the northern vista point parking lot. At the upper end of the parking lot, climb over the gate and follow the contours of the jagged coastline on the low bluffs. Pass a series of beach pockets, tidepools, and outcroppings. Wind through low dunes covered with ice plants. To avoid ending up on the beach and disturbing the elephant seals, stay on the inland side of the dunes. The lighthouse is in full view on Point Piedras Blancas. The trail fades across the blufftop meadow. Pick your own path towards the lighthouse through pockets of ice plant, reaching the lighthouse road by the powerpoles. This is a good turn-around spot.

To extend the hike, follow the road left towards the lighthouse. Near the buildings, leave the road and head north along the fence. Continue on the faint path covered with ice plants to a pocket beach where the coastline nears the highway.

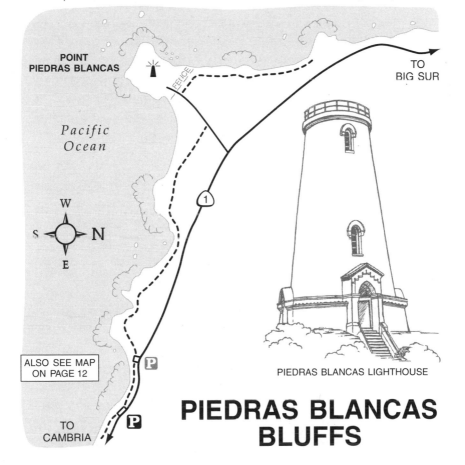

PIEDRAS BLANCAS LIGHTHOUSE

PIEDRAS BLANCAS BLUFFS

Hike 15
San Simeon Point
WILLIAM R. HEARST STATE BEACH

Hiking distance: 2.5 miles round trip
Hiking time: 1 hour
Elevation gain: 50 feet
Maps: U.S.G.S. San Simeon

Summary of hike: The San Simeon Bay Trail begins at William R. Hearst State Beach along a crescent of white sand. The hike leads from the protected bay to the tip of San Simeon Point, a peninsula of striated sandstone extending a half mile into the ocean (back cover photo). The bluff top trails are on the private property of the Hearst Ranch, and although the trails are frequently used, there are no public easements to the point. At the point are beach coves, dramatic rock formations, natural arches, tidepools, and coastal views to Point Estero and Point Buchon. The trail follows the bluffs through a beautiful forest of eucalyptus, pine, cedar, and cypress trees. Portions of the bluff top cliffs are unstable and caution is advised.

Driving directions: From Cambria, drive 8 miles north on Highway 1 to William R. Hearst State Beach on the left, across from the turnoff to Hearst Castle. Turn left on San Simeon Road, and turn left again at 0.1 miles into the state park parking lot by the pier. An alternative trailhead starts from the parking pullouts 0.1 miles ahead (before crossing the bridge). Pullouts are on both sides of the road by the eucalyptus grove.

Hiking directions: From the parking lot, walk down to the sandy beach between the pier and Arroyo del Puerto Creek. From the pullouts, walk through the gated entrance in the chain-link fence, and follow the path through the eucalyptus grove to the ocean, just west of the pier. Head west along the sand and cross Arroyo del Puerto Creek. Continue towards the forested point. As the beach curves south, take the distinct footpath up to the wooded bluffs. Follow the path through the eucalyptus grove along the edge of the bluffs overlooking the ocean. At the beginning of San Simeon Point, the path joins an unpaved road. Head south across the promontory to the southeast tip. Various trails lead around the headland to endless vistas, beach coves, rock formations, and tidepools. The trail continues around the west side of the peninsula through a shady tunnel of tall cedar, juniper, and cypress trees. This is the turn-around spot. Return along the same path.

To hike further, the trail emerges on an open coastal plateau with views of the Piedras Blancas Lighthouse, then descends onto dunes to the beach.

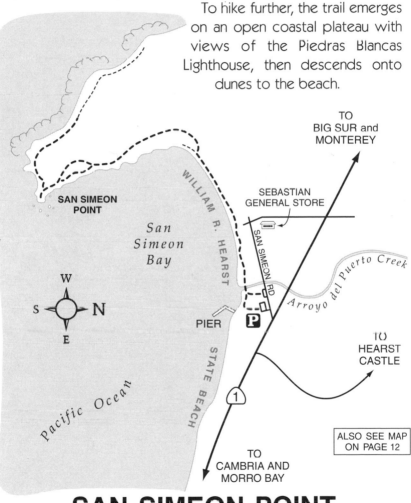

SAN SIMEON POINT
WILLIAM R. HEARST STATE BEACH

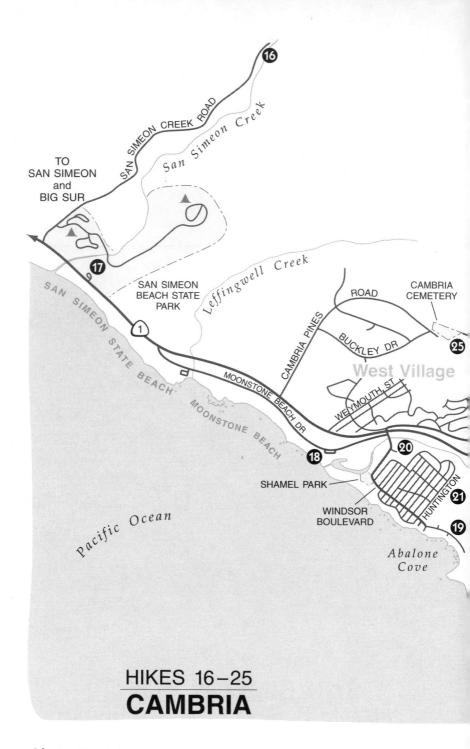

TO
SAN SIMEON
and
BIG SUR

16

SAN SIMEON CREEK ROAD

San Simeon Creek

17

SAN SIMEON
BEACH STATE
PARK

Leffingwell Creek

ROAD

CAMBRIA
CEMETERY

25

BUCKLEY DR

CAMBRIA PINES

West Village

1

SAN SIMEON STATE BEACH

MOONSTONE BEACH DR

WEYMOUTH ST

MOONSTONE BEACH

18

20

SHAMEL PARK

HUNTINGTON

21

WINDSOR
BOULEVARD

19

Pacific Ocean

Abalone
Cove

HIKES 16–25
CAMBRIA

N
W   E
S

SANTA ROSA CREEK ROAD

BRIDGE STREET

MAIN STREET

Creek

Santa Rosa

BURTON

MAIN STREET

ETON RD

East
Village

TO
CAYUCOS,
MORRO BAY
and
SAN LUIS OBISPO

1

1

BURTON DRIVE

23

22

EAST WEST
RANCH

WARREN

ARDATH DRIVE

BERWICK

24

RANDALL

CAMBRIA

19

MARLBOROUGH

WINDSOR BLVD

Otter
Cove

ALSO SEE MAP
ON PAGE 12

1 MILE

2 KILOMETERS

Hike 16
San Simeon Creek Road

Hiking distance: 2—7 miles round trip
Hiking time: 1—3.5 hours
Elevation gain: Level to 400 feet
Maps: U.S.G.S. Cambria and Pebblestone Shut-In

Summary of hike: San Simeon Creek Road begins 2.5 miles north of Cambria, adjacent to San Simeon State Park Campground. The idyllic, dead-end country road heads inland parallel to San Simeon Creek, passing cattle ranches, orchards, and farms. The hike begins two miles up the road and meanders through the verdant valley land. The rural ranch road climbs up the canyon deep into the Santa Lucia Range beneath Red Mountain and Rocky Butte. Along the way are large rock outcroppings and scenic vistas of the surrounding mountains.

Driving directions: From Highway 1 in Cambria, drive 2.4 miles north of Windsor Boulevard to San Simeon Creek Road. The turnoff is just across the highway bridge over San Simeon Creek. Turn right and continue 2.2 miles, passing the San Simeon Creek Campground, to the first bridge over San Simeon Creek. Park alongside the road.

Hiking directions: Walk across the bridge and curve left on the narrow road. Follow the south side of San Simeon Creek, weaving through a mixed forest of oaks, eucalyptus, sycamores, maples, willows, and bay laurels. Stroll through the rolling valley hills, viewing the pastoral ranchland with cattle grazing on the grassy slopes. Cross a bridge over San Simeon Creek at Palmer Flats. At 1.5 miles, enter the canyon, following the course of the creek. Cross a third bridge at 2.2 miles by Rioly Run, a side canyon with a seasonal waterfall dropping off the rock ledge. Continue past corrals on the left, and wind through groves of oak trees. At just over 3 miles, cross another bridge over the creek at the confluence of the North Fork and South Fork of San Simeon Creek. Climb out of the canyon, and leave the creek to the open grassy meadows with beautiful rock outcroppings and vistas of the surrounding mountains. This is a good turn-around spot. To hike further, the road winds two more miles uphill, staying close to the North Fork along the east flank of Red Mountain and Rocky Butte.

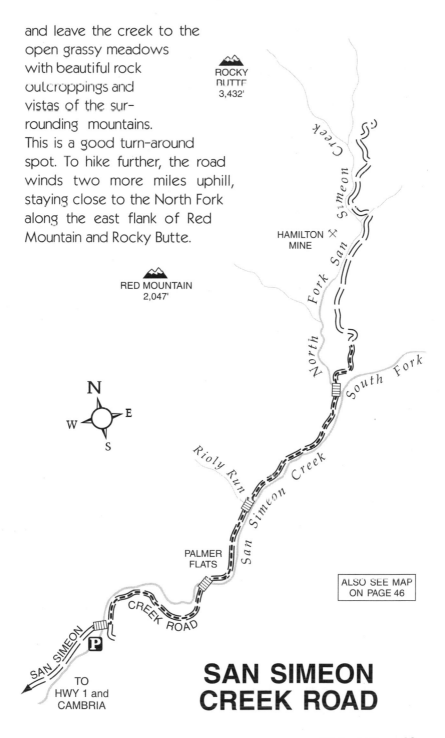

ROCKY BUTTE
3,432'

HAMILTON ✕ MINE

RED MOUNTAIN
2,047'

N
W — E
S

North Fork San Simeon Creek

South Fork

Rioly Run

San Simeon Creek

PALMER FLATS

CREEK ROAD

SAN SIMEON

P

TO
HWY 1 and
CAMBRIA

ALSO SEE MAP
ON PAGE 46

SAN SIMEON CREEK ROAD

Hike 17
San Simeon Trail
SAN SIMEON BEACH STATE PARK

Hiking distance: 4 mile loop
Hiking time: 2 hours
Elevation gain: 200 feet
Maps: U.S.G.S. Cambria

Summary of hike: The San Simeon Trail loops through the state park with a diverse landscape of coastal scrub, grassy meadows, wetlands, a Monterey pine forest, a eucalyptus grove, and riparian woodlands. This loop hike includes foot-bridges and boardwalks, interpretive displays, outcroppings, vernal pools of winter rainfall, benches, and Whitaker Flats, an old dairy ranch dating back to the 1860s.

Driving directions: From Highway 1 in Cambria, drive 2 miles north to the San Simeon Beach State Park turnoff on the right. Turn right and park in the Washburn Day Use Area parking lot.

Hiking directions: From the boardwalk, detour left and head west under Highway 1 to sandy San Simeon Beach along the south bank of San Simeon Creek. Return and follow the boardwalk east to the campground access road and bridge. Bear right on the signed gravel path through the coastal scrub. Cross a footbridge over the wetlands to the edge of the forested hillside. Ascend steps and follow Pine Ridge east through the forest of Monterey pines. At one mile, descend the hillside into Fern Gully, a lush riparian area. Cross the valley floor on Willow Bridge, a 500-foot bridge over the stream and marshland under a canopy of trees. Continue across the grassy slope along the eastern park boundary to a trail fork at the Washburn Campground. The left fork parallels the campground road, returning to the trailhead. Take the right fork across a grassy mesa to a bench and overlook at the Mima Mounds and vernal pools. Bear left, traversing the hillside above San Simeon Creek to a massive forested outcropping. Continue past the formation and head downhill into a eucalyptus grove at the old Whitaker Ranch site. Ascend the hillside, joining the trail from the campground. Bear right, parallel to the campground road, back to the trailhead.

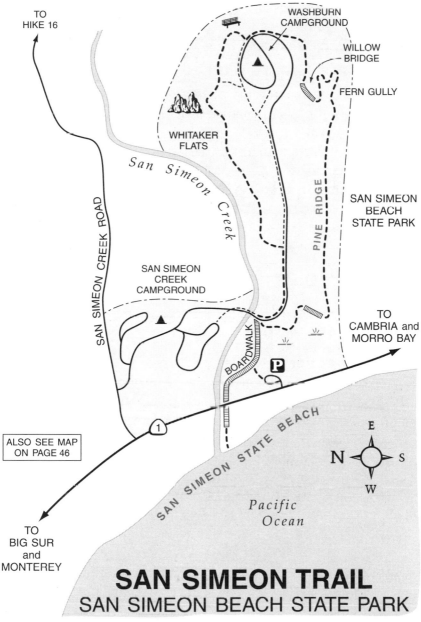

TO
HIKE 16

WASHBURN
CAMPGROUND

WILLOW
BRIDGE

FERN GULLY

WHITAKER
FLATS

San Simeon Creek

PINE RIDGE

SAN SIMEON
BEACH
STATE PARK

SAN SIMEON CREEK ROAD

SAN SIMEON
CREEK
CAMPGROUND

TO
CAMBRIA and
MORRO BAY

BOARDWALK

P

1

ALSO SEE MAP
ON PAGE 46

SAN SIMEON STATE BEACH

E

N — S

W

TO
BIG SUR
and
MONTEREY

Pacific
Ocean

SAN SIMEON TRAIL
SAN SIMEON BEACH STATE PARK

Hike 18
Moonstone Beach Trail

Hiking distance: 2.5 miles round trip
Hiking time: 1.5 hours
Elevation gain: Level
Maps: U.S.G.S. Cambria

Summary of hike: The Moonstone Beach Trail follows the rocky shoreline at the edge of the windswept ocean cliffs in Cambria. On the 20-foot eroded bluffs along the oceanfront corridor, several staircases lead down to the sandy beach. Along the shore are smooth, translucent, milky white moonstone agates. The trail leads past small coves, rock formations, and tidepools to scenic overlooks. There are views up the coast to San Simeon Point and the Piedras Blancas Lighthouse. This is an excellent vantage point to watch migrating gray whales.

Driving directions: From Highway 1 in Cambria, turn west on Windsor Boulevard and a quick right onto Moonstone Beach Drive. Continue 0.3 miles to the Santa Rosa Creek parking lot on the left. Turn left and park.

Hiking directions: The trail begins near the mouth of Santa Rosa Creek on the north end of the parking lot. Head north on the sandstone bluffs overlooking the ocean and offshore rocks, parallel to Moonstone Beach Drive. Steps descend to the sandy beach. Return up to the bluffs, crossing small wooden foot-bridges. At one mile, the old highway bridge spans Leffingwell Creek. Bear left down a ramp to the beach and cross the sand. Ascend the grassy slope to a picnic area and cypress grove at Leffingwell Landing, part of San Simeon Beach State Park. Cross the parking lot, picking up the trail again on the bluffs, and wind through groves of Monterey pine and cypress. At 1.5 miles is an overlook on the left at the north end of Moonstone Beach Drive. Past the overlook, steps lead down to the beach. Return along the same path.

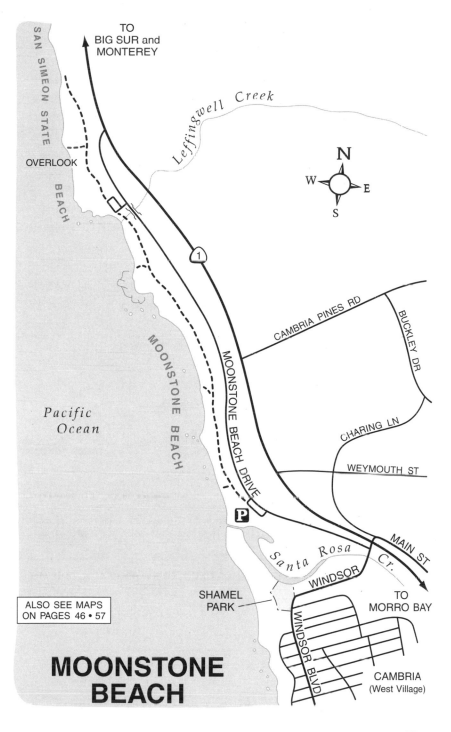

TO
BIG SUR and
MONTEREY

SAN SIMEON STATE

Leffingwell Creek

N
W E
S

OVERLOOK

BEACH

1

CAMBRIA PINES RD

BUCKLEY DR

MOONSTONE BEACH

MOONSTONE BEACH DRIVE

Pacific Ocean

CHARING LN

WEYMOUTH ST

P

Santa Rosa Cr.

MAIN ST

WINDSOR

ALSO SEE MAPS
ON PAGES 46 • 57

SHAMEL PARK

TO
MORRO BAY

WINDSOR BLVD

MOONSTONE
BEACH

CAMBRIA
(West Village)

East West Ranch
HIKES 19—22

East West Ranch is a 436-acre reserve sitting in the middle of Cambria. The undeveloped open space extends from the oceanfront bluffs to the east side of Highway 1. The protected parkland was once a prehistoric Chumash Indian site. It now divides Cambria into north and south residential areas, connecting Park Hill and Seaclift Estates in the north with Marine Terrace and Lodge Hill in the south. Santa Rosa Creek, running 1.5 miles through the ranch, is one of the few remaining wildlife corridors in the area, connecting the coastal Santa Lucia Range with the sea. The dog-friendly public land has a network of trails weaving through coastal bluffs, marine terraces, riparian creek habitats, rolling grasslands, and tree-covered hills, including stands of coast live oaks and rare native Monterey pines.

Hike 19
Bluff Trail
EAST WEST RANCH

Hiking distance: 2 miles round trip
Hiking time: 1 hour
Elevation gain: 50 feet
Maps: U.S.G.S. Cambria

map
next page

Summary of hike: The Bluff Trail follows the edge of eroded 40-foot bluffs above the rocky shoreline and tidepools. En route are two bridge crossings, a handcrafted wooden shelter, and several unique driftwood benches. The mile-long trail crosses the ranch, connecting the two ends of Windsor Boulevard. There is no beach access along the trail, but the views are fantastic. During the winter migration, gray whales swim within 200 yards of the shoreline.

Driving directions: SOUTH TRAILHEAD: From Highway 1 in Cambria, wind 1.6 miles west on Ardath Drive to Marlborough

Lane. Turn right and continue a half mile to Wedgewood Street. Turn left and go one block to Windsor Boulevard. Turn right and park in the trailhead spaces.

NORTH TRAILHEAD: From Highway 1, drive 1 mile southwest on Windsor Boulevard to the trailhead at the end of the road. Park along the curb.

Hiking directions: Starting from the southern trailhead, walk north from the end of Windsor Boulevard through the trailhead gate. Cross the flat grassy bluffs that overlook the jagged shoreline, tidepools, and the ocean. Cross the wooden footbridge over a stream, curving along the edge of the eroded bluffs. Cross a second bridge over a small arroyo, then head past benches and a wooden shelter. The trail ends by a fenceline at the southern end of Windsor Boulevard by Abalone Cove and Seaclift Estates. Return along the same trail.

Hike 20
Santa Rosa Creek Trail
EAST WEST RANCH AREA

Hiking distance: 2 miles round trip
Hiking time: 1 hour
Elevation gain: 200 feet
Maps: U.S.G.S. Cambria

map
next page

Summary of hike: The headwaters of Santa Rosa Creek begin high in the Santa Lucia Range on Black Mountain. The creek flows through Cambria to the sea at the south end of Moonstone Beach. The Santa Rosa Creek Trail begins by Windsor Bridge and follows the west bank of the creek through a lush riparian corridor. The trail ends at Highway 1, where the creek heads east. The path connects with the network of hiking trails in East West Ranch.

Driving directions: From Highway 1 in Cambria, turn west on Windsor Boulevard. Drive 0.1 miles, crossing the bridge over

Santa Rosa Creek, to Heath Lane. Turn left and park in the dirt pullout on the left.

Hiking directions: Walk a short distance northeast along Windsor Boulevard to Santa Rosa Creek. Veer to the right on the grassy path, passing through a vehicle gate. Follow the creek upstream through a lush riparian corridor with eucalyptus trees, bay laurel, and oaks draped with tufts of moss. Ascend the hillside, overlooking the slow-rolling creek. The undulating path passes a side canyon on the right and follows the 20-foot bluffs above the creek. Curve right, away from the creek, and climb the hill towards the homes. Just before reaching the homes, at a circular cement sewer access, curve left and descend, returning to the creek. Skirt around the left side of a fenced utility building and take the dirt road, staying close to Santa Rosa Creek on the left and the hillside on the right. The dirt road passes an old rock foundation and ends at a gate by Highway 1, just south of the highway bridge crossing the creek. A distinct trail veers right, 15 yards shy of the gate. Head up the hillside, passing an old wood shed to a horseshoe left bend. To the right, a path climbs the sloping meadow to Huntington Ridge (Hike 21). To the left, the main trail connects with the Bill Kerr Trail (Hike 22). Return by retracing your steps.

HIKES 19 • 20
BLUFF TRAIL
SANTA ROSA CREEK TRAIL
EAST WEST RANCH

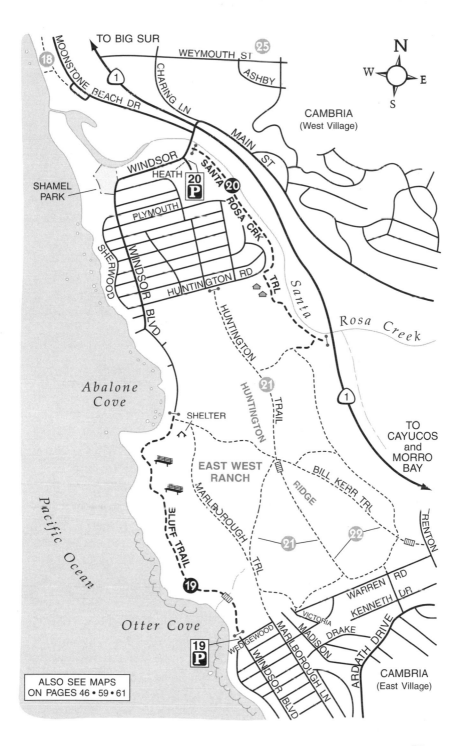

TO BIG SUR

WEYMOUTH ST

25

ASHBY

N
W   E
S

18

MOONSTONE BEACH DR

1

CHARING LN

MAIN ST

CAMBRIA
(West Village)

WINDSOR

HEATH

20
P

20

SANTA ROSA CRK

SHAMEL
PARK

PLYMOUTH

WINDSOR BLVD

SHERWOOD

HUNTINGTON RD

TRL

Santa

Rosa Creek

Abalone
Cove

HUNTINGTON

HUNTINGTON

TRAIL

21

1

TO
CAYUCOS
and
MORRO
BAY

SHELTER

EAST WEST
RANCH

MARLBOROUGH TRL

RIDGE

BILL KERR TRL

RENTON

Pacific Ocean

BLUFF TRAIL

21

22

19

WARREN RD

KENNETH DR

Otter Cove

VICTORIA

MADISON

DRAKE

ARDATH DRIVE

19
P

WEDGEWOOD

MARLBOROUGH LN

WINDSOR BLVD

CAMBRIA
(East Village)

ALSO SEE MAPS
ON PAGES 46 • 59 • 61

Hike 21
Huntington—Marlborough Loop
EAST WEST RANCH

Hiking distance: 2 mile loop
Hiking time: 1 hour
Elevation gain: 200 feet
Maps: U.S.G.S. Cambria

Summary of hike: The Huntington Trail follows the 200-foot ridge across the rolling grasslands of East West Ranch between Seaclift Estates and Lodge Hill. The scenic trail overlooks the crenulated coastline; the bluff-top marine terrace; small, craggy canyons; tree-covered hills; the town of Cambria; and the coastal mountains. The hike returns on the lower marine terrace above the bluffs and weaves through a small arroyo.

Driving directions: From Highway 1 in Cambria, drive 0.7 miles southwest on Windsor Boulevard to Huntington Road. Turn left and continue a quarter mile to the posted trailhead on the right. Park alongside the street.

Hiking directions: Head south across the open rolling grasslands, marveling at the coast-to-mountain vistas. Follow the level ridge, with Monterey pines bordering the east edge of the meadow and views of Cambria. Pass a trail on the right, dropping down the hill into the draw. Stay atop the ridge, passing a trail on the left that leads into the forest. A short distance ahead is a 4-way trail split at the head of the draw by a wooden footbridge. The Bill Kerr Trail bears left and leads through the forest to Trenton Avenue (Hike 22). Cross the bridge and meander along the rolling scenic terrain, skirting the edge of the pine forest. Stay to the right at a Y-fork, curving toward the sea near the homes along Warren Road. Descend to the trailhead at Warren Road and Victoria Way. A few yards before the park boundary, bear right on a footpath. Descend the hill to a wide path on the marine terrace, an unpaved extension of Marlborough Lane. Bear right and head north, parallel to the Bluff Trail. Walk 200 yards and veer right on the footpath, climbing the grassy slope. Traverse the hillside and cross over the ridge on the gently rolling landscape. Complete the loop on Huntington Ridge by the footbridge. Return along the ridge to the left.

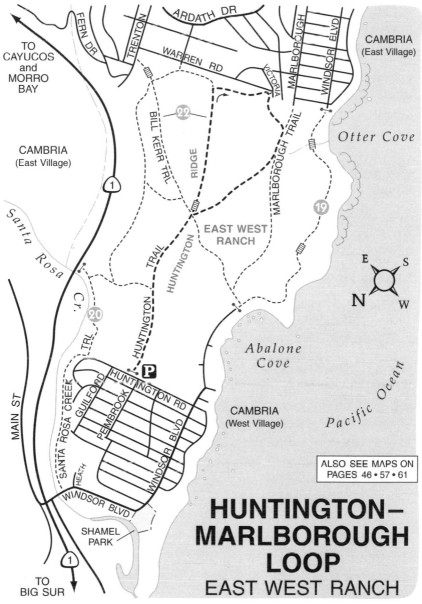

TO
CAYUCOS
and
MORRO
BAY

CAMBRIA
(East Village)

CAMBRIA
(East Village)

FERN DR

TRENTON

ARDATH DR

WARREN RD

MARLBOROUGH

WINDSOR BLVD

VICTORIA

Otter Cove

BILL KERR TRL

RIDGE

22

MARLBOROUGH TRAIL

19

EAST WEST
RANCH

Santa Rosa Cr.

1

HUNTINGTON TRAIL

20

E   S

N   W

TRL

HUNTINGTON

Abalone
Cove

P

GUILFORD

PEMBROOK

HUNTINGTON RD

WINDSOR BLVD

SANTA ROSA CREEK

HEATH

MAIN ST

CAMBRIA
(West Village)

Pacific Ocean

ALSO SEE MAPS ON
PAGES 46 • 57 • 61

WINDSOR BLVD

SHAMEL
PARK

1

TO
BIG SUR

HUNTINGTON–
MARLBOROUGH
LOOP
EAST WEST RANCH

Hike 22
Bill Kerr Loop from Trenton Avenue
EAST WEST RANCH

Hiking distance: 1.5 mile loop
Hiking time: 45 minutes
Elevation gain: 150 feet
Maps: U.S.G.S. Cambria

Summary of hike: The Bill Kerr Trail sits on the southeast corner of East West Ranch. The path weaves through a 70-acre native stand of Monterey pines, ancient oaks, and a lush understory of ferns. The Monterey pine grove is one of three remaining native stands in California and the world. (The other two are located in San Mateo County and near Monterey.) Wildlife moving between the coastal range and ocean bluffs use the grove as a habitat and protective cover. The trail returns along the edge of the forest, overlooking the rolling grasslands, the coastal cliffs, and the ocean.

Driving directions: From Highway 1 in Cambria, wind 0.9 miles west on Ardath Drive to Trenton Avenue. Turn right and proceed 0.15 miles to the forested trailhead on the left. Park alongside the road.

Hiking directions: Descend into a dense pine forest on the Bill Kerr Trail, a footpath cushioned with pine needles. Cross a wooden bridge over a seasonal stream to a Y-fork. Twenty yards ahead, veer right on the upper path and cross a sloping meadow. Return to the shade of the pines, and stroll along the level ridge to the north end of the forest and a Y-fork. Views extend across the rolling grasslands to the sea. Curve left along the edge of the forest and merge with the Huntington Trail. Continue south toward the homes on Warren Road. Slowly curve inland (east) and away from the homes. Weave through the forest to a junction where the trail is lined with logs. Curve right, completing the loop by the bridge. Cross the bridge and return to the left.

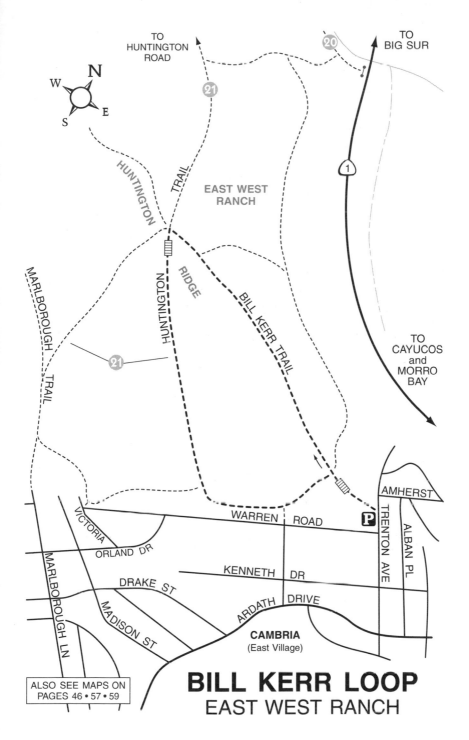

TO
HUNTINGTON
ROAD

TO
BIG SUR

20

N
W   E
S

21

EAST WEST
RANCH

1

HUNTINGTON   TRAIL

TO
CAYUCOS
and
MORRO
BAY

MARLBOROUGH   TRAIL

HUNTINGTON   RIDGE

BILL KERR TRAIL

21

AMHERST

VICTORIA

WARREN   ROAD

P

TRENTON AVE

ALBAN PL

ORLAND DR

MARLBOROUGH LN

KENNETH   DR

DRAKE ST

ARDATH   DRIVE

MADISON ST

CAMBRIA
(East Village)

ALSO SEE MAPS ON
PAGES 46 • 57 • 59

BILL KERR LOOP
EAST WEST RANCH

Hike 23
Fern Canyon

Hiking distance: 0.5 miles round trip
Hiking time: 20 minutes
Elevation gain: 50 feet
Maps: U.S.G.S. Cambria

Summary of hike: The forested town of Cambria is filled with small pastoral gems, quietly tucked away for the locals to enjoy. Lush Fern Canyon is one of the gorgeous riparian respites. The small preserve, purchased by the Land Conservancy of San Luis Obispo County, lies within the neighborhood of Lodge Hill between Highway 1 and Ardath Drive. The trail follows the forested enclave a quarter mile. Although the preserve is surrounded by homes, it has a remote, isolated atmosphere.

Driving directions: From Highway 1 in Cambria, head south on Burton Drive to the first corner. Turn right on Fern Drive and continue 0.15 miles to a horseshoe right bend in the road. Park in the small pullout on the left in the bend by the Fern Canyon trail sign.

Hiking directions: Walk south past the trailhead sign and into the pine forest. Meander along the east side of the drainage on an easy uphill grade. Follow the fern-lined stream through the lush, riparian habitat. Cross the drainage and continue upstream to the end of the short path. The trail ends on Camborne Place, just shy of Ardath Drive. Return by retracing your steps.

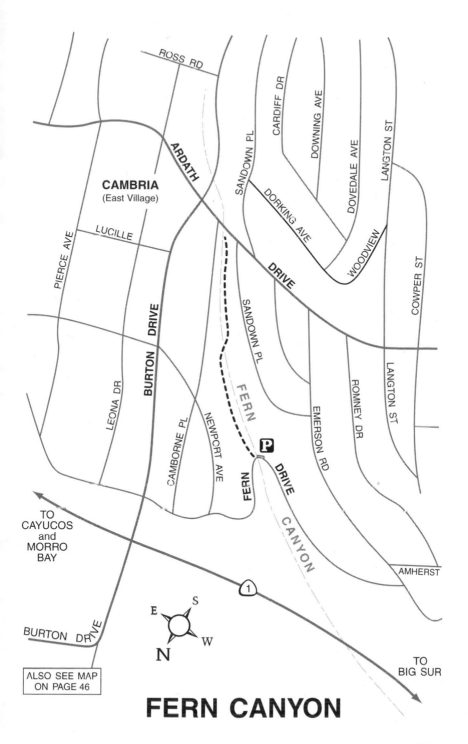

FERN CANYON

Hike 24
Strawberry Canyon

Hiking distance: 0.8 mile loop
Hiking time: 30 minutes
Elevation gain: 50 feet
Maps: U.S.G.S. Cambria

Summary of hike: Strawberry Canyon was acquired by Greenspace, the Cambria Land Trust, and is tucked into the southern end of Cambria. Named for the strawberries planted in the 1930s, the small area is a charming getaway. The loop trail meanders through a lush forest, across a hilltop with views and sitting benches, and into a small canyon and seasonal drainage.

Driving directions: From Highway 1 in Cambria, head 0.75 miles south on Burton Drive to Kay Street on the left. Park on the right side of Burton Drive.

Hiking directions: The posted Strawberry Canyon Trail is on the right, directly across from Kay Street. Drop into the pine forest and walk 75 yards to a junction, bench, and trail sign. Begin the loop to the left, hiking clockwise. Traverse the hillside, strolling through the lush, dense forest. Pass memorial benches in a meadow atop the hill. Loop right and descend into the shady forest to a T-junction. The right fork is the return route. Detour left along the canyon floor, and curve right up the slope. The path ends near the top of the slope at private property. Return to the junction and continue straight ahead along the north edge of the Strawberry Canyon drainage, completing the loop. Return to the left.

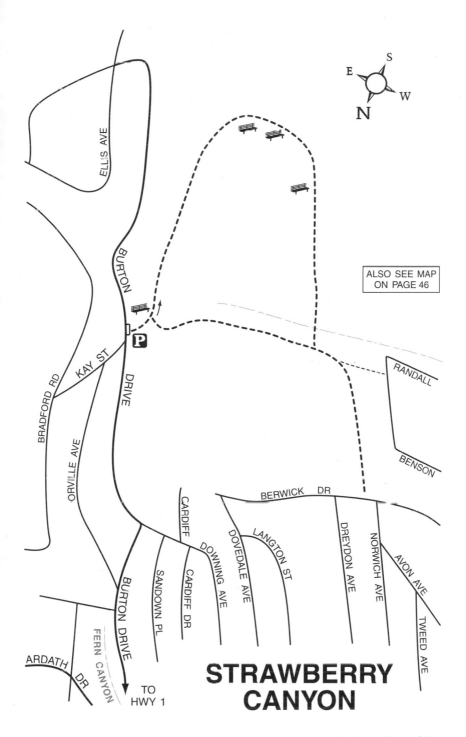

STRAWBERRY CANYON

ALSO SEE MAP
ON PAGE 46

Hike 25
Cambria Cemetery—Pine Knolls Loop

Hiking distance: 1 mile round trip heading north
1.5 mile loop heading south
Hiking time: 1.5 hours
Elevation gain: 120 feet
Maps: U.S.G.S. Cambria

Summary of hike: The Cambria Cemetery, dating back to the 1870s, encompasses 12 acres in the forested hills northwest of the town. Adjacent to the cemetery is densely forested green space, bordered by development. This hike loops through the greenbelt in a forest of pines, toyon, and ceanothus.

Driving directions: From Main Street in the East Village of Cambria, drive one mile north on Bridge Street to the Cambria Cemetery. (Bridge Street is the second left turn east of Burton Drive.) Park in the area on the right, just before entering the cemetery.

Hiking directions: First, enter the cemetery to the north. Stroll through the old burial ground, exploring on a level 0.3-mile loop. Return to the parking area, and walk 100 yards down Bridge Street, past the office buildings, to the trailhead on the right. Enter the forest on the wide path for 50 yards to a Y-fork. Begin on the right (north) fork, skirting the edge of the cemetery through the forest. Pass a stucco wall along the homes fronting Buckley Drive. The trail follows the east side of the large grassy meadow along the hillside. During the week, the meadow is part of Camp Keep (a private school) and is trespassing. During the weekend, it is leased by Camp Yeager for public recreation. A short distance ahead is a trail split. Both paths lead into the campground. The right fork loops around the outside of the cabins to Weymouth Street and Ashby Lane, reaching the camp entrance at a half mile.

Return to the first Y-fork by the trailhead. Take the left (south) fork 30 yards to another Y-fork. All the trails heading south loop and reconnect but are not marked. For this hike, go straight on the right fork and slowly descend, curving left. Continue downhill, staying left at numerous side trails. At a half mile is a triangle-shaped junction. The left fork leads 50 yards to Bridge Street at a horseshoe bend. Take the right fork, passing more side paths. At 0.75 miles, the main path loops to the right and begins the return to the north. The side paths on the left lead to the Pine Knolls development. Stay to the right, steadily climbing at an easy grade and completing the loop.

NOTE: The southern route has many unmarked side paths. Keep in mind that the trails parallel Bridge Street. If you feel confused, take a side path east until you reach Bridge Street.

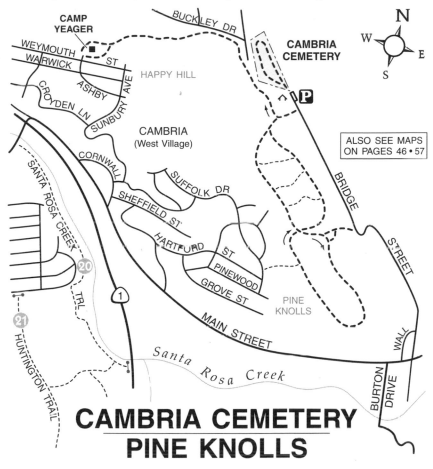

ALSO SEE MAPS
ON PAGES 46 • 57

CAMBRIA CEMETERY
PINE KNOLLS

Hike 26
Harmony Valley

Hiking distance: 2 miles round trip
Hiking time: 1 hour
Elevation gain: 60 feet
Maps: U.S.G.S. Cambria

Summary of hike: The historic town of Harmony began as a dairy cooperative in the 1860s. With a current population of 18, the charming community is now an artists' colony with a post office, wedding chapel, and art shops in the old creamery buildings. Harmony Valley is quietly tucked away in the hills behind Harmony. A one-mile dirt road winds inland from the tiny settlement through pristine rolling farmland along the south side of Perry Creek. The route can be driven, but it is a great place for an easy, picturesque walk, away from the highway and with very few vehicles.

Driving directions: From Cayucos, drive 8 miles north on Highway 1 to the small artist community of Harmony on the right. Turn right on Harmony Valley Road and drive 0.1 miles. Park alongside the road, just before Harmony Cellars Winery near the end of the paved road.

From Cambria, drive 5 miles south to the signed Harmony turnoff on the left.

Hiking directions: Walk up the dirt road, top the rise, and descend into the grassy, rolling hills. Meander through the open pastureland, passing pockets of oak trees, corrals, small sheds, quaint farmhouses, barns, grazing cows, and Perry Creek, slowly snaking through the verdant valley. The road ends at one mile by the entrance to a ranch. Return along the same route.

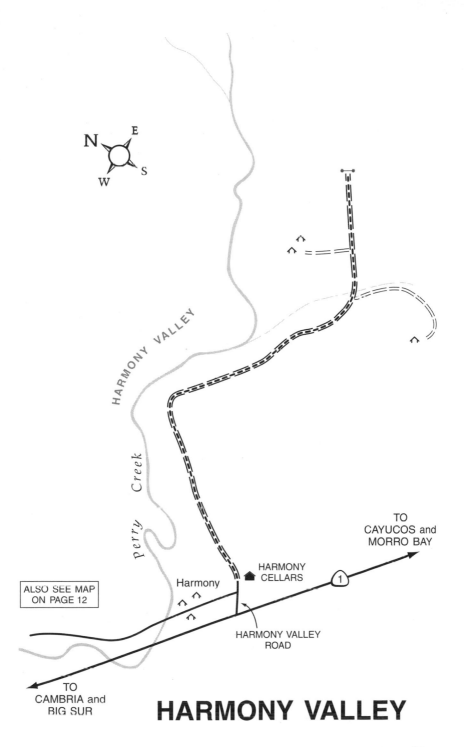

N E S W

HARMONY VALLEY

Perry Creek

ALSO SEE MAP
ON PAGE 12

Harmony

HARMONY
CELLARS

1

TO
CAYUCOS and
MORRO BAY

HARMONY VALLEY
ROAD

TO
CAMBRIA and
BIG SUR

HARMONY VALLEY

Hike 27
Estero Bluffs State Park

Hiking distance: 5 miles round trip
Hiking time: 2.5 hours
Elevation gain: 50 feet
Maps: U.S.G.S. Cayucos

Summary of hike: Estero Bluffs State Park encompasses 355 acres at the north end of crescent-shaped Estero Bay, between the town of Cayucos and Villa Creek. The undeveloped park stretches 3.5 miles along the grassy coastal terrace and rocky shoreline from Highway 1 to the ocean. Six waterways flow from the Santa Lucia foothills through the marine terrace. The hike follows the craggy, windswept palisade, passing sea-battered rocks, sheltered coves, small sandy beaches, promontories, clefts, and rolling knolls.

Driving directions: From downtown Cayucos, drive 1 mile north on Highway 1 to the large dirt pullout on the left—the southern access to Estero Bluffs. The pullout is 0.1 miles past the end of the divided section of Highway 1. Heading north, four additional trailheads access the coastal bluffs over the next 1.6 miles. The northern access is located 1.6 miles south of Villa Creek Road.

Hiking directions: From the southern access, descend the slope from the south end of the parking area. Follow the path across the grassy marine terrace to the edge of the 40-foot bluffs. Take the path to the right, and stroll along the scalloped coastline. Cross an eroded gully and continue past coves, pocket beaches, offshore rocks, and tidepools. Cross San Geronimo Creek in a recessed sandy cove. Climb back to the bluffs by three huge eucalyptus trees. Pass a rounded 100-foot grassy knoll on the right to Red Rock, a 30-foot weather-sculpted rock formation surrounded by a jumble of boulders. A short distance ahead is Cayucos Point by an offshore sea stack. Cross a gully and pass more small sandy coves and numerous rocks jutting out of the sea. Walk by eroding cliffs with finger-shaped points of land and a huge offshore rock with a grassy slope. Curve north, following the contours of the coastline toward Highway 1. Veer west toward the prominent 120-foot rounded hill on the vertical bluffs. Cross three minor draws along the south flank of the hill. At the west end of the knoll, a distinct path heads inland, parallel to Swallow Creek on the northern trail access. This is the turn-around spot.

To extend the hike, stay on the blufftop trail or beach. The wetland terrace from Swallow Creek to Villa Creek is closed for resource protection, except for the blufftop trail.

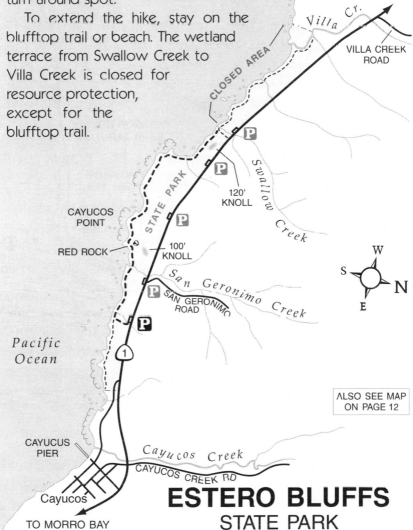

ESTERO BLUFFS
STATE PARK

Hike 28
Whale Rock Reservoir
Open from the last Saturday in April—November 15
Wednesday—Sunday and holidays

Hiking distance: 3.8 miles round trip
Hiking time: 2 hours
Elevation gain: 50 feet
Maps: U.S.G.S. Morro Bay North and Cayucos

Summary of hike: Whale Rock Reservoir sits in the hills above Cayucos surrounded by grassy rolling hills. The Whale Rock Dam was built in 1961, creating the 1,350-acre reservoir. It is a domestic water supply used as a source of drinking water. The lake is fed from Old Creek and Cottontail Creek at the two northern points. The reservoir is open to the public during the trout fishing season. A trail along the eastern side of the lake is primarily used as a fishing access, but it is also a beautiful area for hiking and picnicking.

Driving directions: From Highway 1 at the south end of Cayucos, take Old Creek Road 1.5 miles northeast to the Whale Rock Reservoir parking area on the left, just before the PG&E substation. An entrance fee is required.

Hiking directions: Walk through the entrance gate to the trailhead sign. The left fork leads 0.2 miles on the wide grassy path to the fenced border at Johnson Cove. The right fork leads past a picnic area, then follows the curves of the lake parallel to the shoreline. The path frequently rises above the lake and drops back to the waterline. At 1.3 miles, the trail curves around Dead Horse Cove to a trail split. The right fork is a secondary fishing access from a parking lot by Old Creek Road. Bear left and loop around the perimeter of Dead Horse Point. The trail ends at a fenceline north of the point. Return on the same trail.

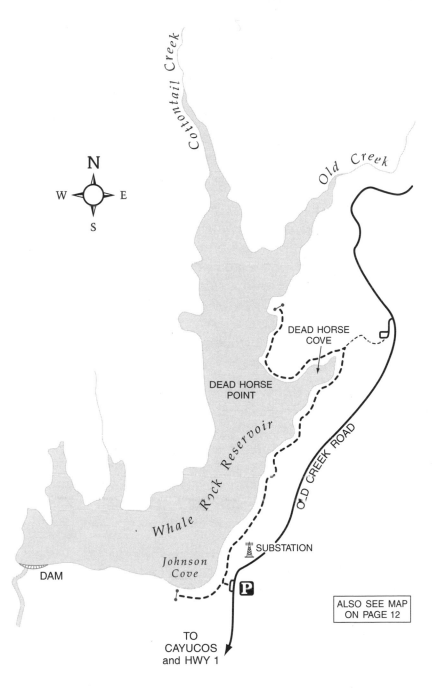

Cottontail Creek

Old Creek

N
W   E
S

DEAD HORSE
COVE

DEAD HORSE
POINT

Whale Rock Reservoir

OLD CREEK ROAD

SUBSTATION

Johnson
Cove

P

DAM

ALSO SEE MAP
ON PAGE 12

TO
CAYUCOS
and HWY 1

WHALE ROCK RESERVOIR

Hike 29
Oak Knoll and Quail's Roost Trail
LAKE NACIMIENTO

Hiking distance: 1.5 miles round trip
Hiking time: 45 minutes
Elevation gain: 100 feet
Maps: U.S.G.S. Tierra Redonda Mountain
Lake Nacimiento Resort trail map

Summary of hike: Located at the far north end of the county, Lake Nacimiento is the county's largest reservoir. The 16-mile-long lake, nestled in a tree-studded valley, was formed by a dam on the Nacimiento River. It is a popular area with 165 miles of shoreline and is surrounded by an 18,000-acre recreation area. The Oak Knoll and Quail's Roost Trail is a connector trail to the various lakeside campgrounds. The trail winds through beautiful stands of oaks and pines, with great views of Lake Nacimiento and the Nacimiento Dam.

Driving directions: From Highway 101 in Paso Robles, take the 24th Street/Highway 46 East exit. Head west on 24th Street through Paso Robles, and drive 16 miles to the Lake Nacimiento Dam at a road fork. (24th Street becomes Nacimiento Lake Drive outside of Paso Robles.) Bear left and drive 0.7 miles to the entrance station. Continue 0.8 miles to the boat launch parking lot. Park at the east end of the lot, farthest from the water's edge. An entrance fee is required.

Hiking directions: Walk across the park road, and enter the restricted parking lot to the signed trailhead. The wide path winds around the hillside through groves of ponderosa pine and oak trees. Curve around several drainages and lake overlooks to the park road. Take the road 50 yards to the right, picking up the signed trail on the left. Follow the forested path east on the narrow fire road. The trail ends at the road by the Oak Knoll and Quail's Roost Campgrounds. Return by following the same path back.

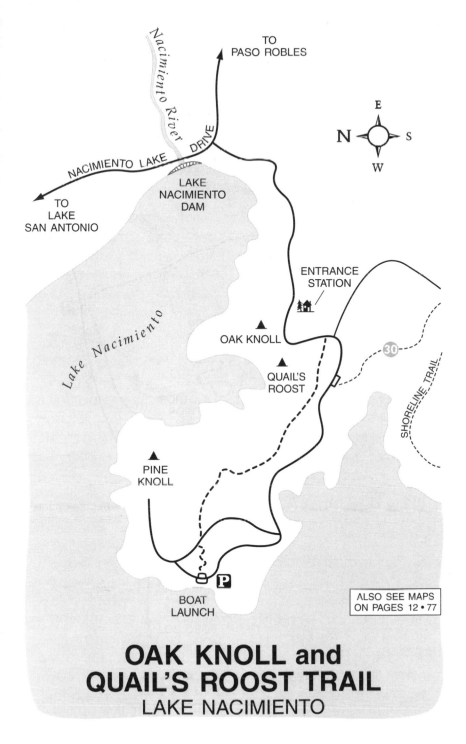

TO
PASO ROBLES

E
N — S
W

Nacimiento River

NACIMIENTO LAKE — DRIVE

LAKE
NACIMIENTO
DAM

TO
LAKE
SAN ANTONIO

ENTRANCE
STATION

Lake Nacimiento

▲
OAK KNOLL

▲
QUAIL'S
ROOST

30

SHORELINE TRAIL

▲
PINE
KNOLL

P

BOAT
LAUNCH

ALSO SEE MAPS
ON PAGES 12 • 77

OAK KNOLL and
QUAIL'S ROOST TRAIL
LAKE NACIMIENTO

Hike 30
Shoreline Trail
LAKE NACIMIENTO

Hiking distance: 4.6 miles round trip
Hiking time: 2.5 hours
Elevation gain: 400 feet
Maps: U.S.G.S. Tierra Redonda Mountain and Lime Mountain
Lake Nacimiento Resort trail map

Summary of hike: The Shoreline Trail follows the contours of the serene rolling hills above the east side of Lake Nacimiento. The pastoral grassy countryside is spotted with ponderosa pines and oak trees. The trail rarely gets close to the shoreline but always overlooks the coves and inlets of the beautiful lake.

Driving directions: From Highway 101 in Paso Robles, take the 24th Street/Highway 46 East exit. Head west on 24th Street through Paso Robles, and drive 16 miles to the Lake Nacimiento Dam at a road fork. (24th Street becomes Nacimiento Lake Drive outside of Paso Robles.) Bear left and drive 0.7 miles to the entrance station. Continue a quarter mile to the trailhead parking pullout on the left at a vista point. An entrance fee is required.

Hiking directions: Walk past the trail sign, heading up a short rise while overlooking the lake. Cross the rolling meadow dotted with trees. Loop around the edge of a forested ravine to an unpaved ranch road. Bear right and pick up the footpath on the right 30 yards ahead. Descend through an oak grove, and follow the hillside trail 150 feet above the lake. At one mile is a signed junction. The right fork descends to the shoreline to a fishing access. The main trail curves left to a saddle and rejoins the old road. Bear right along the road to a footpath at the base of a hill. The path zigzags down to a beach in a secluded cove. The main trail follows the road a short distance to a road fork.

Curve right and follow the ridge to a vista point on a peninsula. Head downhill to the flat beach area at the point. Return along the same trail.

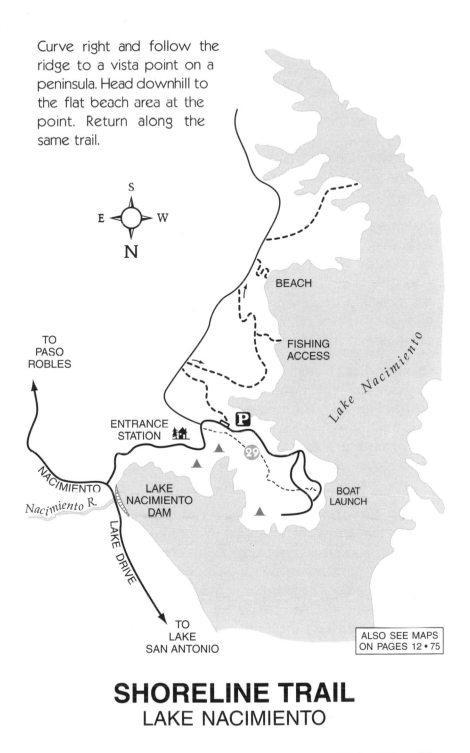

S

E W

N

BEACH

TO
PASO
ROBLES

FISHING
ACCESS

Lake Nacimiento

ENTRANCE
STATION

P

29

NACIMIENTO

Nacimiento R.

LAKE
NACIMIENTO
DAM

BOAT
LAUNCH

LAKE DRIVE

TO
LAKE
SAN ANTONIO

ALSO SEE MAPS
ON PAGES 12 • 75

SHORELINE TRAIL
LAKE NACIMIENTO

Hike 31
Salinas River
from LAWRENCE MOORE PARK

Hiking distance: 1 mile round trip
Hiking time: 40 minutes
Elevation: Level
Maps: U.S.G.S. Templeton
The Thomas Guide—San Luis Obispo County

Summary of hike: The Salinas River slowly flows through Paso Robles on the east side of Highway 101. Migrating birds frequent the riparian habitat during the winter and spring. This popular bird observation area begins in Lawrence Moore Park and heads downstream to Niblick Bridge. The path leads through groves of cottonwood, sycamore, and willow trees along the banks of the river.

Driving directions: From Highway 101 in Paso Robles, take the Spring Street exit and drive 0.5 miles to Niblick Road. Turn right and go 0.6 miles, crossing over the Salinas River to South River Road. Turn right and continue 0.3 miles to Riverbank Lane. Turn right and drive 0.4 miles through a residential neighborhood to Lawrence Moore Park on the right. Park alongside the curb across from Bridgegate Lane.

Hiking directions: Take the unsigned but well-defined trail across the grassy flat towards the Salinas River. Descend through scrub brush, oaks, and sycamores to the streambed. Follow the Salinas River downstream 0.4 miles north to the trail's end at the Niblick Road bridge on the banks of the river. Just before trail's end, a side path bears right to a wide sandy path, extending the hike a short distance through a forested grove. On the return, watch for a distinct trail on the left, which crosses the grassy flat to a paved walking path at the north end of Lawrence Moore Park. The left fork ends at a circular turnaround by the mall. The right fork returns to the trailhead.

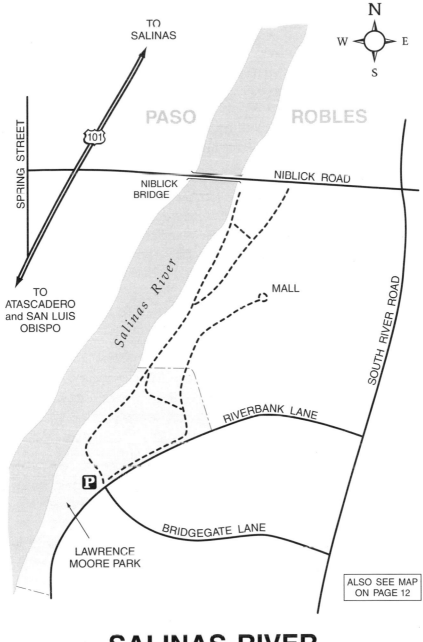

SALINAS RIVER
from LAWRENCE MOORE PARK

Hike 32
Anza National Historic Trail
NORTH ROUTE

Hiking distance: 5.8 miles round trip
Hiking time: 3 hours
Elevation: Level
Maps: U.S.G.S. Atascadero and Templeton
Juan Bautista de Anza National Historic Trail map

Summary of hike: The Anza National Historic Trail follows a portion of the original route led by Juan Bautista de Anza in 1776. The expedition brought hundreds of settlers and more than a thousand head of livestock from Sonora, Mexico to Alta, California. This hike follows the path along the designated northern segment of the multi-purpose hiking, biking, birding, and equestrian trail. The trail winds through stands of cottonwoods, oaks, sycamores, and willows, parallel to the southern banks of the Salinas River. Spanish moss hangs over the limbs of the trees.

Driving directions: From Highway 101 in Atascadero, take the Curbaril Avenue exit and head 1.3 miles east, crossing the railroad tracks to Sycamore Road. Bear left and drive 1.7 miles to the signed trailhead access on the right, on the north side of 4545 Sycamore Road. Park alongside the road.

Hiking directions: Take the water company access road east (between the houses) to the trailhead gate. Bear left on the unpaved road and head northwest. At one mile is a road split at a well house. Take the left fork a hundred yards to a fenced home and trail fork. Bear right, continuing northwest. Various side paths branch off the main route. At 2.7 miles, pass through a shady oak grove to a trail loop near the railroad tracks. Return along the same path.

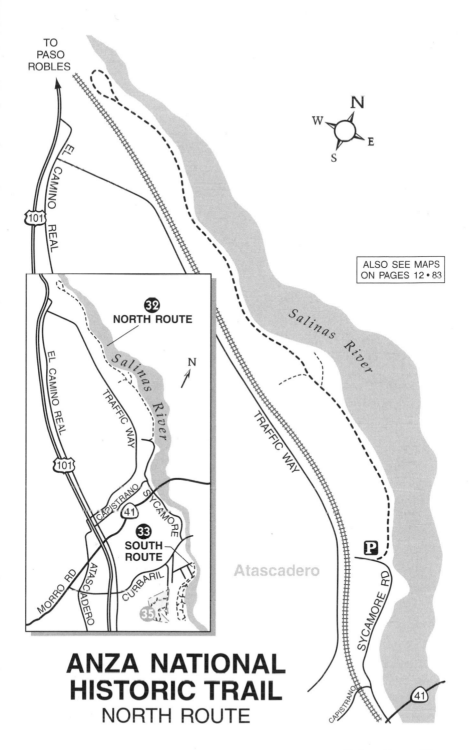

TO
PASO
ROBLES

EL CAMINO REAL

101

N
W   E
S

ALSO SEE MAPS
ON PAGES 12 • 83

Salinas River

32
NORTH ROUTE

Salinas River

N

EL CAMINO REAL

101

TRAFFIC WAY

TRAFFIC WAY

Salinas River

CAPISTRANO

SYCAMORE

41

33
SOUTH
ROUTE

P

MORRO RD

ATASCADERO

CURBARIL

35

Atascadero

SYCAMORE RD

CAPISTRANO

41

ANZA NATIONAL
HISTORIC TRAIL
NORTH ROUTE

Hike 33
Anza National Historic Trail
SOUTH ROUTE

Hiking distance: 2.2 miles round trip
Hiking time: 1.5 hours
Elevation: Level
Maps: U.S.G.S. Atascadero
      Juan Bautista de Anza National Historic Trail map

Summary of hike: The Anza National Historic Trail follows a portion of the original route from Sonora, Mexico to Alta, California led by Juan Bautista de Anza in 1776 (as described in Hike 32). This hike follows the designated southern segment of the multi-purpose hiking, biking, and equestrian trail in Atascadero. The trail meanders along the south bank of the Salinas River through riparian vegetation with stands of oaks, sycamores, cottonwoods, and willows.

Driving directions: From Highway 101 in Atascadero, exit on Curbaril Avenue and drive 1.1 miles east to Garbada Road, the first road after crossing the railroad tracks. Turn right and drive 0.2 miles to Tampico Road—turn left. Continue 0.2 miles to Aragon Road. Turn right and park on the left in the Wranglerette Arena parking area. The trailhead is on Aragon Road near the end of the block.

Hiking directions: Walk to the end of Aragon Road and through the opening in the brush. Take the well-defined path a hundred yards to a trail split. The left fork leads 0.3 miles downstream, dropping into a sandy streambed and ending at the river's edge. The right fork bears south 0.2 miles to another junction. These two trails parallel each other and intertwine with numerous connector trails. Both trails meander upstream between the disposal ponds on the west and the Salinas River on the east. Side paths lead to the river's edge. At 0.8 miles, the trail drops into a sandy creekbed between two ranches. This is a good turn-around spot.

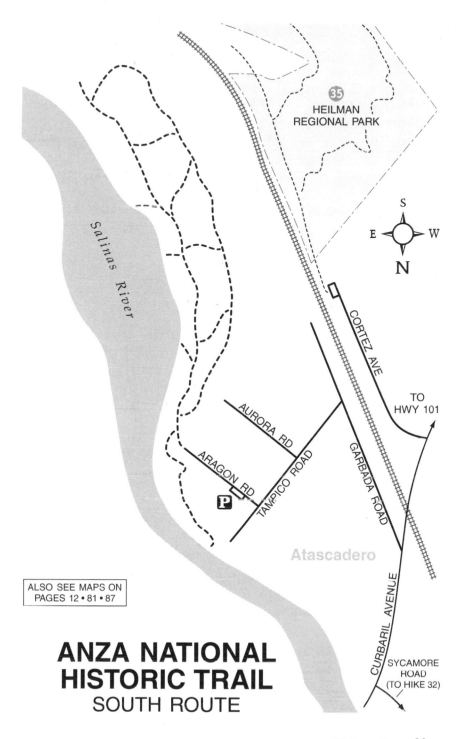

HEILMAN
REGIONAL PARK

35

Salinas River

S
E ✧ W
N

CORTEZ AVE

TO
HWY 101

AURORA RD

GARBADA ROAD

ARAGON RD

TAMPICO ROAD

P

Atascadero

CURBARIL AVENUE

SYCAMORE
ROAD
(TO HIKE 32)

ALSO SEE MAPS ON
PAGES 12 • 81 • 87

ANZA NATIONAL
HISTORIC TRAIL
SOUTH ROUTE

Hike 34
Blue Oak Trail
STADIUM PARK

Hiking distance: 1.3 mile loop
Hiking time: 30 minutes
Elevation gain: 160 feet
Maps: U.S.G.S. Atascadero

Summary of hike: Stadium Park is an undiscovered 26-acre gem tucked away in the heart of Atascadero. Located minutes from downtown, the pristine, bowl-shaped park has a natural amphitheater and sits among a forest of blue oaks. The Blue Oak Trail weaves through the canyon on the southwest flank of Pine Mountain and forms a loop around the hillsides surrounding the beautiful canyon.

Driving directions: From Highway 101 in Atascadero, exit on Morro Road/Highway 41. Head north on Highway 41 to Capistrano Avenue, the first left after El Camino Real. Turn left and continue a quarter mile to Hospital Drive. Turn right and drive 0.1 miles under the Highway 41 bridge to the park and parking area at the end of the road.

Hiking directions: Walk up the wide gravel road into the canyon covered in oaks and draped with lace lichen. A foot-path on the north hillside parallels the dirt road. The road and path end by a posted junction with the Blue Oak Trail in Stadium Canyon, a large, natural amphitheater. Bear left and head up the grassy canyon. At the head of the canyon floor, curve right, following the trail sign, and make a horseshoe right bend. Traverse the hillside through the oak forest along the contours of the hill, with several overlooks of the canyon and surrounding hills. Loop around the head of the canyon by a trail access from Pinal Avenue and Escarpa Avenue. Curve around to the west slope through groves of twisted oaks, returning to the canyon floor. Complete the loop and bear left to the trailhead.

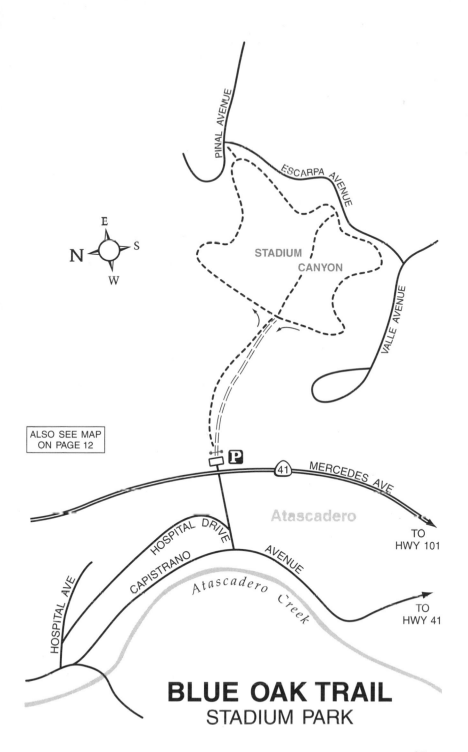

ALSO SEE MAP
ON PAGE 12

PINAL AVENUE

ESCARPA AVENUE

STADIUM
CANYON

VALLE AVENUE

E
N — S
W

P 41 MERCEDES AVE

Atascadero

TO
HWY 101

HOSPITAL DRIVE

CAPISTRANO AVENUE

HOSPITAL AVE

Atascadero Creek

TO
HWY 41

BLUE OAK TRAIL
STADIUM PARK

Hike 35
Jim Green Trail
HEILMAN REGIONAL PARK

Hiking distance: 1.5 mile loop
Hiking time: 1 hour
Elevation: 150 feet
Maps: U.S.G.S. Atascadero
  The Thomas Guide—San Luis Obispo County

Summary of hike: Heilman Regional Park sits in the southeast corner of Atascadero east of Highway 101. The forested park encompasses 315 acres with equestrian and hiking trails. The Jim Green Trail is accessed from the northern end of the park, off of Curbaril Avenue. The trail loops around the contours of the hillsides to scenic overlooks of Chalk Mountain Golf Course, the Salinas River, southern Atascadero, and the surrounding mountains. The path weaves through grassy meadows and groves of oak trees draped with strands of hanging moss.

Driving directions: From Highway 101 in Atascadero, exit on Curbaril Avenue, and drive one mile east to Cortez Avenue. Turn right and drive 0.2 miles to the parking lot on the left at the end of the road.

Hiking directions: Hike south past the trail sign between the railroad tracks and the pole-rail fence to a trail fork. The right fork is the return path. Continue straight ahead to a second trail split. The left fork continues parallel to the railroad tracks and ends at the golf course a short distance ahead. Take the right fork, gaining elevation across the oak-covered grassy hillside. Skirt the north edge of Chalk Mountain Golf Course to the ridge and a bench overlooking southern Atascadero, the surrounding mountains, sycamore-lined Salinas River, and the disposal ponds. The trail loops back along the ridge, descends through the forest, and crosses a meadow, completing the loop. Bear to the left, returning to the trailhead.

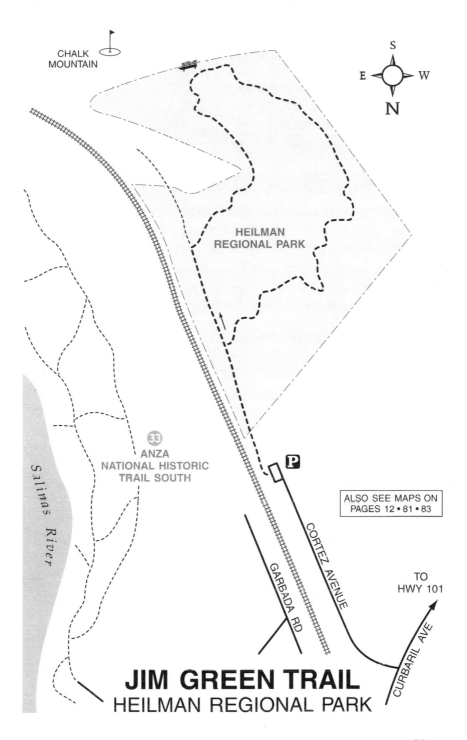

CHALK
MOUNTAIN

S
E ◇ W
N

HEILMAN
REGIONAL PARK

㉝
ANZA
NATIONAL HISTORIC
TRAIL SOUTH

Salinas River

P

ALSO SEE MAPS ON
PAGES 12 • 81 • 83

CORTEZ AVENUE

GARBADA RD

CURBARIL AVE

TO
HWY 101

JIM GREEN TRAIL
HEILMAN REGIONAL PARK

Hike 36
Atascadero Lake Loop

Hiking distance: 1.3 mile loop
Hiking time: 40 minutes
Elevation gain: Level
Maps: U.S.G.S. Atascadero

Summary of hike: Atascadero Lake Park is a popular desti-
nation for the community of Atascadero. The 35-acre park is
home to the 5-acre Charles Paddock Zoo (dating back to
1955), sports fields, a tree-filled grassy picnic area with a playground, and the centerpiece of the park, Atascadero Lake. The
lake has a fishing pier and boat rentals. This hike follows a
popular walking path that circles the lake. The hike is not a backcountry experience but is a charming respite within the city.

Driving directions: From Highway 101 in Atascadero, exit
on Morro Road/Highway 41. Head 1.4 miles southwest to Lago
Avenue on the left, located 0.1 miles past Portola Road. Turn
left into the Atascadero Lake Park and zoo parking lot.

From the south end of Atascadero, exit Highway 101 at Santa
Rosa Road. Drive 1.3 miles west on Santa Rosa Road to Morro
Road/Highway 41, passing the south end of Atascadero Lake
en route. Turn right and continue 0.1 miles to Lago Avenue. Turn
right into the parking lot.

Hiking directions: Walk past Charles Paddock Zoo into the
grassy parkland dotted with a mix of pine, spruce, maple, redwood, oak, cedar, and walnut trees. Straight ahead is the Lake
Pavilion. Bear left, past the bird and tree information boards, to
the wooden bridge by the playground equipment. Cross the
footbridge over the outlet stream of Atascadero Creek, and
cross the dam to the east side of Atascadero Lake. Follow the
east edge of the lake along Lake View Drive. Meander along the
curvature of the lake to the forested island at the south end of
the lake. At 0.7 miles is the southern parking area, just off Santa
Rosa Road. Loop around the south end, with close-up views of

the island. Cross a bridge over the creek's inlet stream, and parallel Santa Rosa Road on the edge of the lake between the island and the shore. Head north, staying close to the shore along Marchant Way. Beyond the island, views open up across the lake. At the lake's north end, return to the Lake Pavilion by Pismo Avenue.

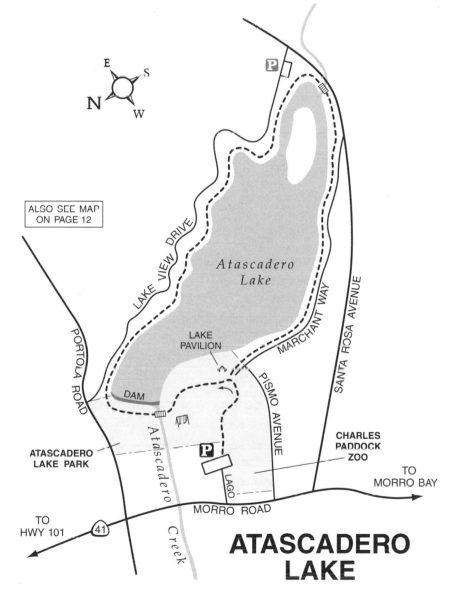

Hike 37
Cerro Alto Peak

Hiking distance: 4 miles round trip
Hiking time: 2.5 hours
Elevation: 1,650 feet
Maps: U.S.G.S. Atascadero
        The Mountain Biking Map for San Luis Obispo

Summary of hike: Cerro Alto Peak has spectacular, unlimited 360-degree vistas of the county's beautiful landscape. The peak rises to 2,624 feet and lies in the Los Padres National Forest between Morro Bay and Atascadero. From the summit the views to the south include Morro Bay, Estero Bay, the Irish Hills, Oceano, and the Guadalupe dunes. The northern view extends to Cambria, San Simeon, and the Piedras Blancas Lighthouse. The line of volcanic morros from Morro Rock to Islay Hill lies to the east, along with Chorro Valley, San Luis Obispo, the Cuesta Ridge, and the Santa Lucia Range.

Driving directions: From Highway 101 in Atascadero, take the Highway 41 West/Morro Bay exit, and head 8.7 miles west to the Cerro Alto Campground turnoff. Turn left and continue 0.9 miles up the winding road to the parking lot at the end of the road. A parking fee is required.
    From Highway 1 in Morro Bay, head 7.2 miles east on Highway 41 to the campground turnoff on the right.

Hiking directions: From the parking area, return back down the road 20 yards to the signed trail on the left by campsite 16. Descend into a forest of bays and live oaks, then cross a wooden bridge over the East Fork of Morro Creek. Switchbacks lead through the forest onto the chaparral-covered hillside. Continue up the drainage to a signed junction with the AT&T Cable Road at 0.7 miles. The right fork leads to the West Cuesta Ridge Trail (Hike 39). Bear left for 200 yards uphill to a signed junction on the right with the Cerro Alto Summit Trail to the peak. The trail curves along the edge of the mountainside, crossing two drainages to a junction. The right fork, straight ahead, follows the Lookout Road to the summit and also connects with the TV Tower Road on West Cuesta Ridge (Hike 87). Bear left, circling the peak 0.3 miles up to the summit. After resting and marveling at the views, return by retracing your steps.

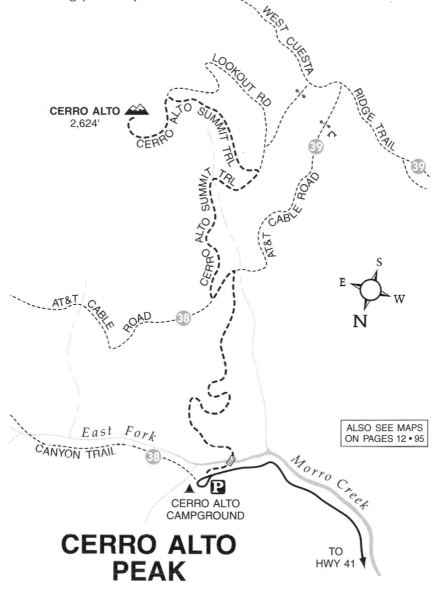

ALSO SEE MAPS
ON PAGES 12 • 95

CERRO ALTO
PEAK

Hike 38
Cerro Alto Loop Trail

Hiking distance: 2.5 mile loop
Hiking time: 1.5 hours
Elevation: 640 feet
Maps: U.S.G.S. Atascadero
  The Mountain Biking Map for San Luis Obispo

map
next page

Summary of hike: For those who wish to enjoy the Cerro Alto area without climbing 1,600 feet to the peak (Hike 37), the Cerro Alto Loop Trail is perfect. The trail parallels the upper East Fork of Morro Creek up a lush narrow canyon with oak, sycamore, and cottonwood. The hike traverses the mountain slopes to various overlooks, then descends into an oak woodland.

Driving directions: From Highway 101 in Atascadero, take the Highway 41 West/Morro Bay exit, and head 8.7 miles west to the Cerro Alto Campground turnoff. Turn left and continue 0.9 miles up the winding road to the parking lot at the end of the road. A parking fee is required.
  From Highway 1 in Morro Bay, head 7.2 miles east on Highway 41 to the campground turnoff on the right.

Hiking directions: From the east end of the parking area by campsite 19, take the signed Cerro Alto Trail. Traverse up the north wall of the canyon through an oak and bay forest above the fern-lined creek. Cross the East Fork of Morro Creek, climbing the west wall to the head of the canyon. At 0.8 miles is a signed junction with the AT&T Cable Road. Go right towards the summit, bearing right past two intersecting trails on the left to an overlook above the canyon. Heading west, follow the contours of Cerro Alto to overlooks of Morro Bay and the estuary. At 1.5 miles is a junction with the Cerro Alto Summit Trail (Hike 37). Stay to the right, heading downhill to a signed junction 200 yards ahead. Bear right (north), down the hillside. Switchbacks lead into a live oak forest. Cross the bridge over the East Fork of Morro Creek, returning to the campground by the parking lot.

Hike 39
Boy Scout—West Cuesta Ridge—AT&T Loop

Hiking distance: 4.8 mile loop
Hiking time: 3 hours
Elevation gain: 1,050 feet
Maps: U.S.G.S. Morro Bay North and Atascadero
       The Mountain Biking Map for San Luis Obispo

map
next page

Summary of hike: The Boy Scout Trail is a connector trail from the Cerro Alto Campground road to West Cuesta Ridge. The trail climbs from the East Fork of Morro Creek in a lush oak-filled forest to the ridge, which overlooks the San Luis Obispo coastline and a string of morros. The hike traverses the ridge through a beautiful eucalyptus grove and descends along the west flank of Cerro Alto in a stream-fed drainage.

Driving directions: From Highway 101 in Atascadero, take the Highway 41 West/Morro Bay exit. Head 8.7 miles west to the Cerro Alto Campground turnoff. Turn left and drive 0.1 miles to the Forest Service kiosk and metal gate. Park in the large pull-outs on either side of the road. A parking fee is required.

From Highway 1 in Morro Bay, head 7.2 miles east on Highway 41 to the posted campground turnoff on the right.

Hiking directions: Take the path along the right side of the road 20 yards. Drop down and cross the East Fork of Morro Creek by a concrete spillway. Walk under a canopy of massive twisted oaks and a poison oak ground cover, following the base of the mountain. Curve left and climb the east wall of the forested canyon. Cross over the drainage, and emerge from the shady canopy to the open slopes. Climb to a finger ridge as coastal views open up. Curve left and follow the spine uphill to the open, rolling flat and a T-junction at the top of the mountain with the West Cuesta Ridge Road at 0.9 miles. The right fork slopes downhill 0.15 miles to an overlook of the coastline, Morro Rock, Morro Bay Estuary, Cerro Cabrillo, Hollister Peak, and the Irish Hills. Bear left and head up the easy incline, passing a side path on the left. Curve right, looping around a hill to sweeping vistas south and west. Descend to a horseshoe left bend by an old mine dump on the right at 1.6 miles. Around the bend is a Y-fork. The right fork leads to Sweetwater Mine. Stay to the left into a draw with a gorgeous eucalyptus grove. Weave through the fragrant grove to a Y-fork. To the left is a grassy meadow rimmed with trees. Continue straight on the main trail, with eastward views of the chain of volcanic morros, to a T-junction at the southwest foot of Cerro Alto at 2.5 miles. The right fork continues on the West Cuesta Ridge Road. The left fork is the Cerro Alto Road at the trail gate. For this hike, walk back 150 yards to the distinct AT&T Cable Road, now on your right. Head north along the base of Cerro Alto, and pass a rusted trail gate and a maintenance shed. Meander through tall brush and descend along the west wall of the stream-fed canyon. Cross the drainage to a posted junction. The Summit Trail to Cerro Alto is straight ahead (Hike 37). Bear left and head downhill, perched on the cliffside. Enter a dense oak forest to the East Fork of Morro Creek. Cross the wooden bridge to the campground near the end of the entrance road. Bear left and walk 0.8 miles down the forested road, completing the loop by the trailhead.

HIKE 38
CERRO ALTO LOOP TRAIL
HIKE 39
BOY SCOUT–WEST CUESTA RIDGE–AT&T LOOP

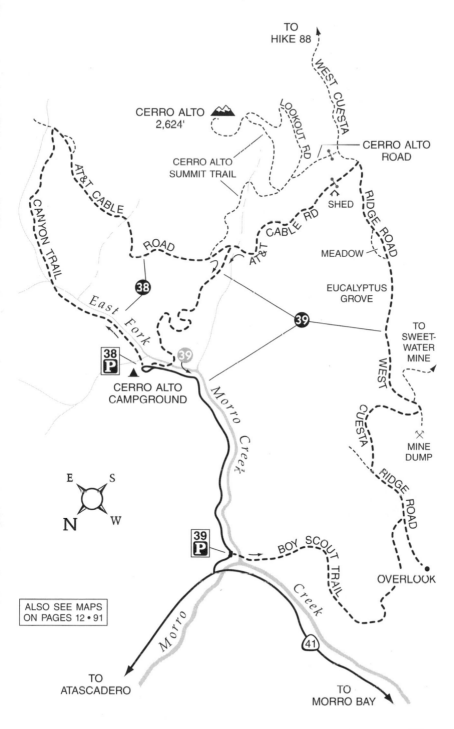

TO
HIKE 88

WEST CUESTA

CERRO ALTO
2,624'

CERRO ALTO
ROAD

LOOKOUT RD

CERRO ALTO
SUMMIT TRAIL

AT&T CABLE
ROAD

SHED

RIDGE ROAD

AT&T CABLE RD

MEADOW

38

EUCALYPTUS
GROVE

CANYON TRAIL

East Fork

39

TO
SWEET-
WATER
MINE

38
P

39

CERRO ALTO
CAMPGROUND

Morro Creek

WEST CUESTA RIDGE ROAD

MINE
DUMP

E   S

N   W

39
P

BOY SCOUT TRAIL

OVERLOOK

ALSO SEE MAPS
ON PAGES 12 • 91

Morro

Creek

41

TO
ATASCADERO

TO
MORRO BAY

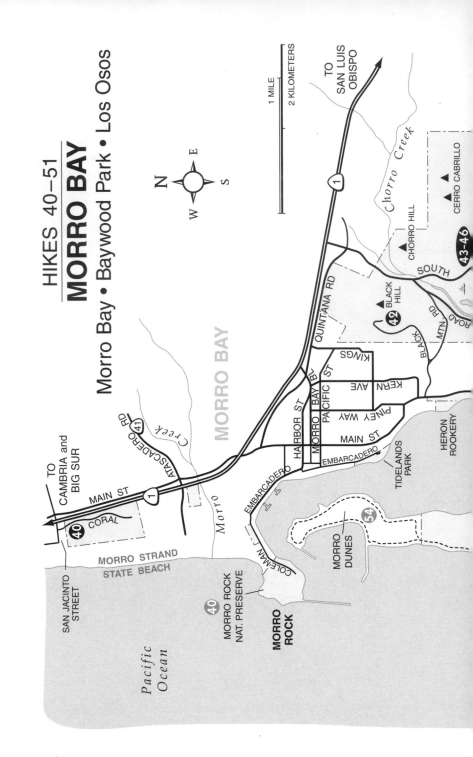

HIKES 40–51
MORRO BAY
Morro Bay • Baywood Park • Los Osos

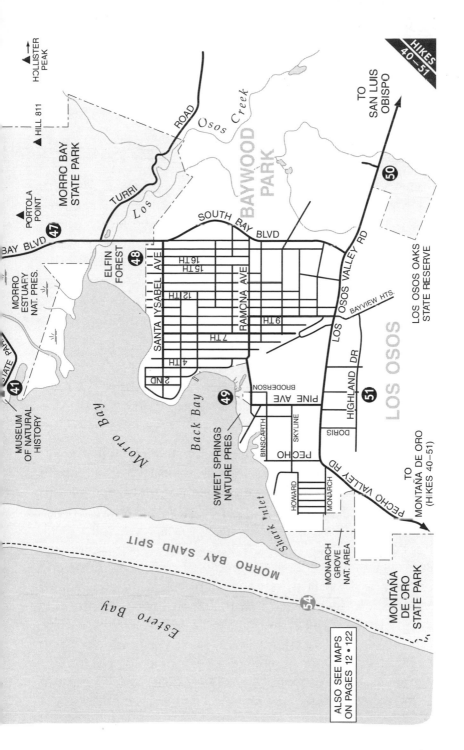

HOLLISTER PEAK

HILL 811

MORRO BAY STATE PARK

PORTOLA POINT

BAY BLVD

47

Osos Creek

Osos

ROAD

TURRI

Los

BAYWOOD PARK

SOUTH BAY BLVD

TO SAN LUIS OBISPO

50

LOS OSOS VALLEY RD

ELFIN FOREST

48

MORRO ESTUAFY NAT. PRES.

SANTA YSABEL AVE

16TH

15TH

12TH

RAMONA AVE

9TH

7TH

4TH

2ND

BAYVIEW HTS.

LOS OSOS OAKS STATE RESERVE

LOS OSOS

LOS

HIGHLAND DR

51

DORIS

STATE PARK

41

MUSEUM OF NATURAL HISTORY

Morro Bay

Back Bay

Shark Inlet

SWEET SPRINGS NATURE PRES.

49

BRODERSON

PINE AVE

BINSCARTH

SKYLINE

PECHO

HOWARD

MONARCH

PECHO VALLEY RD

TO MONTAÑA DE ORO (HIKES 40–51)

MONARCH GROVE NAT. AREA

MONTAÑA DE ORO STATE PARK

Estero Bay

MORRO BAY SAND SPIT

54

ALSO SEE MAPS ON PAGES 12 • 122

Hike 40
Cloisters Wetland to Morro Rock

Hiking distance: 3.5 miles round trip
Hiking time: 1.5 hours
Elevation gain: Level
Maps: U.S.G.S. Morro Bay North and Morro Bay South

Summary of hike: The Cloisters Wetland is a 2.6-acre wildlife habitat with a freshwater lagoon. A trail with interpretive signs circles the lagoon. The hike crosses Morro Strand State Beach to Morro Rock, a dome-shaped volcanic plug rising from the ocean at the mouth of the harbor. This ancient 578-foot monolithic outcropping sits amidst a 30-acre wildlife preserve which is a protected nesting site for the peregrine falcon.

Driving directions: From Highway 1 in Morro Bay, head 2 miles north to San Jacinto Street and turn left. Drive to the first street and turn left again on Coral Avenue. Continue 0.3 miles and park in the Cloisters Community Park parking lot on the right.

Hiking directions: Take the paved path through the developed park along the south side of the lagoon. At the dunes is a junction. The right fork circles the Cloisters Wetland, a freshwater lagoon. Bear left and follow the path between the dunes and the park meadow towards the prominent Morro Rock. The trail curves through the dunes, crossing a wooden footbridge. Bear right and walk parallel to a row of pine trees to the end of the boardwalk at the sandy beach. Follow the shoreline of Morro Strand State Beach directly towards Morro Rock. Cross the sand isthmus to the base of the rock. Walk across the parking area and follow Coleman Drive (the paved road) clockwise around the perimeter of Morro Rock along the edge of the bay. At the west end of the rock is a sandy beach and breakwater at the entrance to the bay. Return along the same route.

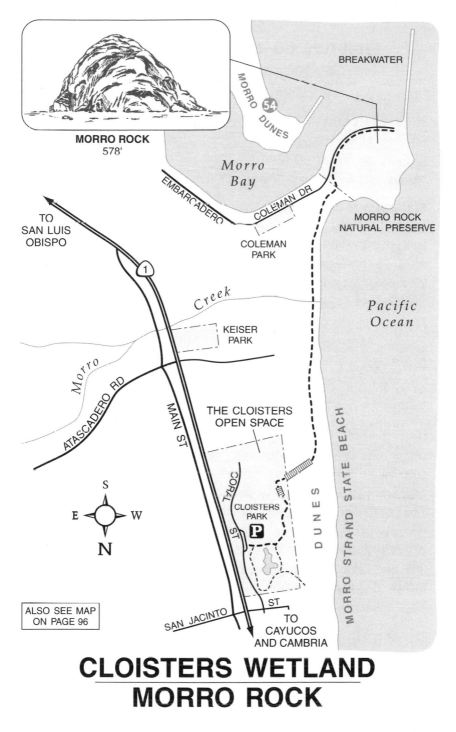

MORRO ROCK
578'

BREAKWATER

MORRO DUNES
54

Morro Bay

EMBARCADERO

COLEMAN DR

MORRO ROCK
NATURAL PRESERVE

TO
SAN LUIS
OBISPO

1

COLEMAN
PARK

Creek

Pacific
Ocean

KEISER
PARK

Morro

ATASCADERO RD

MAIN ST

THE CLOISTERS
OPEN SPACE

CORAL ST

CLOISTERS
PARK
P

MORRO STRAND STATE BEACH

DUNES

S
E W
N

ALSO SEE MAP
ON PAGE 96

SAN JACINTO

ST

TO
CAYUCOS
AND CAMBRIA

CLOISTERS WETLAND
MORRO ROCK

Hike 41
White Point: from the Museum to Heron Rookery and Marina Point
MORRO BAY STATE PARK

Hiking distance: 2 miles round trip
Hiking time: 1 hour
Elevation gain: 80 feet
Maps: U.S.G.S. Morro Bay South

map next page

Summary of hike: Morro Bay State Park is located along the lush inland side of Morro Bay. The 2,345-acre state park includes a massive estuary, a protected bird sanctuary, heron rookery, salt marsh, mudflats, dunes, pines, chaparral and riparian habitats, a golf course, campground, a small boat marina, and a history museum. The Heron Rookery Natural Preserve at Fairbank Point is a refuge for egrets, cormorants, and Great Blue Herons, which nest atop the eucalyptus and cypress trees. The protected rookery is the only remaining large rookery between San Francisco and Mexico. The Museum of Natural History is perched on White Point, overlooking the bay with an observation deck. There are interpretive exhibits about the bay's history, wildlife, ecology, geology, and Native American life. The Morro Estuary Natural Preserve, within the state park, extends four miles, linking the communities of Morro Bay, Baywood Park, and Los Osos. The estuary, where fresh and salt water mix, is fed by Chorro Creek and Los Osos Creek. It is protected from the ocean by the 4-mile-long Morro Dunes Sand Spit. The estuary is among the earth's richest and most productive habitats. This hike begins at the museum and follows the shoreline to the heron rookery and along the northwest corner of the estuary by the marina.

Driving directions: From the intersection of Los Osos Valley Road and South Bay Boulevard in Los Osos, drive 3.2 miles north on South Bay Boulevard to State Park Road. Turn left and continue 1.2 miles, following the north edge of the Morro

Bay Estuary, to the Museum of Natural History. Turn left and park.

From Highway 1 in Morro Bay, take the Los Osos/Baywood Park exit. Drive 0.7 miles south on South Bay Boulevard to State Park Road and turn right.

Hiking directions: After visiting the Museum of Natural History, walk back down the ramp and pick up the footpath in the cypress grove between the park road and Morro Bay. Head north along the bay toward Morro Rock. Climb a slope through the fragrant eucalyptus grove to the east edge of the protected heron rookery on Fairbank Point. The area allows observation, but access into the rookery is closed. Return to the museum and follow the paved, rock-lined walkway around forested White Point, 40 feet above the bay. The paved path ends at the south end of the parking lot. Descend steps toward the Morro Bay State Park Marina, or curve right through the eucalyptus grove, parallel to the park road. At the south end of the marina, pick up the posted footpath on the edge of the estuary. Cross the south end of the marina to a trail split. Begin the loop to the right, and head west to the tip of the spit protecting the marina. Circle Marina Point and return along the estuary on one of the parallel paths, determined by the tide level. Curve left to complete the loop, and return to the museum.

Hike 42
Black Hill
MORRO BAY STATE PARK

Hiking distance: 0.6—2.6 miles round trip
Hiking time: 30 minutes—1.5 hours
Elevation gain: 180—540 feet
Maps: U.S.G.S. Morro Bay South

map
next page

Summary of hike: Black Hill (also known as Black Mountain) is an ancient 661-foot volcanic peak in Morro Bay State Park. It is the second in the chain of nine morros, stretching from Morro

Rock (Hike 40) to Islay Hill (Hike 81) in San Luis Obispo. There is a short easy trail to the rocky summit and a longer forested route. The longer route climbs up the western face through the shade of a eucalyptus forest, an oak woodland, and Monterey pine groves. From the rocky summit are panoramic views of Morro Bay and the estuary, Estero Point, Cayucos, Chorro Valley, and the nearby morros of Cerro Cabrillo and Hollister Peak. The ocean views span from Montaña de Oro to San Simeon.

Driving directions: From Highway 101 south of San Luis Obispo, take the Los Osos Valley Road exit, and head 9.6 miles west to South Bay Boulevard. Turn right and continue 3.2 miles to State Park Road and turn left.

From Highway 1 in Morro Bay, take the Los Osos/Baywood Park exit. Head 0.7 miles south on South Bay Boulevard to State Park Road and turn right.

FOR THE LONG HIKE, bear right 0.1 mile ahead at a road fork, and head up Park View Drive for 0.3 miles to a parking pullout on the left.

FOR THE SHORT HIKE, bear right 0.1 mile ahead at a road fork and head 0.6 miles up Park View Drive to the unsigned Black Mountain Road and turn right. Continue 0.7 miles through the golf course to the trailhead parking area at the end of the road.

Hiking directions: For the long hike, walk 100 yards up the road to the trail on the right with the "no bikes" sign. Head north across a meadow, dropping into a ravine to a T-junction. Bear left through a eucalyptus grove past an intersecting trail on the right. A short distance ahead is a third junction. Bear right, gaining elevation through an oak woodland. At one mile, loop around the right side of a cement water tank to the upper trailhead parking lot. This is where the short hike begins. Head northeast up several switchbacks to the summit. After marveling at the views, return by retracing your steps.

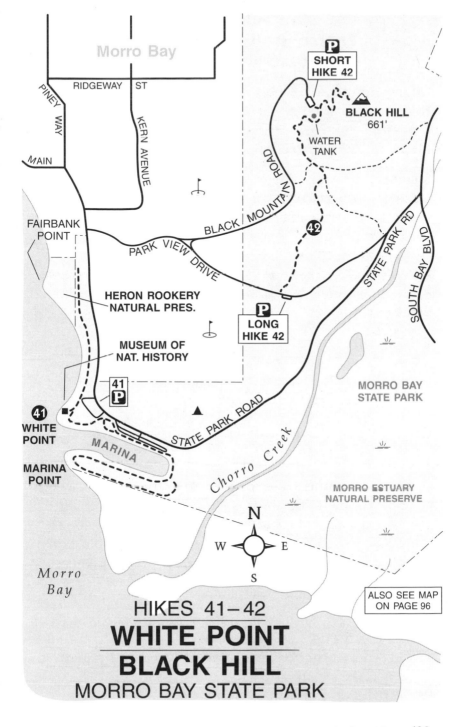

Morro Bay

RIDGEWAY ST

PINEY WAY

KERN AVENUE

MAIN

FAIRBANK POINT

PARK VIEW DRIVE

BLACK MOUNTAIN ROAD

P SHORT HIKE 42

▲ **BLACK HILL** 661'

WATER TANK

42

STATE PARK RD

SOUTH BAY BLVD

HERON ROOKERY NATURAL PRES.

P LONG HIKE 42

MUSEUM OF NAT. HISTORY

41 **P**

41 WHITE POINT

MARINA

MARINA POINT

STATE PARK ROAD

Chorro Creek

MORRO BAY STATE PARK

MORRO ESTUARY NATURAL PRESERVE

N
W • E
S

Morro Bay

ALSO SEE MAP ON PAGE 96

HIKES 41–42
WHITE POINT
BLACK HILL
MORRO BAY STATE PARK

Hike 43
Chorro Trail to Turtle Rock
MORRO BAY STATE PARK

Hiking distance: 1.8 miles round trip
Hiking time: 1 hour
Elevation gain: 200 feet
Maps: U.S.G.S. Morro Bay South

Summary of hike: Chorro Hill (also known as Turtle Rock) is a 209-foot rounded outcropping in Morro Bay State Park. The rocky hill sits to the east of Black Hill (Hike 42) and at the northwest base of Cerro Cabrillo (Hike 46). Monterey pines grow around the rocky peak. The summit overlooks the four-mile expanse of Morro Bay and the Morro Estuary Natural Preserve, a bird and wildlife habitat where the fresh water of Chorro Creek and Los Osos Creek mix with the salt water of the ocean.

Driving directions: From Highway 101 south of San Luis Obispo, take the Los Osos Valley Road exit, and head 9.6 miles west to South Bay Boulevard. Turn right and continue 2.6 miles to the trailhead parking lot on the right.

From Highway 1 in Morro Bay, take the Los Osos/Baywood Park exit. Drive 1.4 miles south on South Bay Boulevard to the trailhead parking lot on the left.

Hiking directions: Take the signed Quarry Trail east up the scrubby slope. At 200 yards is a trail on the left. Bear left on the Chorro Trail, and curve around the lower west slope of Cerro Cabrillo above South Bay Road. Notice the marbled effect of the streams meandering through the Morro Bay estuary. Once around the western flank of Cerro Cabrillo, descend to a fenced service road. Veer to the right, following the road up to Chorro Hill. At the top of the road is a locked gate and fenceline at the park boundary. Take the footpath to the left, winding up to the rocky summit. The final ascent curves around large boulders to the Monterey pines at the summit. After enjoying the views, return on the same trail.

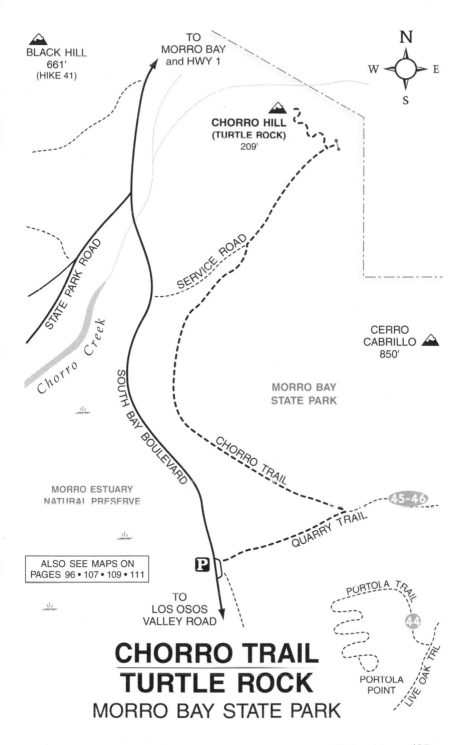

N
W • E
S

BLACK HILL
661'
(HIKE 41)

TO
MORRO BAY
and HWY 1

CHORRO HILL
(TURTLE ROCK)
209'

STATE PARK ROAD

SERVICE ROAD

Chorro Creek

CERRO
CABRILLO
850'

MORRO BAY
STATE PARK

SOUTH BAY BOULEVARD

CHORRO TRAIL

MORRO ESTUARY
NATURAL PRESERVE

45-46

QUARRY TRAIL

ALSO SEE MAPS ON
PAGES 96 • 107 • 109 • 111

P

TO
LOS OSOS
VALLEY ROAD

PORTOLA TRAIL

44

PORTOLA
POINT

LIVE OAK TRL

CHORRO TRAIL
TURTLE ROCK
MORRO BAY STATE PARK

Hike 44
Portola Point
MORRO BAY STATE PARK

Hiking distance: 2 mile loop
Hiking time: 1 hour
Elevation gain: 320 feet
Maps: U.S.G.S. Morro Bay South
The Mountain Biking Map for San Luis Obispo

Summary of hike: Portola Hill is a 329-foot rounded volcanic hill on the east side of Morro Bay State Park. The route loops around the base of the hill. A spur trail leads up to Portola Point, offering sweeping views of the surrounding morros and the Morro Bay area, one of the most vital and productive bird habitats in the country. The hike follows the Quarry and Live Oak Trails across rolling native grassland and through oak groves thriving in the shelter of the hills.

Driving directions: From Highway 101 south of San Luis Obispo, take the Los Osos Valley Road exit, and head 9.6 miles west to South Bay Boulevard. Turn right and continue 2.6 miles to the trailhead parking lot on the right.
From Highway 1 in Morro Bay, take the Los Osos/Baywood Park exit. Drive 1.4 miles south on South Bay Boulevard to the trailhead parking lot on the left.

Hiking directions: Take the signed Quarry Trail uphill through the sage scrub. Head east along the south-facing slopes of Cerro Cabrillo to a signed junction at 0.5 miles. Take the Live Oak Trail to the right, descending across a grassy meadow towards Portola Hill. Near the base of the hill is a signed trail fork. Bear right on the Portola Trail, and ascend the hill past an oak grove. Switchbacks lead up to a trail split, circling the point to various overlooks and a resting bench. Complete the loop and return to the Live Oak Trail. Go right and descend into the draw between Portola Hill and Hill 811. At 1.5

miles is a signed trail split. Bear right, contouring around Portola Hill on the Live Oak Trail. Return to the parking lot.

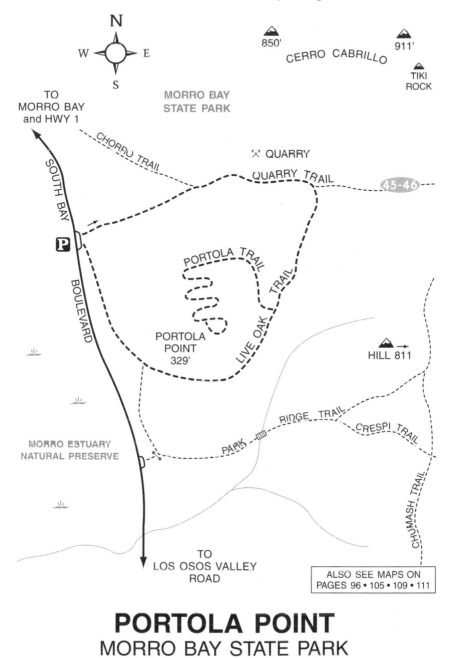

PORTOLA POINT
MORRO BAY STATE PARK

Hike 45
Quarry and Park Ridge Loop
MORRO BAY STATE PARK

Hiking distance: 2.5 mile loop
Hiking time: 1 hour
Elevation gain: 350 feet
Maps: U.S.G.S. Morro Bay South
The Mountain Biking Map for San Luis Obispo

Summary of hike: The Quarry and Park Ridge Trails are on the east side of Morro Bay State Park under the shadow of Cerro Cabrillo, a 911-foot double-peaked ridge. In 1959, volcanic rock was blasted out of the south shoulder of Cerro Cabrillo and used for paving Highway 1. Remnants from the abandoned quarry still remain. The Quarry Trail skirts the southern flank of Cerro Cabrillo past the rubble piles of the old quarry site. Park Ridge is the crested elevation between Cerro Cabrillo and Hollister Peak. The Park Ridge Trail is an old farm road that crosses rolling grasslands over a group of minor rises. From the end of the trail are sweeping vistas of Chorro Valley to the Cuesta Ridge.

Driving directions: From Highway 101 south of San Luis Obispo, take the Los Osos Valley Road exit, and head 9.6 miles west to South Bay Boulevard. Turn right and continue 2.6 miles to the trailhead parking lot on the right.

From Highway 1 in Morro Bay, take the Los Osos/Baywood Park exit. Drive 1.4 miles south on South Bay Boulevard to the trailhead parking lot on the left.

Hiking directions: Take the signed Quarry Trail toward the foot of Cerro Cabrillo. The trail parallels the base of the mountain, passing the quarry site on the left. Continue past the Live Oak Trail on the right (Hike 44) to a junction at 0.9 miles with the Park Ridge Trail on the right. Stay on the Quarry Trail, heading east to the signed junction with the Canet Trail on the right. The Quarry Trail ends 0.2 miles ahead at the fenced park boundary. Take the Canet Trail south, crossing the rolling hill to a saddle and a junction. Bear left on the Park Ridge Trail, and head downhill to a trail split with the Chumash Trail. Veer right and stay right again at a junction with the Crespi Trail (Hike 47). Cross a small bridge, returning to a gate near South Bay Boulevard. Bear right (north) on the Live Oak Trail back to the parking lot.

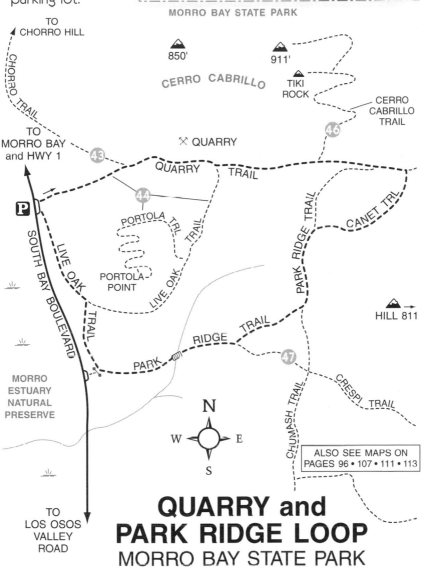

MORRO BAY STATE PARK

TO CHORRO HILL

CHORRO TRAIL

TO MORRO BAY and HWY 1

850'

911'

CERRO CABRILLO

TIKI ROCK

CERRO CABRILLO TRAIL

46

QUARRY

43

QUARRY TRAIL

44

PORTOLA TRL

TRAIL

PARK RIDGE TRAIL

CANET TRL

P

SOUTH BAY BOULEVARD

LIVE OAK

PORTOLA POINT

LIVE OAK

TRAIL

HILL 811

RIDGE TRAIL

PARK

RIDGE TRAIL

47

CHUMASH TRAIL

CRESPI TRAIL

MORRO ESTUARY NATURAL PRESERVE

N

W E

S

ALSO SEE MAPS ON PAGES 96 • 107 • 111 • 113

TO LOS OSOS VALLEY ROAD

QUARRY and PARK RIDGE LOOP
MORRO BAY STATE PARK

Hike 46
Cerro Cabrillo Peak
MORRO BAY STATE PARK

Hiking distance: 3 miles round trip
Hiking time: 2 hours
Elevation gain: 900 feet
Maps: U.S.G.S. Morro Bay South

Summary of hike: Cerro Cabrillo is the third in a chain of nine prehistoric volcanic plugs, stretching in a line from Morro Rock (Hike 40) to Islay Hill in San Luis Obispo (Hike 81). Cerro Cabrillo sits at the base of the Morro Estuary Natural Preserve. The elongated morro is saddle shaped with double peaks of 850 feet and 911 feet. The hike follows the Quarry Trail across rolling grasslands to the east end of Cerro Cabrillo and steeply climbs to the 911-foot summit. From the peak are sweeping 360-degree views from the coastline to the Santa Lucia Mountains.

Driving directions: Same as Hike 45.

Hiking directions: Take the signed Quarry Trail east up the scrubby slope. Pass the Chorro Trail on the left (Hike 43) at the base of Cerro Cabrillo. Traverse the southern base of the 911-foot morro, overlooking the park's trail system to the south and passing the old quarry on the left. Steadily climb on the elevated perch between Cerro Cabrillo and Portola Hill, heading toward prominent Hollister Peak. Continue past the junction with the Live Oak Trail, where Tiki Rock comes into view high on the east slope of Cerro Cabrillo. Cross a large sloping meadow to the Cerro Cabrillo Trail by a distinct 6-foot boulder. Bear left and climb the foothill to the east face of Cerro Cabrillo. At the upper end of the 400-foot meadow are vistas up Chorro Valley to the Santa Lucia Mountains, Morro Bay, Baywood Park, Los Osos, the estuary, and the Irish Hills. This is a good turn-around spot for a rewarding hike. Beyond this point the hike is steep and on the return, the loose gravel can be very slippery. Use good judgment and caution.

To hike further, begin the steep ascent of Cerro Cabrillo beneath Tiki Rock. Three switchbacks lead to the ridge. Curve left and follow the steep ridge. Just below the summit is a Y fork. A narrow side path on the left leads 40 yards to Tiki Rock. The main trail veers right and climbs up a jumble of boulders. Climb the rocks, picking your way to the summit. After savoring the views, carefully return along the same route.

CHORRO HILL

MORRO BAY STATE PARK

CHORRO TRAIL

N
W E
S

850'

911'

CERRO CABRILLO

TIKI ROCK

CERRO CABRILLO TRAIL

TO MORRO BAY and HWY 1

43

QUARRY

QUARRY TRAIL

44

PORTOLA TRL

LIVE OAK TRAIL

PORTOLA POINT

45

PARK RIDGE TRAIL

CANET TRL

SOUTH BAY BOULEVARD

P

HILL 811 and HOLLISTER PEAK

MORRO ESTUARY NATURAL PRESERVE

47

CRESPI TRAIL

TO LOS OSOS VALLEY ROAD

ALSO SEE MAPS ON PAGES 96 • 105 • 107 • 109

CERRO CABRILLO PEAK
MORRO BAY STATE PARK

Hike 47
Crespi Trail
MORRO BAY STATE PARK

Hiking distance: 3.2 mile loop
Hiking time: 1.5 hours
Elevation gain: 300 feet
Maps: U.S.G.S. Morro Bay South
 The Mountain Biking Map For San Luis Obispo

Summary of hike: The verdant rolling grasslands on the eastern portion of Morro Bay State Park were once part of the Baptista and Pedro Ranches. A well-signed trail system weaves through this undeveloped ranchland. The Crespi Trail, south of Cerro Cabrillo, winds across the hills through coastal sage scrub and pockets of coastal live oak. There are sweeping views of the expansive Morro Bay Estuary to the west and 1,409-foot Hollister Peak to the east.

Driving directions: From Highway 101 south of San Luis Obispo, take the Los Osos Valley Road exit, and head 9.6 miles west to South Bay Boulevard. Turn right and continue 2.2 miles to the trailhead parking area on the right.
 From Highway 1 in Morro Bay, take the Los Osos/Baywood Park exit. Drive 1.8 miles south on South Bay Boulevard to the trailhead parking lot on the left.

Hiking directions: Head east on the Park Ridge Trail across the rolling grasslands, and cross a seasonal streambed. Continue past a large outcropping on the left to a signed trail split at 0.3 miles. The left fork is the Park Ridge Trail (Hike 45). Bear right on the Crespi Trail to a 4-way junction with the Chumash Trail at 0.5 miles. Continue straight ahead, staying on the Crespi Trail along the hillside to a saddle. Descend into the drainage to a canopy of coastal live oak. Cross the creek and curve to the right down the drainage. Return up the hillside, curving west to a junction. Bear right on the Chumash Trail, completing the loop at a junction with the Crespi Trail. Go left and return to the trailhead.

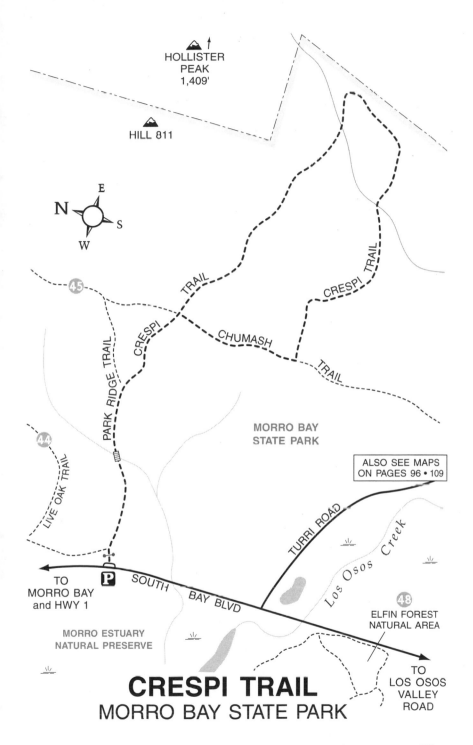

HOLLISTER
PEAK
1,409'

HILL 811

E
N S
W

45

TRAIL

CRESPI TRAIL

PARK RIDGE TRAIL

CRESPI

CHUMASH

TRAIL

44

LIVE OAK TRAIL

MORRO BAY
STATE PARK

ALSO SEE MAPS
ON PAGES 96 • 109

TURRI ROAD

Los Osos Creek

TO
MORRO BAY
and HWY 1

P

SOUTH BAY BLVD

48

ELFIN FOREST
NATURAL AREA

MORRO ESTUARY
NATURAL PRESERVE

TO
LOS OSOS
VALLEY
ROAD

CRESPI TRAIL
MORRO BAY STATE PARK

Hike 48
Elfin Forest Natural Area

Hiking distance: 1.5 miles round trip
Hiking time: 1 hour
Elevation gain: 100 feet
Maps: U.S.G.S. Morro Bay South

Summary of hike: The Elfin Forest Natural Area is a 90-acre refuge on an ancient sand dune on the shore of Morro Bay, abutting the estuary. A mile of wooden walkways with two viewing platforms and overlooks form an oval loop around the coastal slope. The area includes a salt marsh, coastal dune scrub, morro manzanita, riparian woodland, and dense stands of dwarfed 500-year-old pygmy oaks. The gnarled, windswept oaks have room-like openings and are draped with moss and lichens.

Driving directions: From Highway 101 south of San Luis Obispo, take the Los Osos Valley Road exit, and head 9.6 miles west to South Bay Boulevard. Turn right and continue 1.4 miles to Santa Ysabel Avenue on the left. Turn left and drive to 16th Street. Turn right and park at the end of the block. The trail system can also be accessed from the north ends of 11th through 17th Streets.

From Highway 1 in Morro Bay, take the Los Osos/Baywood Park exit. Drive 2.7 miles south on South Bay Boulevard to Santa Ysabel Avenue. Turn right and follow the directions above.

Hiking directions: Head north at the end of 16th Street on the Monterey pine boardwalk. Walk through the dense sage scrub to the ridge overlooking the Morro Bay estuary. Bear left (west), following the Ridge Trail boardwalk to an overlook at the west end. Sandy paths return to the street accesses. From the overlook, return east 150 yards to a junction and bear left. Descend to the Celestial Meadow Trail. The left fork leads to another overlook platform at the edge of the estuary. The right fork heads uphill to a junction with the Ridge Trail. En route,

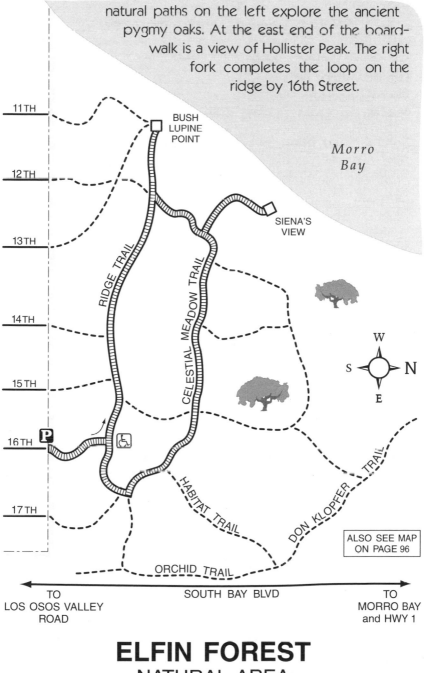

natural paths on the left explore the ancient pygmy oaks. At the east end of the board-walk is a view of Hollister Peak. The right fork completes the loop on the ridge by 16th Street.

11TH

BUSH
LUPINE
POINT

*Morro
Bay*

12TH

SIENA'S
VIEW

13TH

RIDGE TRAIL

CELESTIAL MEADOW TRAIL

14TH

W

S ✦ N

15TH

E

P

16TH

17TH

HABITAT TRAIL

DON KLOPFER TRAIL

ALSO SEE MAP
ON PAGE 96

ORCHID TRAIL

TO
LOS OSOS VALLEY
ROAD

SOUTH BAY BLVD

TO
MORRO BAY
and HWY 1

ELFIN FOREST
NATURAL AREA

Hike 49
Sweet Springs Nature Preserve

Hiking distance: 0.5 to 1 mile round trip
Hiking time: 30 minutes
Elevation gain: Level
Maps: U.S.G.S. Morro Bay South

Summary of hike: Sweet Springs Nature Preserve is a 24-acre wetland sanctuary for nesting and migrating birds. The preserve is located in Baywood Park on the southeast shore of Morro Bay. There are two serene freshwater ponds, a saltwater marsh at the bay, Monterey cypress, and eucalyptus groves. The eucalyptus groves are home to monarch butterflies during the winter months. The preserve is managed by the Morro Coast Audubon Society.

Driving directions: From Highway 101 south of San Luis Obispo, take the Los Osos Valley Road exit, and head 10.1 miles west to 9th Street (0.5 miles past South Bay Boulevard). Turn right and drive 0.6 miles to Ramona Avenue, curving to the left. Continue 0.5 miles to the nature preserve on the right. Park along the road.

From Highway 1 in Morro Bay, take the Los Osos/Baywood Park exit. Drive 4 miles south on South Bay Boulevard to Los Osos Valley Road and turn right. Continue 0.5 miles to 9th Street and turn right. Continue with directions above.

Hiking directions: From the preserve entrance gate, walk past the trail sign and cross a wooden footbridge over the pond. Bear left to a second wooden bridge. Towards the right is a maze of waterways winding through the estuary. After crossing the bridge, the trail weaves through a eucalyptus grove. At the west end of the preserve is a junction. The left fork returns to the road at Broderson Street. The right fork leads to an overlook of the bay and marshy tidelands. Morro Rock can be seen at the north end of the bay. Return to the first bridge. Bear to the left, heading east alongside the pond. The

trail loops back through another eucalyptus grove and returns
to the park entrance.

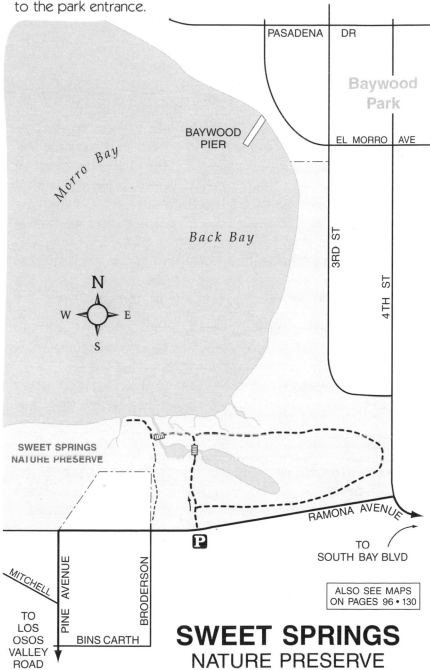

PASADENA DR

Baywood
Park

BAYWOOD
PIER

EL MORRO AVE

Morro Bay

Back Bay

3RD ST

4TH ST

N

W   E

S

SWEET SPRINGS
NATURE PRESERVE

RAMONA AVENUE

TO
SOUTH BAY BLVD

ALSO SEE MAPS
ON PAGES 96 • 130

P

MITCHELL

PINE AVENUE

BRODERSON

TO
LOS
OSOS
VALLEY
ROAD

BINS CARTH

SWEET SPRINGS
NATURE PRESERVE

Hike 50
Los Osos Oaks State Reserve

Hiking distance: 2 miles round trip
Hiking time: 1 hour
Elevation gain: 100 feet
Maps: U.S.G.S. Morro Bay South

Summary of hike: Los Osos Oaks State Reserve encompasses 85 acres of an ancient sand dune that was once home to the Chumash Indians. Located just east of Los Osos, this small reserve has stands of 600- to 800-year-old dwarfed pygmy oaks (coast live oaks). Lace lichen streamers hang from the massive, twisted, and contorted branches. Three short, enchanting loop trails meander under the canopy of these unique old-growth oaks past ferns, mushrooms, and poison oak. Los Osos Creek follows the eastern edge of the preserve under the shade of sycamore, willow, laurel, and cottonwood trees.

Driving directions: From Highway 101 south of San Luis Obispo, take the Los Osos Valley Road exit, and head 8.9 miles west to the signed trailhead parking lot on the left.

From Highway 1 in Morro Bay, take the Los Osos/Baywood Park exit. Drive 4 miles south on South Bay Boulevard to Los Osos Valley Road and turn left. Drive 0.7 miles to the signed trailhead parking lot on the right.

Hiking directions: Head south on the signed trail under the dense forest canopy of coastal live oaks. Cross a wooden bridge over the trickling feeder stream to a four-way junction. All three trails loop back, returning to this junction. To the left is the Los Osos Creek Trail; to the right is the Chumash Loop Trail; straight ahead is the Oak View Trail. The left fork loops around the east border of the park above the perennial Los Osos Creek. It leads into grasslands and native chaparral to an overlook of Los Osos Valley, the Irish Hills, and the Santa Lucia Mountains. Various side paths lead left to creekside overlooks. The trail loops back, reentering the dense forest to junctions with the other two trails. Stroll through the shady reserve on the well-defined trails, choosing your own path.

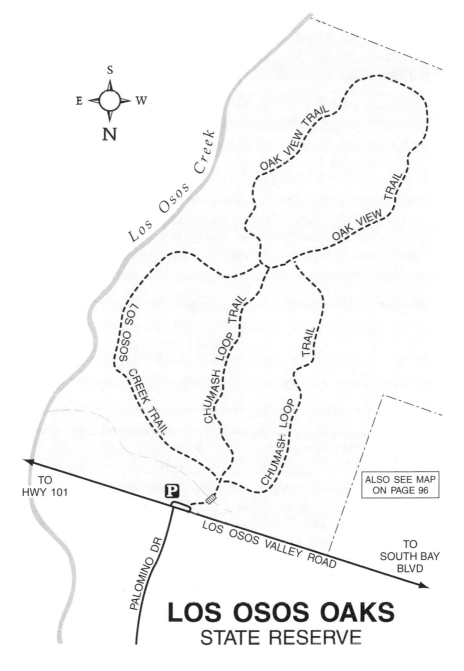

TO
HWY 101

ALSO SEE MAP
ON PAGE 96

P

PALOMINO DR

LOS OSOS VALLEY ROAD

TO
SOUTH BAY
BLVD

LOS OSOS OAKS
STATE RESERVE

Hike 51
Bayview Ecological Reserve

Hiking distance: 3.5 mile loop
Hiking time: 2 hours
Elevation gain: 800 feet
Maps: U.S.G.S. Morro Bay South

Summary of hike: The Bayview Ecological Reserve encompasses 204 acres on the south end of Los Osos on the sloping foothills adjacent to Highland Drive. Formerly known as the Morro Palisades, the pristine, protected coastal dune habitat is a critical link in the contiguous Los Osos Greenbelt, connecting Montaña de Oro State Park with Morro Bay State Park. The paths climb to a ridge at a shaded eucalyptus grove on the north rim of Hazard Canyon in Montaña de Oro State Park. A management plan or formal trail system is not yet in place. For now, stay on the existing trails.

Driving directions: From the intersection of Los Osos Valley Road and South Bay Boulevard in Los Osos, drive one mile west on Los Osos Valley Road to Broderson Avenue. Turn left and continue 0.3 miles to the end of the road, just south of Highland Drive. Park alongside the road.

Hiking directions: Walk past the end of Broderson Avenue. Head south up the grassy slope, passing a cypress tree on the right. The path makes a gradual but steady climb, with a view of Morro Rock, the estuary, and the sand spit protecting the bay. Pass coastal live oaks to the top of the lower slope. Curve left, with views of Hollister Peak, Cerro Cabrillo, Black Hill, and Baywood Park. Curve right and climb through a narrow eroded ravine to a flat grassy area and a 3-way trail split. Begin the loop sharply to the left. Traverse the hillside and curve right along the west edge of a deep canyon. Continue along the rim of the stream-fed canyon, and ascend three short but steep sections to the ridge. Follow the ridge into a huge eucalyptus grove. Walk to a flat grassy area at an overlook of Montaña de Oro on the north rim of Hazard Canyon. Curve right to a junction and sweeping 360-degree vistas. The right fork forms a loop and returns on the same path. Bear left and descend a few log steps to a junction. Straight ahead, the Rim Trail leads to Pecho Valley Road near the Morro Dunes and the entrance to Montaña de Oro. Bear right on the sandy path, and weave down the hill through scrub brush above Cabrillo Estates. Stay to the right, pass a few side paths on the left, and complete the loop at the flat grassy area. Return to Broderson Avenue.

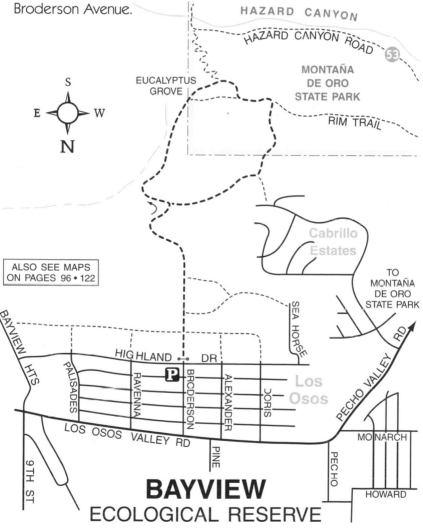

ALSO SEE MAPS
ON PAGES 96 • 122

BAYVIEW
ECOLOGICAL RESERVE

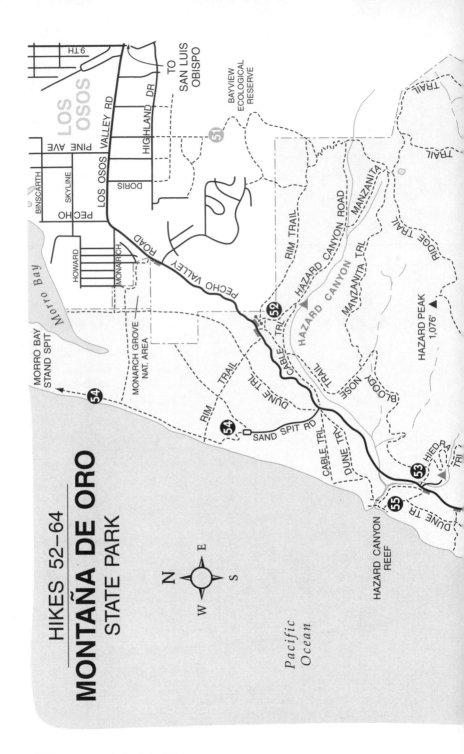

HIKES 52–64
MONTAÑA DE ORO
STATE PARK

N
W–E
S

Pacific
Ocean

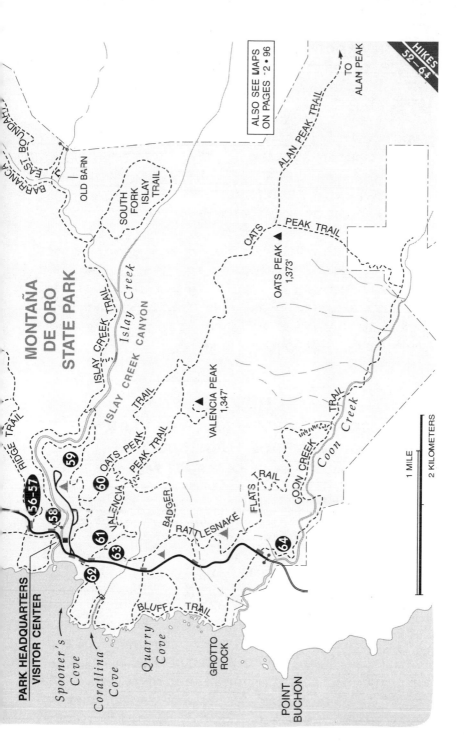

HIKES
52—64

ALSO SEE MAPS
ON PAGES -2 • 96

MONTAÑA
DE ORO
STATE PARK

OLD BARN

EAST BOUNDARY

BARRANCA

SOUTH FORK ISLAY TRAIL

ISLAY CREEK TRAIL

Islay Creek

ISLAY CREEK CANYON

TO ALAN PEAK

ALAN PEAK TRAIL

OATS PEAK TRAIL

OATS PEAK
1,373'

RIDGE TRAIL

59

56-57

58

60

OATS PEAK TRAIL

VALENCIA PEAK
1,347'

VALENCIA PEAK TRAIL

61

63

62

BADGER

RATTLESNAKE

FLATS TRAIL

COON CREEK TRAIL

Coon Creek

64

PARK HEADQUARTERS
VISITOR CENTER

Spooner's
Cove

Corallina
Cove

Quarry
Cove

BLUFF TRAIL

GROTTO
ROCK

POINT
BUCHON

1 MILE

2 KILOMETERS

Montaña de Oro State Park
HIKES 52—64

Located 2.5 miles south of Los Osos, Montaña de Oro State Park (meaning *mountain of gold*) is a protected wilderness area on the west end of the Irish Hills. It is a dramatic meeting of land and sea. Three major creeks drain the interior mountains into the ocean—Coon Creek, Islay Creek, and Hazard Creek. The undeveloped 8,400-acre state park features rugged cliffs, wooded creek canyons, coastal marine terraces, secluded beaches with tidepools, sand dunes, rolling hills, and seven miles of coastline with myriad offshore weather-sculpted sea stacks. The park has primitive and equestrian campsites and more than 50 maintained miles of hiking, biking, and horse trails. The visitor center is housed in the original Spooner Ranch house, dating back to 1892, in a grove of cypress trees overlooking the beach at Spooner's Cove.

Hike 52
Hazard Canyon—East Boundary—
Barranca Trails Loop
MONTAÑA DE ORO STATE PARK

Hiking distance: 7.5 mile loop
Hiking time: 4 hours
Elevation gain: 600 feet
Maps: U.S.G.S. Morro Bay South
     Montaña de Oro State Park map

map
page 129

Summary of hike: This hike explores the northeast end of Montaña de Oro State Park. The hike begins in Hazard Canyon on an old dirt road. The East Boundary Trail weaves through the Irish Hills to Islay Creek Canyon. Atop the East Boundary summit, the path crosses two springs that feed Islay Creek. At the creek, the trail visits the old Spooner Ranch barn, an abandoned tin-roofed barn, then makes a loop back down Hazard Canyon.

Driving directions: From the intersection of Los Osos Valley Road and South Bay Drive in Los Osos, drive 2.5 miles southwest on Los Osos Valley Road to the Montaña de Oro State Park entrance sign. (Los Osos Valley Road becomes Pecho Valley Road en route.) From the entrance sign, continue 0.1 miles to the posted "Horse Camp" turnoff on the left. Park in the dirt pullout next to (but not blocking) the gated road/trail. If the area is full, park just beyond the trailhead in a pullout on the right.

Hiking directions: Pass the trailhead gate and head southeast on the dirt campground road. Walk through a eucalyptus grove on the north wall of Hazard Canyon, and descend to the horse camp on the right. Continue straight, staying in Hazard Canyon. Pass a second trail gate to a posted junction with the Manzanita Trail on the right at 0.8 miles. Both routes head up the drainage and rejoin near the east boundary. The Manzanita Trail follows the north wall of a small side canyon. The Hazard Canyon Road stays on the dirt road through the open brush and chaparral. At the fenced border at the east end of the Hazard Canyon Road, bear right on the East Boundary Trail, and cross over the transient stream. Wind up the south canyon wall, with views down canyon to the ocean. Across the canyon, a zipper-shaped trail with 28 switchbacks can be seen climbing to the Rim Trail at the park's north boundary. At 1.8 miles, pass the upper junction with the Manzanita Trail in a saddle and stay left, leaving Hazard Canyon. One hundred yards ahead the Manzanita Trail goes to the right. Veer left to the Ridge Trail, also on the right. Bear left, staying on the East Boundary Trail, and pass a seasonal pond in a depression on the right. Cross a saddle to the Barranca Trail on the right. Begin the 3.3-mile loop to the left, and stroll through an oak grove high above Islay Creek Canyon. Traverse the rolling grasslands across the head of the canyon near the fenced boundary of the state park. Cross two wood bridges over springs, and follow the contours of the canyon along the cliffs. Descend to the floor of Islay Creek Canyon at the north side of the creek. Go right 200 yards to the old ranch barn, and continue another 200 yards to the posted Barranca Trail. Bear right on the Barranca Trail, and wind up the south-facing wall, following the ridge between two drainages. Near the top, pass oak groves to a trail split. The right fork leads 25 yards to a coastal overlook with a bench on the knoll. Complete the loop on the Barranca Trail, continuing to a saddle at the East Boundary Trail. Retrace your steps to the left (west).

Hike 53
Bloody Nose—Cable—Dune Trail Loop
MONTAÑA DE ORO STATE PARK

Hiking distance: 4 mile loop
Hiking time: 2 hours
Elevation gain: 400 feet
Maps: U.S.G.S. Morro Bay South
      Montaña de Oro State Park map

map
page 129

Summary of hike: This loop hike explores three trails in the northern part of the state park. The descriptive Bloody Nose Trail begins in a dense eucalyptus grove near Hazard Canyon Reef on the west flank of Hazard Peak. The trail weaves through stream-carved drainages and rolling hills, connecting with the Dune Trail in Hazard Canyon. The return route contours through vegetated coastal dunes along the west side of the park road.

Driving directions: From the intersection of Los Osos Valley Road and South Bay Drive in Los Osos, drive 2.5 miles southwest on Los Osos Valley Road to the Montaña de Oro State Park entrance sign. (Los Osos Valley Road becomes Pecho Valley Road en route.) From the entrance sign, continue 1.5 miles to the large parking lot on right, at the south end of the huge eucalyptus grove.

Hiking directions: Walk 50 yards back down the road to the trailhead on the right (east). Climb the slope on the north side of Camp Keep through an enormous eucalyptus grove, and curve left to the posted Bloody Nose Trail. Follow the flat terrace north on a narrow dirt road along the lower west slope of Hazard Peak. At the picnic area and wood kiosk, curve right on the footpath, and drop into a lush, stream-fed drainage. Cross over the ephemeral stream, and ascend the canyon wall to an overlook of the coastline to the Santa Lucia Mountains. Weave through the rolling scrub-covered hills, and traverse the south wall of another stream-fed canyon. Descend to the canyon floor in a riparian corridor with ferns, vines, and poison oak. Cross the seasonal stream and climb the north canyon wall. Follow the canyon rim on a downward slope through groves of eucalyptus to a T-junction. The Cable Trail, named to commemorate the fiber optic cable buried along the path, is a wide, sandy path. The right fork leads to the horse camp in Hazard Canyon. Bear left and head south through the forest, parallel to the park road. The trail crosses Pecho Valley Road by Sand Spit Road. Cross the road and pick up the posted Dune Trail. Curve south, weaving through the dunes for 0.6 miles to an overlook of Hazard Canyon Reef, a rocky beach cove with tidepools. Cross and climb the narrow drainage on long, wide steps back to the trailhead parking lot.

Hike 54
Morro Bay Sand Spit
MORRO DUNES NATURAL PRESERVE
MONTAÑA DE ORO STATE PARK

Hiking distance: 8—9.5 miles round trip
Hiking time: 3—5 hours
Elevation gain: 50 feet
Maps: U.S.G.S. Morro Bay South
  Montaña de Oro State Park map

map
page 130

Summary of hike: The Morro Dunes Natural Preserve, known as the Morro Bay Sand Spit, is a three-mile-long narrow vein of land that separates Morro Bay and the estuary from the waters of Estero Bay and the Pacific Ocean. A fragile 80-foot sand dune ridge, stabilized by scrubs, grasses, and succulents, runs the length of the preserve. Along the striated dunes are ancient Chumash Indian shell mounds known as middens. This hike follows the remote sand spit, offering solitude along the ocean side of the dunes.

Driving directions: From the intersection of Los Osos Valley Road and South Bay Drive in Los Osos, drive 2.5 miles southwest on Los Osos Valley Road to the Montaña de Oro State Park entrance sign. (Los Osos Valley Road becomes Pecho Valley Road en route.) From the entrance sign, continue 0.8 miles to Sand Spit Road and turn right. Drive 0.5 miles to the parking lot at the end of the road.

Hiking directions: Take the footpath past the information boards, and head west across the scrub-covered sand dunes. The path reaches the ocean at 0.2 miles. Head north along the hard-packed sand, staying close to the shoreline for easier walking. The coastline has an abundance of sea shells. At 4 miles is the first of two breakwaters guarding the bay entrance. Morro Rock, a 578-foot volcanic rock, dominates the landscape. This is a good turn-around spot. To add an additional 1.5 miles to the hike, continue following the shoreline to a second breakwater. Curve east towards Morro Bay, and follow the bay south about one mile. The trail curves west, crossing the soft sands of the dunes back to the ocean. Return along the same route.

HIKE 52
HAZARD CANYON–EAST BOUNDARY–BARRANCA LOOP

HIKE 53
BLOODY NOSE–CABLE–DUNE TRAIL LOOP
MONTAÑA DE ORO STATE PARK

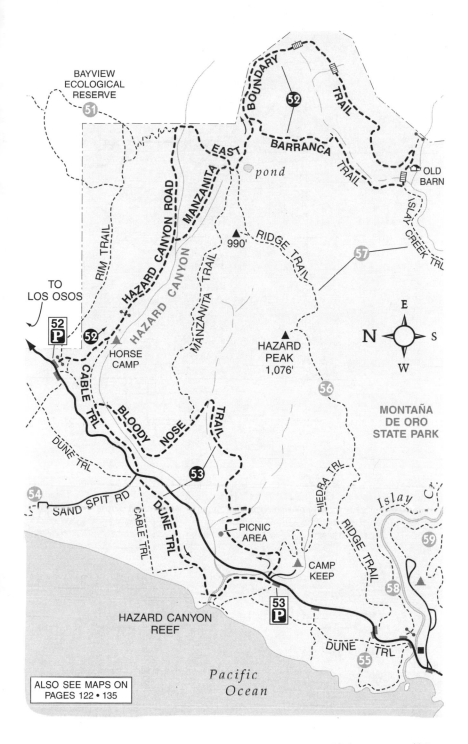

BAYVIEW
ECOLOGICAL
RESERVE

51

TO
LOS OSOS

52
P

52

HORSE
CAMP

RIM TRAIL

HAZARD CANYON ROAD

MANZANITA

HAZARD CANYON

MANZANITA TRAIL

EAST

BOUNDARY

52

BARRANCA

TRAIL

pond

990'

RIDGE TRAIL

HAZARD
PEAK
1,076'

OLD
BARN

ISLAY CREEK TRL

57

56

MONTAÑA
DE ORO
STATE PARK

E

N

S

W

CABLE TRL

BLOODY

NOSE

TRAIL

53

DUNE TRL

54

SAND SPIT RD

CABLE TRL

DUNE TRL

PICNIC
AREA

CAMP
KEEP

YEDRA TRL

RIDGE TRAIL

Islay Cr.

59

58

HAZARD CANYON
REEF

53
P

DUNE TRL

55

Pacific
Ocean

ALSO SEE MAPS ON
PAGES 122 • 135

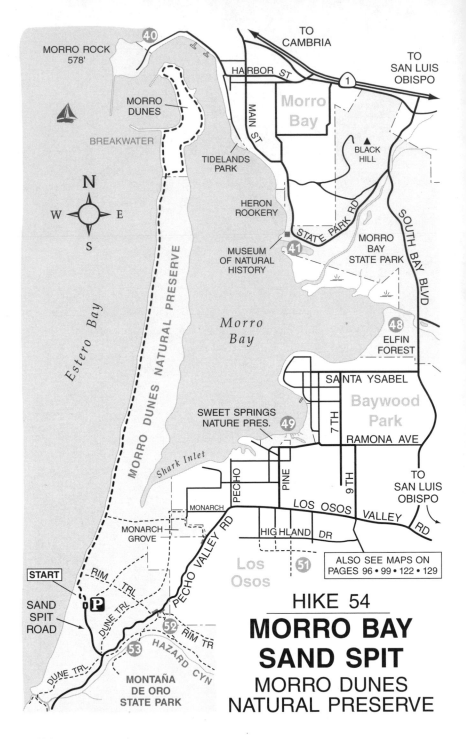

HIKE 54
MORRO BAY
SAND SPIT
MORRO DUNES
NATURAL PRESERVE

ALSO SEE MAPS ON
PAGES 96 • 99 • 122 • 129

Hike 55
Dune Trail to Hazard Canyon Reef
MONTAÑA DE ORO STATE PARK

Hiking distance: 2.6 miles round trip
Hiking time: 1.5 hours
Elevation gain: 50 feet
Maps: U.S.G.S. Morro Bay South
Montaña de Oro State Park map

map
page 135

Summary of hike: The Dune Trail parallels the ocean bluffs across scrub-covered dunes from Spooner's Cove. The trail leads down narrow Hazard Canyon in a eucalyptus-lined drainage to Hazard Canyon Reef, a rocky beach cove with superb tidepools at the base of the cliffs. It is a popular surfing beach. Above Hazard Canyon Reef is a stunning overlook of the scalloped coastline.

Driving directions: From the intersection of Los Osos Valley Road and South Bay Drive in Los Osos, drive 2.5 miles southwest on Los Osos Valley Road to the Montaña de Oro State Park entrance sign. (Los Osos Valley Road becomes Pecho Valley Road en route.) From the entrance sign, continue 2.5 miles to the trailhead parking area on the right, just north of Spooner's Cove. The visitor center is 0.1 mile ahead on the left.

Hiking directions: At the signed trailhead are two trails. The left fork is a loop that curves around Spooner's Cove and the bluffs before reconnecting with the Dune Trail a short distance ahead. The right fork is the Dune Trail, heading north across the scrub-covered sand dunes. The sandy trail parallels the coastline between the bluffs and Pecho Valley Road. At 0.5 miles, the trail crosses a junction. To the right is a parking area by the park road. The left route heads across the rolling dunes to a surfing beach. Continue straight ahead to another trail split at one mile. Bear right to a parking area in a eucalyptus grove. Pick up the trail again on the left. Long, wide steps descend into narrow Hazard Canyon. Cross a wooden boardwalk alongside a small creek to Hazard Canyon Reef, another surfing beach. This is a great spot for beachcombing and enjoying the tide-pools along the base of the cliffs. The Hazard Reef Trail heads up to the bluffs to an overlook of the rugged coastline. This is the turn-around spot. Return along the same path.

Hike 56
Ridge Trail to Hazard Peak
MONTAÑA DE ORO STATE PARK

Hiking distance: 4.6 miles round trip

Hiking time: 2 hours

Elevation gain: 1,000 feet

Maps: U.S.G.S. Morro Bay South
Montaña de Oro State Park map

map
page 135

Summary of hike: The Ridge Trail crosses the shoulder of the mountain to Hazard Peak, a 1,076-foot grassy summit. The trail follows the scrub-covered ridge east while overlooking Islay Creek Canyon, half-moon shaped Spooner's Cove, the scalloped bluffs, and the dunes. The hike ends at an overlook just beyond Hazard Peak. From the overlook are views into Hazard Canyon and across the sand spit to Morro Rock and the bay, from Point Buchon to Point Estero.

Driving directions: From the intersection of Los Osos Valley Road and South Bay Drive in Los Osos, drive 2.5 miles southwest on Los Osos Valley Road to the Montaña de Oro State Park entrance sign. (Los Osos Valley Road becomes Pecho Valley Road en route.) From the entrance sign, continue 2.3 miles to the signed trailhead on the left. There are parking areas on both sides of the road. The visitor center is 0.3 miles ahead.

Hiking directions: Hike east past the trail sign on the wide path. Cross the rolling foothills through a dense thicket of scrub up to a ridge. Curve north, then east up the hillside towards a large, rounded 781-foot hill. The trail traverses the hillside to the right, 600 feet above Islay Creek Canyon, with views of Valencia Peak and the coastal bluffs. Continue ascending the hill to a saddle. At 2.2 miles, a ridge leads to Hazard Peak on the left. From Hazard Peak, follow the narrow, grassy ridge between two steep drainages to an overlook at a fenceline and survey pin. This is the turn-around spot. To hike further, continue with Hike 57, which makes a loop back through Islay Creek Canyon.

Hike 57
Ridge—Barranca—Islay Creek Loop
MONTAÑA DE ORO STATE PARK

Hiking distance: 7.9 mile loop
Hiking time: 4 hours
Elevation gain: 1,050 feet
Maps: U.S.G.S. Morro Bay South
Montaña de Oro State Park map

map
page 135

Summary of hike: This hike connects Hikes 56 and 58 to make a large loop through the center of Montaña de Oro State Park, traversing from a panoramic ridge to a lush canyon bottom. The Ridge Trail follows the ridgeline between Islay Creek Canyon and Hazard Canyon. En route, the trail crosses 1,076-foot Hazard Peak before descending to the Barranca Trail. The Barranca Trail descends a side drainage to the floor of Islay Creek Canyon. The Islay Creek Trail follows a wooded ranch road along Islay Creek to the old Spooner Ranch house, now the park headquarters. The hike offers scenic mountain stretches and sweeping coastal vistas.

Driving directions: From the intersection of Los Osos Valley Road and South Bay Drive in Los Osos, drive 2.5 miles southwest on Los Osos Valley Road to the Montaña de Oro State Park entrance sign. (Los Osos Valley Road becomes Pecho Valley Road en route.) From the entrance, continue 2.3 miles to the signed trailhead on the left. There are parking areas on both sides of the road. The visitor center is 0.3 miles ahead.

Hiking directions: Head up the posted footpath on an easy uphill grade. Weave through coastal scrub with views of Spooner's Cove, Valencia Peak, Oats Peak, and the campground. Continue the ascent to the west base of a rounded 781-foot hill. Curve right, circling around the hill, and traverse the south-facing slope above Islay Creek Canyon. Climb to the ridge over-looking Morro Bay and the estuary by a 4-foot cairn. Follow the ridge and cross a saddle between two steep canyons. Ascend the west slope to 1,076-foot Hazard Peak. After savoring the views, continue on the narrow spine. Sweep downhill to the left, and cross two more saddles to a trail split. The left fork detours 100 yards to a 990-foot overlook of Hazard Canyon and the coastline to the Santa Lucia Range. From the junction, descend and pass a seasonal pond on the right to the end of the Ridge Trail at a junction with the East Boundary Trail at 3.2 miles. Bear right and stroll through the rolling valley surrounded by hills to a posted junction with the Barranca Trail. Go to the right (south), weaving through coastal scrub and pockets of oak trees on the east side of Hazard Peak. Top the upper north slope of Islay Creek Canyon past a junction on the left that leads to a coastal overlook with a picnic table. Stay right and descend for a mile to the canyon floor, 200 yards downstream from the abandoned ranch barn. Bear right on the Islay Creek Trail, and follow the old ranch road 3 miles down-stream along the north edge of the creek. Along the way, pass a waterfall (see Hike 58) and the Reservoir Flats Trail on the left to the park road. Follow the road to the right 0.1 miles back to the trailhead.

HIKE 55
DUNE TRAIL to REEF

HIKES 56–57
HAZARD PEAK
RIDGE TRAIL–ISLAY LOOP
MONTAÑA DE ORO STATE PARK

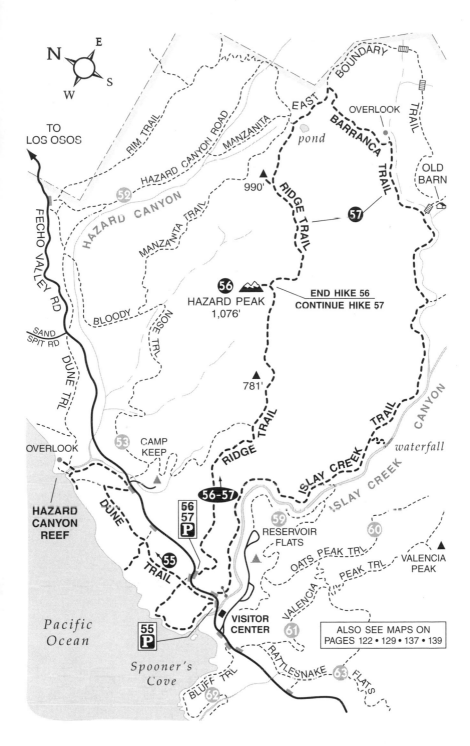

Hike 58
Islay Creek Trail
MONTAÑA DE ORO STATE PARK

Hiking distance: 6 miles round trip
Hiking time: 3 hours
Elevation gain: 300 feet
Maps: U.S.G.S. Morro Bay South
　　　　 Montaña de Oro State Park map

Summary of hike: Islay Creek is a major drainage on the west end of the Irish Hills. The creek flows through the heart of Montaña de Oro, entering the sea in Spooner's Cove. The Islay Creek Trail begins across the creek from the old Spooner Ranch house, now used as the visitor center. The trail follows the old ranch road up the north side of the wooded canyon beneath the shadow of Valencia Peak and Oats Peak. The road parallels the creek on an easy grade to an abandoned tin-roofed barn in the mountainous interior. En route, the trail passes a waterfall tumbling out of a rock outcropping.

Driving directions: From the intersection of Los Osos Valley Road and South Bay Drive in Los Osos, drive 2.5 miles southwest on Los Osos Valley Road to the Montaña de Oro State Park entrance sign. (Los Osos Valley Road becomes Pecho Valley Road en route.) From the entrance sign, continue 2.4 miles to the trailhead parking area on the left by the signed trailhead. The visitor center is 0.2 miles ahead.

Hiking directions: Hike past the metal gate on the unpaved ranch road. The road winds along the south-facing hillside above Islay Creek and the campground. At a quarter mile, weathered Monterey shale forms a beautiful rock wall along the cliff side of the trail. At one mile is a signed junction with the Reservoir Flats Trail on the right (Hike 59). This short detour descends 50 yards down to the creek. Back on the main trail, continue to a narrow unsigned trail on the right at 1.3 miles. This footpath leads down the steep cliff to a waterfall. (The scramble is not easy, and the waterfall can be seen from the main trail before reaching the footpath.) At two miles, Islay Creek forks. Just beyond the fork is a signed junction with the South Fork Islay Trail, a small loop to the right. Stay on the main road, passing the Barranca Trail on the left. Cross a bridge to the old ranch barn at 2.9 miles. The Islay Creek Trail ends at the gated eastern border of the park. Return on the same trail.

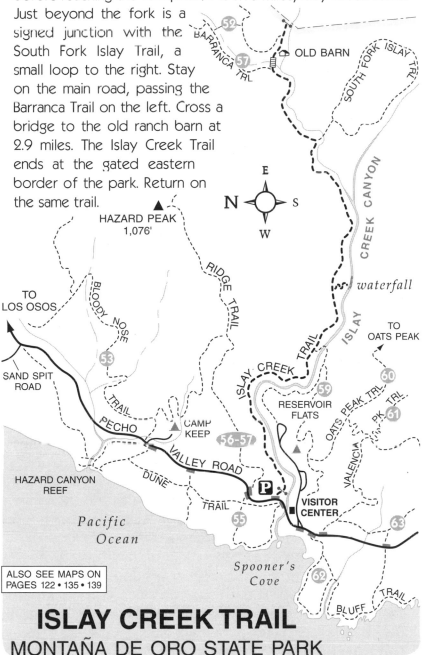

ALSO SEE MAPS ON
PAGES 122 • 135 • 139

ISLAY CREEK TRAIL
MONTAÑA DE ORO STATE PARK

Hike 59
Reservoir Flats Trail
MONTAÑA DE ORO STATE PARK

Hiking distance: 2.1 mile loop
Hiking time: 1 hour
Elevation gain: 250 feet
Maps: U.S.G.S. Morro Bay South
Montaña de Oro State Park map

Summary of hike: The Reservoir Flats Trail follows Islay Creek along the south wall of the canyon. Ferns and moss carpet the lush canyon, willows and cottonwoods line the creek, and lichen streamers hang from the branches of the pine trees. After leaving the canyon, the trail reaches a ridge along the grassy hillside to the seasonal, one-acre reservoir site fed by springs. From the ridge are views of Islay Canyon, the bluffs, Spooner's Cove, and the Pacific Ocean.

Driving directions: From the intersection of Los Osos Valley Road and South Bay Drive in Los Osos, drive 2.5 miles southwest on Los Osos Valley Road to the Montaña de Oro State Park entrance sign. (Los Osos Valley Road becomes Pecho Valley Road en route.) From the entrance sign, continue 2.6 miles to the visitor center on the left and park.

Hiking directions: From the visitor center, walk east up the Islay Creek Campground road 0.4 miles to the Reservoir Flats Trail by campsite 40. Continue east on the footpath up the lush drainage dense with willows. Traverse the hillside above the riparian vegetation and meandering Islay Creek. At 1.1 miles is a junction. The left fork is a short detour to the creek. Return and bear left on the main trail, heading out of the shady canyon to an overlook of the canyon and Spooner's Cove. Descend from the ridge to Reservoir Flats, an open grassy bowl. Continue past the shallow basin, and stay to the right at the signed Oats Peak Trail (Hike 60), high above the campground. Cross the scrub-covered hill, and descend back to the visitor center.

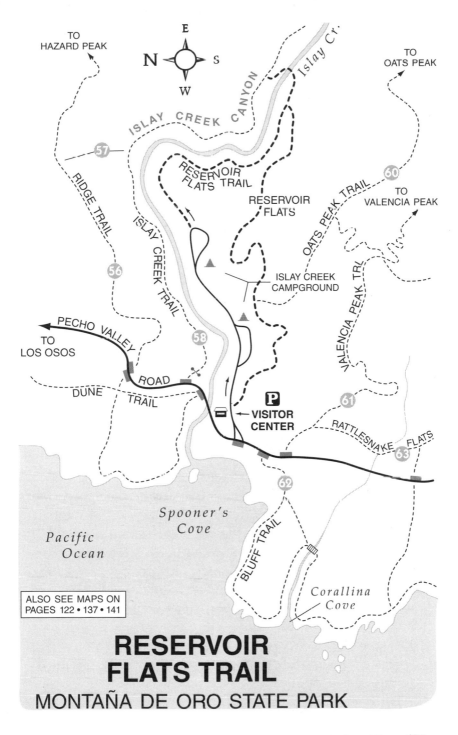

RESERVOIR
FLATS TRAIL
MONTAÑA DE ORO STATE PARK

ALSO SEE MAPS ON
PAGES 122 • 137 • 141

Hike 60
Oats Peak Trail
MONTAÑA DE ORO STATE PARK

Hiking distance: 5.5 miles round trip
Hiking time: 3 hours
Elevation gain: 1,300 feet
Maps: U.S.G.S. Morro Bay South
Montaña de Oro State Park map

Summary of hike: The Oats Peak Trail climbs from the ocean by Spooner's Cove to the second highest peak in the park at 1,373 feet. The trail crosses chaparral, thick brush, and grassy meadows under the shadow of Valencia Peak. There are great views into the Coon Creek drainage, the folded interior canyons, and the ridges of the Irish Hills backcountry. To the north are views from Morro Bay to San Simeon .

Driving directions: From the intersection of Los Osos Valley Road and South Bay Drive in Los Osos, drive 2.5 miles southwest on Los Osos Valley Road to the Montaña de Oro State Park entrance sign. (Los Osos Valley Road becomes Pecho Valley Road en route.) From the entrance sign, continue 2.6 miles to the visitor center on the left and park.

Hiking directions: Walk 50 yards east on the campground road, and take the signed Reservoir Flats Trail on the right by the maintenance buildings. Head uphill across the dry hillside to a signed trail split at 0.3 miles. The Reservoir Flats Trail (Hike 59) veers left. Go right on the Oats Peak Trail. At 0.6 miles is the Badger Trail, the first of two connector trails to Valencia Peak (Hike 61). Stay to the left, curving around to the east side of Valencia Peak to a saddle and signed junction. Bear left, following the ridge south to a second saddle near the summit of a 1,295-foot peak. Descend a short distance and begin the final half-mile ascent to Oats Peak. After enjoying the views, return along the same path.

To hike further, just beyond the peak is a junction. The Alan Peak Trail heads east for several miles to the peak. The Oats Peak Trail drops steeply into Coon Creek Canyon to the right (Hike 64).

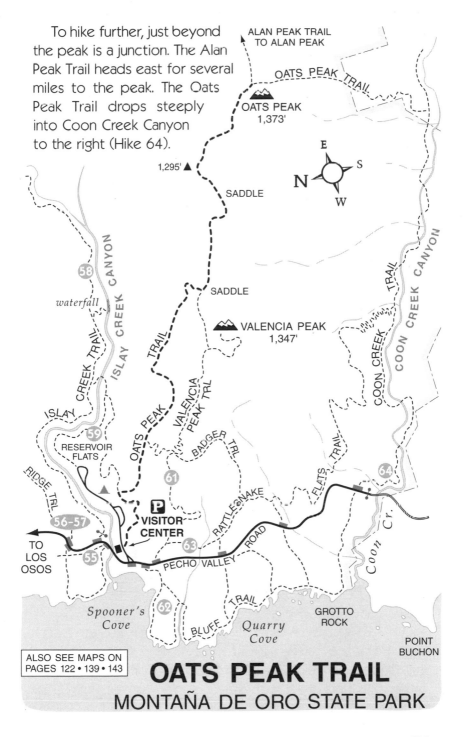

ALAN PEAK TRAIL
TO ALAN PEAK

OATS PEAK TRAIL

OATS PEAK
1,373'

1,295' ▲

SADDLE

N E S W

ISLAY CREEK CANYON

58

waterfall

CREEK TRAIL

SADDLE

VALENCIA PEAK
1,347'

COON CREEK TRAIL

COON CREEK CANYON

ISLAY

TRAIL

OATS PEAK

VALENCIA PEAK TRL

BADGER TRL

59

RESERVOIR
FLATS

RIDGE TRL

56-57

61

FLATS TRAIL

64

P
VISITOR
CENTER

RATTLESNAKE

ROAD

Coon Cr.

55

63

TO
LOS
OSOS

PECHO VALLEY

62

BLUFF TRAIL

*Spooner's
Cove*

*Quarry
Cove*

GROTTO
ROCK

POINT
BUCHON

ALSO SEE MAPS ON
PAGES 122 • 139 • 143

OATS PEAK TRAIL
MONTAÑA DE ORO STATE PARK

Hike 61
Valencia Peak Trail
MONTAÑA DE ORO STATE PARK

Hiking distance: 4 miles round trip
Hiking time: 2 hours
Elevation gain: 1,150 feet
Maps: U.S.G.S. Morro Bay South
  Montaña de Oro State Park map

Summary of hike: Valencia Peak, at 1,347 feet, has spectacular 360-degree views of Montaña de Oro, Morro Bay, Los Osos Valley, and the rugged coastline from Point Sal to Piedras Blancas. The chain of morros leading from Morro Rock to San Luis Obispo are in view. The trail crosses grasslands and straddles a ridge between two canyons before climbing directly up to the coastal peak.

Driving directions: From the intersection of Los Osos Valley Road and South Bay Drive in Los Osos, drive 2.5 miles southwest on Los Osos Valley Road to the Montaña de Oro State Park entrance sign. (Los Osos Valley Road becomes Pecho Valley Road en route.) From the entrance sign, continue 2.6 miles to the visitor center on the left. Drive another 100 yards past the visitor center on Pecho Valley Road to the trailhead parking area on the left.

Hiking directions: Hike east across the broad chaparral-covered marine terrace on the signed trail. Head toward the base of the mountain, passing the Rattlesnake Flats Trail on the right (Hike 63). As the trail begins to climb, views emerge of the scenic coastal plain. Switchbacks lead up to the first ridge above Spooner's Cove and the bluffs. Cross the grassy flat, in full view of Valencia Peak, to a junction with the Badger Trail at the base of the cone-shaped mountain. The left fork leads to the Oats Peak Trail (Hike 60). The right fork descends to Rattlesnake Flats (Hike 63). Stay on the Valencia Peak Trail, climbing the edge of the mountain to a narrow ridge. Follow the ridge east up two steep sections with loose shale. At the base of the final ascent is another connector trail to the Oaks Peak Trail—stay to the right. Continue uphill, reaching the summit at two miles. After savoring the views, return along the same route.

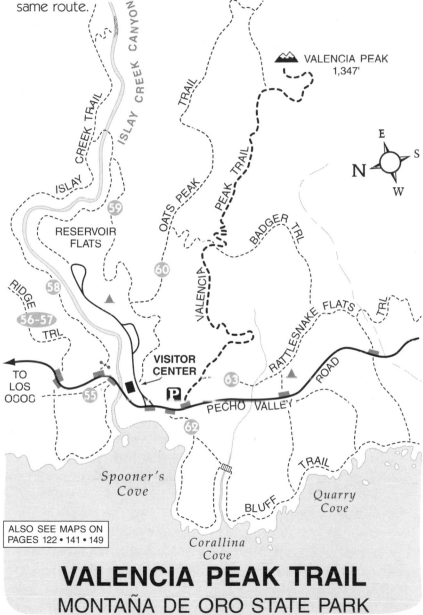

ALSO SEE MAPS ON
PAGES 122 • 141 • 149

VALENCIA PEAK TRAIL
MONTAÑA DE ORO STATE PARK

Hike 62
Bluff Trail
MONTAÑA DE ORO STATE PARK

Hiking distance: 3.4 miles round trip
Hiking time: 1.5 hours
Elevation gain: Level
Maps: U.S.G.S. Morro Bay South
   Montaña de Oro State Park map

Summary of hike: The Bluff Trail is an easy hike along one of the premier locations on the central California coastline. The popular trail snakes along the contours of a rugged network of eroding sandstone cliffs on a grassy marine terrace. Land extensions jut out into the ocean like fingers. There are hidden coves, sea caves, arches, sandy beaches, reefs, offshore outcroppings, clear tidepools, crashing surf, and basking seals and otters.

Driving directions: From the intersection of Los Osos Valley Road and South Bay Drive in Los Osos, drive 2.5 miles southwest on Los Osos Valley Road to the Montaña de Oro State Park entrance sign. (Los Osos Valley Road becomes Pecho Valley Road en route.) From the entrance sign, continue 2.6 miles to the visitor center on the left. Drive another 100 yards past the visitor center on Pecho Valley Road to the trailhead parking area on the right.

Hiking directions: Head west on the wide trail, and cross a wooden bridge over an arroyo to a trail fork. Take the right branch, following the cliff's edge along Spooner's Cove. Spur trails intersect the main trail throughout the hike, leading back to the road. The main path generally follows the cliff's edge, passing coves and rocky reefs. At Corallina Cove, a sandy beach, curve inland. Cross a footbridge over a narrow ravine, and return to the oceanfront cliffs. Continue south past dramatic fingers of water-carved land to Quarry Cove, another sandy beach with tidepools. At 1.7 miles, is Grotto Rock, a prominent castle-shaped rock with caves. Near the PG&E fenceline is the mouth of Coon Creek. This is the turn-around spot. The trail leaves the coastline here and heads east to Pecho Valley Road and the Coon Creek Trail (Hike 64). To return, retrace your steps.

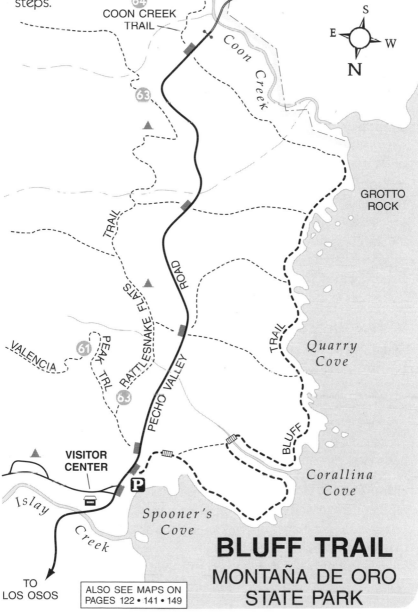

COON CREEK
TRAIL

Coon Creek

GROTTO
ROCK

TRAIL

ROAD

RATTLESNAKE FLATS

TRAIL

VALENCIA

PEAK TRL

Quarry
Cove

PECHO VALLEY

BLUFF

VISITOR
CENTER

Corallina
Cove

Islay

Creek

Spooner's
Cove

BLUFF TRAIL
MONTAÑA DE ORO
STATE PARK

TO
LOS OSOS

ALSO SEE MAPS ON
PAGES 122 • 141 • 149

Hike 63
Rattlesnake Flats—Coon Creek—
Bluff Trail Loop
MONTAÑA DE ORO STATE PARK

Hiking distance: 6.5 mile loop
Hiking time: 3 hours
Elevation gain: 550 feet
Maps: U.S.G.S. Morro Bay South
Montaña de Oro State Park map

*map
next page*

Summary of hike: This hike makes a loop across Rattlesnake Flats, down the Coon Creek drainage, and back along the incredible Bluff Trail. Rattlesnake Flats is an uplifted marine terrace on the west flank of Valencia Peak. Beginning near Spooner's Cove, the trail follows the coastal slope into Coon Creek Canyon. The Coon Creek Trail heads downstream through the lush riparian corridor with bridge crossings. The hike returns atop the 40-foot wave-sculpted terrace on the Bluff Trail, passing tilted and twisted strata, jagged layered rocks with tidepools, and sandy beach pockets.

Driving directions: From the intersection of Los Osos Valley Road and South Bay Drive in Los Osos, drive 2.5 miles southwest on Los Osos Valley Road to the Montaña de Oro State Park entrance sign. (Los Osos Valley Road becomes Pecho Valley Road en route.) From the entrance sign, continue 2.6 miles to the visitor center on the left. Drive another 100 yards past the visitor center on Pecho Valley Road to the trailhead parking area on the left.

Hiking directions: Head up the sloping hill through chaparral and coastal scrub on the posted Valencia Peak Trail. At 175 yards, bear right on the signed Rattlesnake Flats Trail. Cross the marine terrace, weaving beneath the west flank of Valencia Peak, and cross a water-carved drainage. Pass the Badger Trail on the left, connecting with Valencia Peak, and cross a second drainage. Curve around a west-facing finger of land between two canyons. Descend the hillside on a couple of switchbacks to a trailhead on the right by the park road at 1.5 miles. Bend left, cross a gully into the rolling mountains, and traverse the north wall of a side canyon. Loop back on the south wall, and climb to the north ridge of Coon Creek Canyon. Slowly descend and curve clockwise around the east side of a distinct 600-foot rounded knoll. Zigzag down the canyon wall with the aid of 15 switchbacks to a T-junction by Coon Creek at 3.2 miles. Bear right and head downstream between the steep canyon walls, passing eroded rock formations with caves. Cross a bridge over perennial Coon Creek, and wind through a tall tunnel of foliage. Cross a second bridge over the creek, returning to the north bank. At the mouth of the canyon, curve right and climb to the Coon Creek parking lot at Pecho Valley Road. Cross the road and head west on the Bluff Trail, crossing the marine terrace along the park boundary to the ocean. Follow the oceanfront cliffs to Spooner's Cove, and veer right to the trailhead. To shorten the hike by one mile, from the Coon Creek parking lot, follow Pecho Valley Road 1.2 miles to the trailhead.

Hike 64
Coon Creek Trail
MONTAÑA DE ORO STATE PARK

Hiking distance: 5 miles round trip
Hiking time: 2.5 hours
Elevation gain: 250 feet
Maps: U.S.G.S. Morro Bay South and Port San Luis
      Montaña de Oro State Park map

map
next page

Summary of hike: The Coon Creek Trail, at the south end of Montaña de Oro, heads up Coon Creek Canyon alongside the winding watercourse of the perennial stream. The trail crosses six bridges over the creek through the shade of the lush riparian corridor. Willows, maples, cottonwoods, coast live oaks, cedars, and cypress grow in the canyon, with lace lichen draped from the branches.

Driving directions: From the intersection of Los Osos Valley Road and South Bay Drive in Los Osos, drive 2.5 miles southwest on Los Osos Valley Road to the Montaña de Oro State Park entrance sign. (Los Osos Valley Road becomes Pecho Valley Road en route.) From the entrance sign, continue 3.9 miles to the trailhead parking area on the left at the end of the road. It is 1.2 miles past the visitor center.

Hiking directions: Hike east past the trail sign and over a small ridge to a ravine. Bear right down wide steps, and follow the path along the fenced park boundary to Coon Creek at 0.3 miles. Head up the canyon through the forest along the north side of the creek. Cross the first two of six bridges over the willow-lined creek past beautiful rock outcroppings. At 1.2 miles, the trail rises to an overlook of Coon Creek Canyon at a signed trail junction with the Rattlesnake Flats Trail on the left (Hike 63). Continue straight ahead up the shady canyon, and cross four more bridges. At 2.4 miles is a junction on the left with the Oats Peak Trail. Continue a short distance ahead to the trail's end in a grove of cypress trees and large, twisted oaks at an old homestead cabin site from the 1920s. Return by retracing your steps.

HIKE 63
RATTLESNAKE FLATS– COON CREEK–BLUFF TRAIL LOOP

HIKE 64
COON CREEK TRAIL
MONTAÑA DE ORO STATE PARK

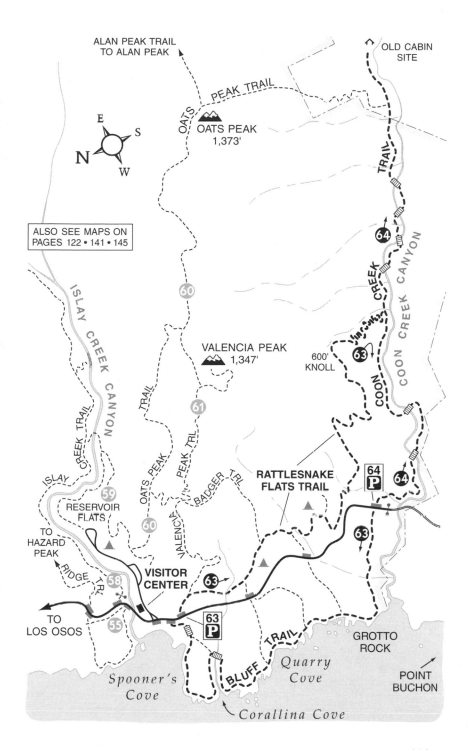

ALAN PEAK TRAIL
TO ALAN PEAK

OLD CABIN
SITE

PEAK TRAIL

OATS

OATS PEAK
1,373'

TRAIL

E
N   S
W

ALSO SEE MAPS ON
PAGES 122 • 141 • 145

60

COON CREEK CANYON

CREEK

64

VALENCIA PEAK
1,347'

600'
KNOLL

63

ISLAY CREEK CANYON

TRAIL

61

COON

CREEK TRAIL

OATS PEAK   PEAK TRL

BADGER TRL

RATTLESNAKE
FLATS TRAIL

ISLAY

64
P

64

59

RESERVOIR
FLATS

VALENCIA

60

63

TO
HAZARD
PEAK

RIDGE TRL

58

VISITOR
CENTER

63

TO
LOS OSOS

55

63
P

BLUFF TRAIL

GROTTO
ROCK

Quarry
Cove

POINT
BUCHON

Spooner's
Cove

Corallina Cove

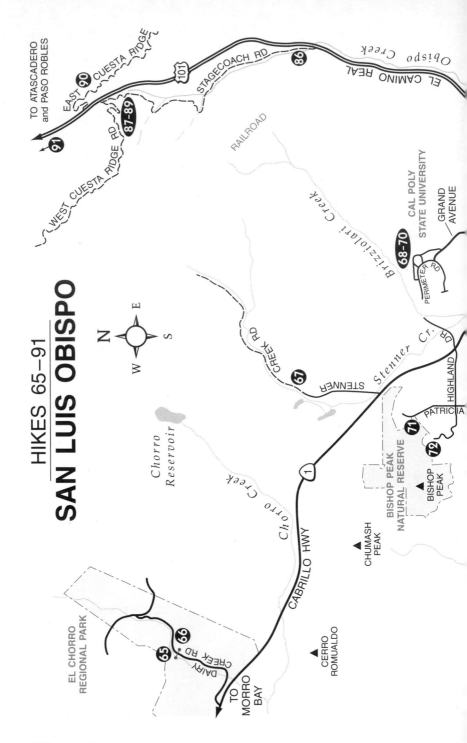

HIKES 65–91
SAN LUIS OBISPO

TO ATASCADERO
and PASO ROBLES

CUESTA RIDGE

EAST **90**

91

87-89

WEST CUESTA RIDGE RD

STAGECOACH RD

86

101

RAILROAD

Obispo Creek

EL CAMINO REAL

N
W E
S

CAL POLY
STATE UNIVERSITY

68-70

GRAND
AVENUE

PERIMETER RD

Brizziolari Creek

Chorro
Reservoir

Stenner Cr.

CREEK RD

61

STENNER

HIGHLAND DR

PATRICIA

71

72

BISHOP PEAK
NATURAL RESERVE

BISHOP
PEAK

Chorro Creek

1

CABRILLO HWY

CHUMASH
PEAK

EL CHORRO
REGIONAL PARK

66

65

DAIRY CREEK RD

TO
MORRO
BAY

CERRO
ROMUALDO

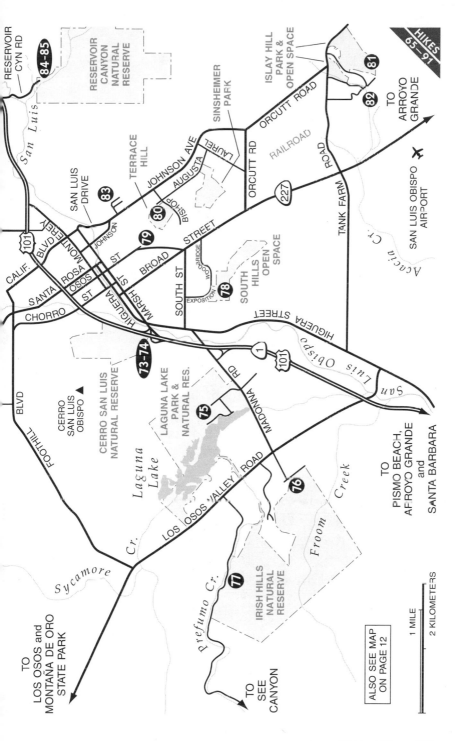

HIKES 65 – 91

RESERVOIR CYN RD

84-85

RESERVOIR CANYON NATURAL RESERVE

ISLAY HILL PARK & OPEN SPACE

81

82

TO ARROYO GRANDE

San Luis

SINSHEIMER PARK

ORCUTT ROAD

ORCUTT RD

RAILROAD

SAN LUIS DRIVE

TERRACE HILL

JOHNSON AVE

LAUREL

AUGUSTA

83

ROAD

TANK FARM

227

SAN LUIS OBISPO AIRPORT

Acacia Cr.

JOHNSON

80

BISHOP

79

STREET

BROAD

BRIDGE

WOOD

SOUTH HILLS OPEN SPACE

CALIF.

101

MONTEREY

BLVD

ST

OSOS

ROSA

SANTA

MARSH ST

HIGUERA ST

SOUTH ST

EXPOSITION

78

CHORRO

HIGUERA STREET

13-74

1

101

San Luis Obispo

FOOTHILL BLVD

CERRO SAN LUIS OBISPO

CERRO SAN LUIS NATURAL RESERVE

LAGUNA LAKE PARK & NATURAL RES.

75

MADONNA RD

TO PISMO BEACH, ARROYO GRANDE and SANTA BARBARA

Laguna Lake

76

Froom Creek

Cr.

Sycamore

LOS OSOS VALLEY ROAD

TO LOS OSOS and MONTAÑA DE ORO STATE PARK

Prefumo Cr.

71

IRISH HILLS NATURAL RESERVE

TO SEE CANYON

ALSO SEE MAP ON PAGE 12

1 MILE

2 KILOMETERS

128 Great Hikes – **151**

Hike 65
Dairy Creek—El Chorro Park Loop
EL CHORRO REGIONAL PARK

Hiking distance: 3 miles round trip
Hiking time: 1.5 hours
Elevation gain: 300 feet
Maps: U.S.G.S. San Luis Obispo

Summary of hike: El Chorro Regional Park encompasses more than 700 acres in El Chorro Valley at the base of the Santa Lucia Range. The park has shady oak and sycamore groves, hillside pastures, a botanical garden, a campground, and miles of hiking and equestrian trails. Dairy Creek, a year-round creek, flows through the park. It is a tributary of Chorro Creek, which empties into the Morro Esturary. This hike follows Dairy Creek up the valley and across the rolling hills to an overlook.

Driving directions: From Highway 101 in San Luis Obispo, take the Morro Bay/Highway 1 exit, and drive 5.5 miles northwest towards Morro Bay to El Chorro Regional Park on the right. It is located across the highway from Cuesta College. Turn right on the park road, and continue 0.8 miles to the Dairy Creek parking lot on the left by the locked gate.

Hiking directions: Hike up Dairy Creek Road past the locked trailhead gate. Follow the road through the rolling hillsides parallel to Dairy Creek to a junction at 0.8 miles. Bear left on the paved road, crossing the bridge over Dairy Creek. Pass a locked vehicle gate at one mile, and continue to an unpaved road on the left near the top of the hill. The road straight ahead continues along Pennington Creek back to Highway 1 at Cuesta College. Take the path to the left, heading up the grassy hillside past several outcroppings to a trail split. Begin the loop on the right fork, reaching the top of a 664-foot hill at 1.6 miles. After enjoying the panoramic views, descend on the footpath to the left towards the water tank. A hundred yards before reaching the tank, bear left on the grassy road, heading east towards

Dairy Creek Road. The trail curves left, completing the loop back at the trail split. Bear right, returning to the paved road. Retrace your steps back to the trailhead.

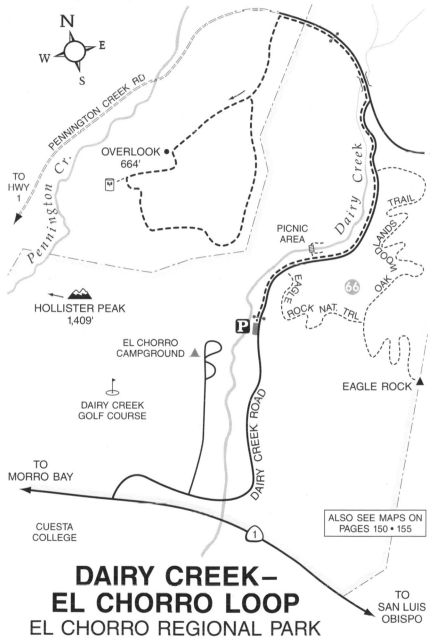

N
E
W
S

PENNINGTON CREEK RD.

Pennington Cr.

OVERLOOK •
664'

TO
HWY
1

Dairy Creek

TRAIL

PICNIC
AREA

WOODLANDS

OAK

EAGLE

66

ROCK NAT. TRL.

HOLLISTER PEAK
1,409'

EL CHORRO
CAMPGROUND ▲

EAGLE ROCK ▲

DAIRY CREEK
GOLF COURSE

P

DAIRY CREEK ROAD

TO
MORRO BAY

CUESTA
COLLEGE

1

ALSO SEE MAPS ON
PAGES 150 • 155

DAIRY CREEK–
EL CHORRO LOOP
EL CHORRO REGIONAL PARK

TO
SAN LUIS
OBISPO

Hike 66
Eagle Rock—Oak Woodlands Loop
EL CHORRO REGIONAL PARK

Hiking distance: 2.5 mile loop
Hiking time: 1.5 hours
Elevation gain: 300 feet
Maps: U.S.G.S. San Luis Obispo

Summary of hike: The Eagle Rock Trail leads up a grassy hillside past Chumash mortar bowls to an overlook at a large rock outcropping. There are beautiful views of Chorro Valley, West Cuesta Ridge, Cuesta College, Camp San Luis Obispo (a training ground for the National Guard), Dairy Creek Golf Course, and the volcanic morros of Cerro Romualdo, Hollister Peak, and Cerro Cabrillo. Leashed dogs are allowed on the trails.

Driving directions: Same as Hike 65.

Hiking directions: Hike up Dairy Creek Road, past the trailhead gate, to the signed Eagle Rock Nature Trail on the right by a huge, twisted oak tree. Leave the road and curve up the hillside through an oak forest on the well-defined footpath. Beyond the forest, beautiful vistas open up of the surrounding area. At 0.4 miles the trail reaches a saddle at signpost 3. To the left of the trail is a rock slab with bowl-shaped holes. These holes were created by the Chumash Indians by grinding acorns into meal for bread. From the saddle, head east toward the prominent Eagle Rock to a signed junction. The left fork is the return route on the Oak Woodlands Trail. Take the right fork and pass a gate. Switchbacks lead up the grassy slope through scrub oak and chaparral to the overlook at Eagle Rock. Return 0.3 miles back to the junction, and head north on the Oak Woodlands Trail. The trail winds its way downhill through a forest of coast live oaks, with an understory of ferns and lichen-covered rocks, to Dairy Creek Road at 1.9 miles. The road to the right heads up canyon, connecting with Pennington Creek Road and Hike 65. Bear left and head down the canyon between oak trees to the left and sycamore trees along the creek. Down the road 0.3 miles is a shady picnic area on the right at a wooden bridge across Dairy Creek. Continue 100 yards, completing the loop.

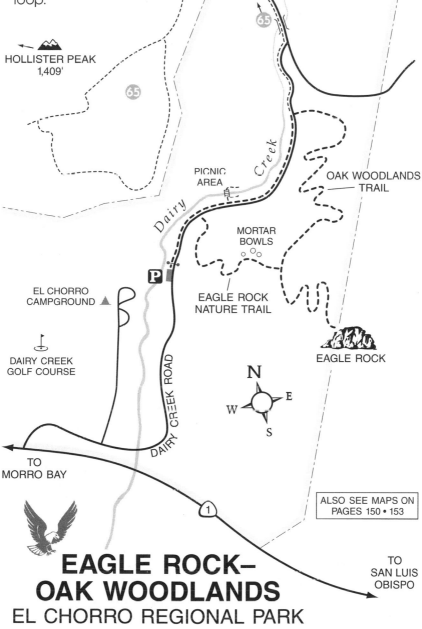

EAGLE ROCK–
OAK WOODLANDS
EL CHORRO REGIONAL PARK

Hike 67
Stenner Creek Canyon

Hiking distance: 4.8 miles round trip
Hiking time: 2.5 hours
Elevation gain: 450 feet
Maps: U.S.G.S. San Luis Obispo

map
next page

Summary of hike: Stenner Creek Canyon sits in the lower foothills beneath West Cuesta Ridge, just north of Cal Poly in San Luis Obispo. The trail along the perennial stream-fed drainage connects with Poly Canyon via an old ranch road over the rolling grassland hills. The hike begins at the old Stenner train trestle, built in the 1880s, and follows the stream up canyon through lush riparian habitat to Stenner Creek Ranch and the head of Poly Canyon. Throughout the hike are great vistas of West Cuesta Ridge and Chorro Valley.

Driving directions: From Santa Rosa Street (Highway 1) and Foothill Blvd, at the north end of San Luis Obispo, drive 1.2 miles northwest on Santa Rosa Street to Stenner Creek Road. Turn right and continue 0.75 miles to the end of the paved road, just before crossing under the Stenner train trestle. Park along the side of the road.

Hiking directions: Walk under the train trestle and enter the mouth of Stenner Creek Canyon. Stroll between the grassy slopes dotted with oaks and Stenner Creek. Cross a bridge over Stenner Creek at a half mile. Curve left and follow the course of the creek. Gradually gain elevation to the top of the hill by the water tanks at one mile. Weave through a pocket of oaks, and pass a junction on the right with the Stenner Creek Ranch. Meander through the rolling grasslands with close-up vistas of West Cuesta Ridge. Cross a cattle guard by a grove of cactus to the end of Stenner Creek Road by two homes at 1.8 miles. Go to the right and cross the bridge to a gate. Pass the gate and follow the old ranch road through stands of eucalyptus. Curve right around the old barn, and pass through another gate. Continue on the dirt road, curving uphill to the left. Cross a spring-fed drainage, and climb to the railroad tracks. Curve right and parallel the tracks on the undulating road. Descend and cross three more drainages in a grove of oaks to a gate at the head of Poly Canyon. This is the turn-around spot.

To hike further, the road parallels Brizziolari Creek through Poly Canyon to the Cal Poly campus (Hike 68) for a 5.6-mile shuttle hike.

Hike 68
Poly Canyon

Hiking distance: 5.5 miles round trip
Hiking time: 2.5 hours
Elevation gain: 700 feet
Maps: U.S.G.S. San Luis Obispo
  The Mountain Biking Map for San Luis Obispo

map
next page

Summary of hike: The Poly Canyon Trail follows a ranch road through the pastoral rolling hills alongside Brizziolari Creek behind the Cal Poly campus. The trail winds through the open space and rock outcroppings to the railroad tracks below West Cuesta Ridge, connecting with Stenner Creek Canyon (Hike 67). The return route follows the north ridge of the canyon through beautiful oak groves overlooking the canyon.

Driving directions: MONDAY—FRIDAY: From Highway 101 in San Luis Obispo, take the Grand Avenue/Cal Poly exit. Turn left onto Grand Avenue, and drive a quarter mile to the Cal Poly entrance station. Obtain a parking permit and parking directions. A parking fee is required.

WEEKENDS: From the Cal Poly entrance station, drive 0.4 miles to Perimeter Road. Turn right and park 0.2 miles ahead in the H-4 parking lot on the right, just after crossing Poly Canyon Road (no fee required).

Hiking directions: Walk a short distance up Poly Canyon Road, and take the unpaved jogging road on the left. Head up the canyon through the eucalyptus grove, parallel to Brizziolari

Creek on the left. At 0.9 miles is a stone arch on the left, the entrance of the architectural design village (Hike 69). Continue straight ahead on the road, passing the university ranch houses, barn, and the first in a series of cattle gates. The trail heads up canyon parallel to Brizziolari Creek. Curve around the hillsides across the open rolling grasslands dotted with trees. Cross over the creek to a corral. Curve left, paralleling a barbed wire fence as the grade steepens. Near the top of the hill, the trail curves left to a metal gate below the railroad tracks on a saddle between Poly Canyon and Stenner Creek Canyon. Take the well-defined footpath to the left, following the fenceline along the edge of the hillside. Cross through a beautiful oak grove and pass a barbed wire gate. Continue to an unsigned junction at a metal gate. Both routes return to the canyon floor. Straight ahead past the gate, the road gently curves down to the canyon and exits at the north end of Via Carta by the horse stables and equine center, located 0.6 miles from Perimeter Road. The footpath to the left descends rather steeply along the fenceline to the canyon. Bear right, returning to the trailhead.

WATER TANKS

Stenner Creek

67

STENNER TRAIN TRESTLE

67
P

ALSO SEE MAPS ON
PAGES 150 • 161 • 163

TO
MORRO BAY

SANTA ROSA STREET

STENNER CREEK RD

HIKE 67

STENNER CREEK CANYON

HIKE 68

POLY CANYON

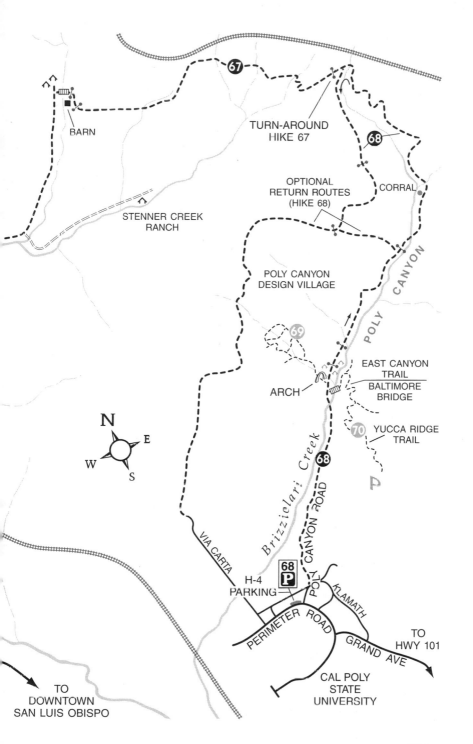

BARN

STENNER CREEK
RANCH

TURN-AROUND
HIKE 67

OPTIONAL
RETURN ROUTES
(HIKE 68)

CORRAL

POLY CANYON
DESIGN VILLAGE

POLY CANYON

EAST CANYON
TRAIL

BALTIMORE
BRIDGE

ARCH

YUCCA RIDGE
TRAIL

P

Brizziclari Creek

POLY CANYON ROAD

VIA CARTA

N
W — E
S

H-4
PARKING

PERIMETER ROAD

KLAMATH

GRAND AVE

TO
HWY 101

TO
DOWNTOWN
SAN LUIS OBISPO

CAL POLY
STATE
UNIVERSITY

Hike 69
Poly Canyon Design Village

Hiking distance: 3 miles round trip
Hiking time: 1.5 hours
Elevation gain: 300 feet
Maps: U.S.G.S. San Luis Obispo

Summary of hike: Poly Canyon Design Village is a collection of artistic, futuristic, and sometimes humorous monuments from the architectural and engineering departments of Cal Poly. These monuments are works of art, attractively set among the rolling hills and grassy meadows in Poly Canyon. The experimental housing projects include a geodesic dome, an underground house, a shell house, a stick house, a greenhouse, and a cantilevered platform in the shape of a ship bow. The trail to the village parallels Brizziolari Creek up the shady canyon.

Driving directions: MONDAY—FRIDAY: From Highway 101 in San Luis Obispo, take the Grand Avenue/Cal Poly exit. Turn left onto Grand Avenue, and drive a quarter mile to the Cal Poly entrance station. Obtain a parking permit and parking directions. A parking fee is required.

WEEKENDS: From the Cal Poly entrance station, drive 0.4 miles to Perimeter Road. Turn right and park 0.2 miles ahead in the H-4 parking lot on the right, just after crossing Poly Canyon Road (no fee required).

Hiking directions: Walk up Poly Canyon Road, bearing left on the jogging road. (See map on next page.) Enter the mouth of the canyon, and follow the unpaved canyon road northeast through the eucalyptus grove along the east side of Brizziolari Creek. At 0.9 miles is a junction with a beautiful stone arch on the left. Bear left under the arch and pass the trail map. Walk up the stone-lined path, and cross the techtite bridge over the stream. Head up the draw past a picnic ground, large art sculptures, and fascinating experimental structures. There are several looping routes and bridges across the rolling grassy meadows.

Oak groves line the trickling streams through the village. The trails connect and return to the bridge and stone arch.

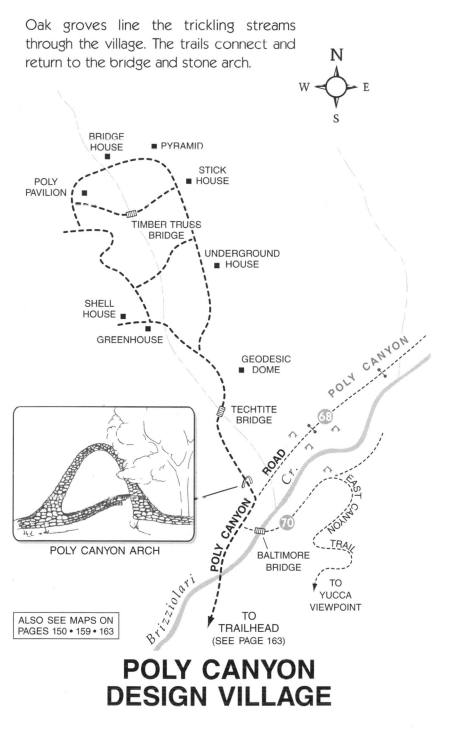

N
W E
S

BRIDGE HOUSE
■ PYRAMID

POLY PAVILION
■

STICK HOUSE ■

TIMBER TRUSS BRIDGE

UNDERGROUND HOUSE ■

SHELL HOUSE ■

GREENHOUSE

GEODESIC DOME ■

POLY CANYON

TECHTITE BRIDGE

ROAD

Cr.

68

POLY CANYON ARCH

POLY CANYON ROAD

Brizziolari

70

BALTIMORE BRIDGE

EAST CANYON TRAIL

TO YUCCA VIEWPOINT

ALSO SEE MAPS ON PAGES 150 • 159 • 163

TO TRAILHEAD
(SEE PAGE 163)

POLY CANYON DESIGN VILLAGE

Hike 70
Yucca Ridge Trail

Hiking distance: 3 miles round trip
Hiking time: 1.5 hours
Elevation gain: 700 feet
Maps: U.S.G.S. San Luis Obispo

Summary of hike: The Yucca Ridge Trail in Poly Canyon winds through an unmaintained botanical garden covered with yucca plants (the *laughing plants of the desert*). The trail ascends a ridge to the 1,139-foot Yucca Viewpoint, above the Poly "P." From the top are panoramic views of Poly Canyon, San Luis Obispo, and the chain of nine morros from Islay Hill to Morro Rock.

Driving directions: From Highway 101 in San Luis Obispo, take the Grand Avenue/Cal Poly exit. Turn left onto Grand Avenue, and drive 0.7 miles to Perimeter Road in Cal Poly. Turn right and park 0.2 miles ahead in the H-4 parking lot on the right, just after crossing Poly Canyon Road. A parking fee is required.

Hiking directions: Walk a short distance up Poly Canyon Road, and take the unpaved jogging road on the left. Continue up the canyon through a eucalyptus grove alongside Brizziolari Creek. At 0.9 miles is the university ranch and a beautiful rock arch. Twenty yards before reaching the arch is Baltimore Bridge, a wooden footbridge crossing the creek on the right. Cross the bridge, taking the East Canyon Trail through a shady woodland. Near a wooden structure on the left, the trail curves right and climbs up the east canyon wall. Switchbacks and steps lead up to a signed junction with the Yucca Ridge Trail on the right. Go right, heading up the hillside on rock steps through a field of yuccas in an unmaintained botanical garden. The trail continues uphill to a saddle on the north flank of the mountain. Follow the path up the ridge to the 1,139-foot peak. From the peak are great 360-degree views. Return along the same path.

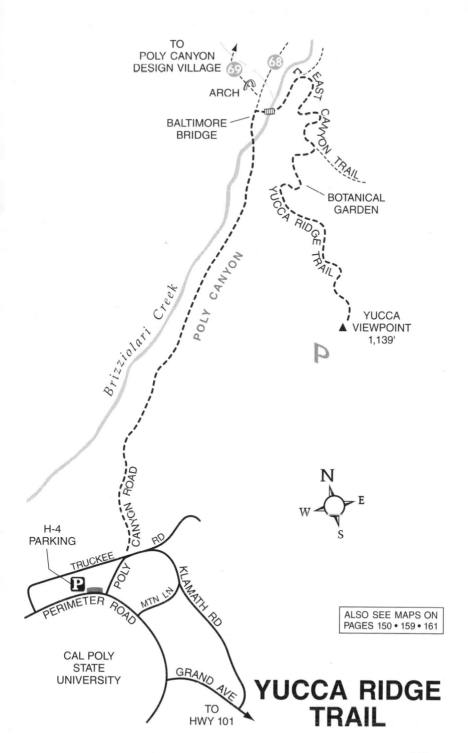

TO
POLY CANYON
DESIGN VILLAGE

69 68

ARCH

BALTIMORE
BRIDGE

EAST CANYON TRAIL

BOTANICAL
GARDEN

YUCCA RIDGE TRAIL

Brizziolari Creek

POLY CANYON

YUCCA
▲ VIEWPOINT
1,139'

P

N
W E
S

POLY CANYON ROAD

H-4
PARKING

P

TRUCKEE RD

MTN LN

KLAMATH RD

PERIMETER ROAD

CAL POLY
STATE
UNIVERSITY

GRAND AVE

TO
HWY 101

ALSO SEE MAPS ON
PAGES 150 • 159 • 161

YUCCA RIDGE
TRAIL

Hike 71
Felsman Loop

Hiking distance: 3.2 miles round trip
Hiking time: 1.5 hours
Elevation gain: 520 feet
Maps: U.S.G.S. San Luis Obispo
Bishop Peak Natural Reserve map

Summary of hike: Bishop Peak Natural Reserve encompasses 352 acres with live oak woodlands, mixed scrub-chaparral,
and perennial native grassland. Two main trails and two trailheads access the natural preserve. The Bishop Peak Trail (Hike
72) climbs to the 1,559-foot summit. This hike traverses the
northern flank of Bishop Peak. The sinuous path meanders across
open pastures and shaded forests, with views of the city and
surrounding hills. At the northern end of the reserve, the path
follows a ridge overlooking the Santa Lucia Mountains, Poly
Canyon, West Cuesta Ridge, San Luis Obispo, and the string of
volcanic morros.

Driving directions: From downtown San Luis Obispo, head
west on Foothill Boulevard to Patricia Drive and turn right.
Continue 0.7 miles to the signed trailhead on the left. Park
alongside the road.

From Los Osos Valley Road, take Foothill Boulevard 2.1 miles
east to Patricia Drive on the left, then follow the directions
above.

Hiking directions: Head west past the trail sign on the
wide path. At 150 yards, cross through the gate into a grove of
coastal live oak. An asphalt road leads up to a water tank on the
right. Bear left on the signed Bishop Peak Trail. Switchbacks lead
uphill past an overlook of San Luis Obispo to a saddle, a cattle
pond, and a junction. The left fork leads to the upper trailhead
on Highland Drive. Bear right and zigzag up to a saddle at a
fenceline, trail gate, and junction. The left fork leads to Bishop
Peak (Hike 72). Go right on the Felsman Loop, joining an old

ranch road. Head across the grassy hills and tree groves past two junctions. Follow the Felsman Loop along a ridge heading north to a signed footpath on the right. Bear right, traverse the hillside and cross the ravine. Switchbacks lead down to a trail gate. Continue around the contours of the hillside and around the left side of the water tank, completing the loop. Return to the trailhead on the left.

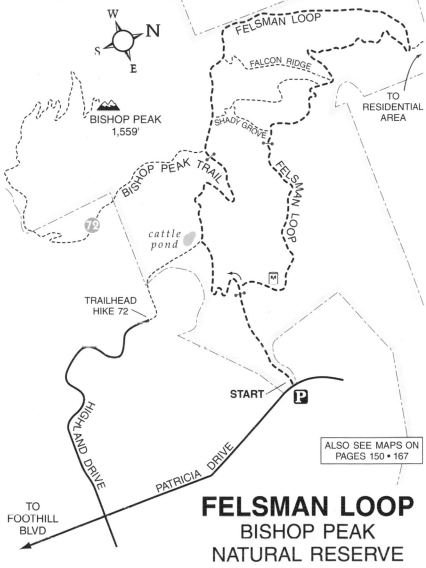

FELSMAN LOOP
BISHOP PEAK
NATURAL RESERVE

Hike 72
Bishop Peak Trail

Hiking distance: 4.5 miles round trip
Hiking time: 2 hours
Elevation gain: 950 feet
Maps: U.S.G.S. San Luis Obispo
Bishop Peak Natural Reserve map

Summary of hike: Bishop Peak is the seventh in a string of nine extinct volcanoes (known as morros) stretching from Morro Bay to San Luis Obispo. The peak, which stands at 1,559 feet, has three distinctive peaks and is the highest morro in the chain. It is the signature backdrop for the city of San Luis Obispo (cover photo), sitting between Chumash Peak and Cerro San Luis Obispo. The climb to the rocky peak winds through perennial native grasslands and live oak woodlands. Near the summit, the trail becomes a scramble over massive granite boulders. From the peak is a panoramic, 360-degree bird's-eye view from the mountains to the coast, including San Luis Obispo and the entire chain of morros.

Driving directions: From downtown San Luis Obispo, head west on Foothill Boulevard to Patricia Drive and turn right. Continue 0.3 miles to Highland Drive and turn left. Drive 0.6 miles up to the signed trailhead at the end of the road.

From Los Osos Valley Road, take Foothill Boulevard 2.1 miles to Patricia Drive on the left, then follow the directions above.

Hiking directions: Walk up the signed trail, following the fenceline into the shade of an oak forest. As you exit the forest, the trail merges with the path from the lower trailhead near a cattle pond. Wind up the grassy hillside beneath the peak to a ridge. Follow the ridge west to a fenceline. Pass through the gate stile and bear left. (The right fork is the Felsman Loop, Hike 71.) Head left through the woodland, passing a V-gate, and traverse the base of the mountain to the south. Switchbacks zigzag up the mountain while passing beautiful rock formations.

The trail wraps around to the west side of Bishop Peak to the upper ridge. Weave up, over, and around the jumble of boulders to the peak. Numerous paths reach the top. After marveling at the views, return along the same path.

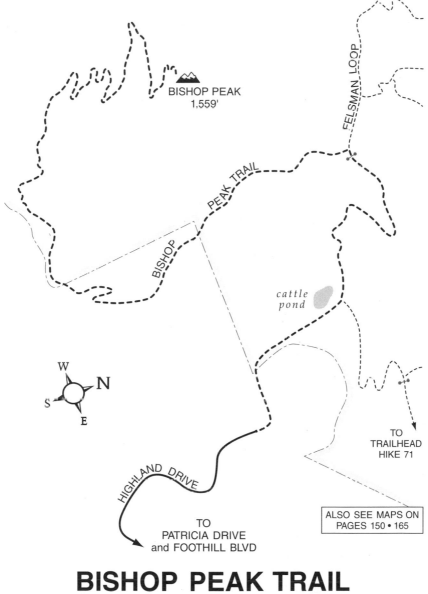

BISHOP PEAK TRAIL
BISHOP PEAK NATURAL RESERVE

Hike 73
Lemon Grove Loop Trail
CERRO SAN LUIS OBISPO NATURAL RESERVE

Hiking distance: 2.2 mile loop
Hiking time: 1 hour
Elevation gain: 400 feet
Maps: U.S.G.S. San Luis Obispo

map
next page

Summary of hike: Cerro San Luis Obispo Natural Reserve encompasses 118 acres on the eastern slope of Cerro San Luis Obispo. The prominent 1,292-foot volcanic landmark, with the letter "M" on its east face, overlooks San Luis Obispo and the Santa Lucia Mountains. The Lemon Grove Loop Trail is named for a 100-year-old abandoned lemon grove, which still survives on the north end of the open space. This hike traverses the east slope of the mountain, following the contour of the foothill en route to the lemon grove. The trail offers panoramic views of the city, Bishop Peak, the Irish Hills, Terrace Hill, Islay Hill, South Hills, and the Santa Lucia Mountains.

Driving directions: From downtown San Luis Obispo, take Higuera Street to the Highway 101 South on-ramp. Just before entering the freeway, turn right onto Fernandez Road (a dirt road) and into the trailhead parking area on the right.

From Highway 101, exit on Marsh Street, and cross the Marsh Street/Higuera Street intersection. Double back to Higuera by turning left on Carmel Street and left again on Higuera Street, then continue with the directions above.

Hiking directions: Head north past the trailhead gate on an old dirt road, up the rolling grasslands. At 300 yards is a posted junction with the Lemon Grove Loop Trail on the right. Begin the loop straight ahead, staying on the wide main trail. Continue uphill past a large prickly pear patch and a bench to the left. The sweeping vistas extend across San Luis Obispo to the surrounding morros and mountains. At the west boundary of the reserve, make a horseshoe right bend to a second posted junction 150 yards shy of the base of the mountain. The main trail continues out of the reserve and climbs to the summit of Cerro San Luis Obispo (Hike 74). Bear right on the Lemon Grove Loop Trail, and traverse the chaparral-covered east face of the mountain while overlooking the city. Cross a seasonal stream in a small oak grove. At the north boundary (0.9 miles) is the historic lemon grove with a pedestrian gate on the left. A faint path loops through the grove. After the lemon grove, take the path north through a eucalyptus grove, past another trail gate, and leave the open space. The trail traverses the hillside to a bench and overlook on the right with great views of Bishop Peak, Cal Poly, and West Cuesta Ridge. Return to the Lemon Grove Loop, and continue along a grove of towering eucalyptus trees. Zigzag down the hillside, passing a draw with a large rock outcropping on the left. A side path leads to the top of the formation. Weave down the slope, crossing a rocky seasonal drainage, and complete the loop. Return to the left.

Hike 74
Cerro San Luis Obispo

Hiking distance: 3 miles round trip
Hiking time: 1.5 hours
Elevation gain: 1,100 feet
Maps: U.S.G.S. San Luis Obispo

map
next page

Summary of hike: Cerro San Luis Obispo is the large morro looming over San Luis Obispo with the big "M." It stands for Mission School. Cerro San Luis Obispo is the eighth of nine volcanic peaks that form a craggy ridge between the cities of Morro Bay and San Luis Obispo, dividing Los Osos Valley and Chorro Valley. The trail up to the peak begins in Cerro San Luis Obispo Natural Reserve, then crosses into private land owned by the Madonna family. The hike has great views of Laguna Lake (Hike 75) and Bishop Peak (Hike 72). From the summit are sweeping views of San Luis Obispo, the Santa Lucia Mountains, and the chain of morros.

Driving directions: Same as Hike 73.

Hiking directions: Follow the hiking directions for Hike 73 to the second junction with the Lemon Grove Loop Trail. The Lemon Grove Loop—Hike 73—goes to the right. Go left on the main trail to the base of the mountain, leaving the reserve and heading westward. Cross a seasonal creek and wind up the west flank of the mountain, with views of Laguna Lake, Bishop Peak, and Los Osos Valley. At the final approach to the summit, there is a trail fork. The trail loops around a knoll and returns to this spot. Take the left fork, hiking clockwise to a platform just below the final scramble to the rocky peak. After marveling at the views, return back to the main trail and continue circling the knoll. Return along the same route.

CERRO
SAN LUIS OBISPO
1,292'

HIKE 73
LEMON GROVE LOOP TRAIL
CERRO SAN LUIS OBISPO
NATURAL RESERVE

HIKE 74
CERRO SAN LUIS OBISPO

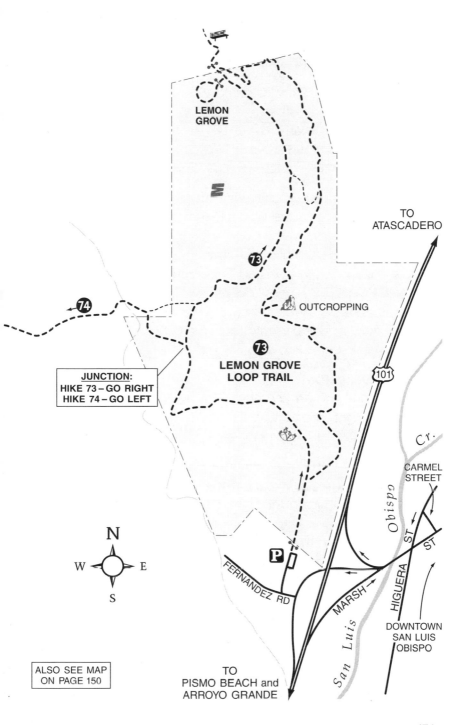

LEMON GROVE

TO
ATASCADERO

74

73

OUTCROPPING

73
LEMON GROVE
LOOP TRAIL

{101}

JUNCTION:
HIKE 73 – GO RIGHT
HIKE 74 – GO LEFT

Cr.

CARMEL
STREET

Obispo

ST

HIGUERA ST

ST

N
W — E
S

P

FERNANDEZ RD

MARSH

DOWNTOWN
SAN LUIS
OBISPO

San Luis

ALSO SEE MAP
ON PAGE 150

TO
PISMO BEACH and
ARROYO GRANDE

Hike 75
Laguna Lake Trail
LAGUNA LAKE PARK AND NATURAL RESERVE

Hiking distance: 1.5 miles round trip
Hiking time: 45 minutes
Elevation gain: Level
Maps: U.S.G.S. San Luis Obispo
      The Thomas Guide—San Luis Obispo County

Summary of hike: Laguna Lake Park encompasses 450 acres, including a 25-acre natural lake and a large, undeveloped open space with hiking trails. The popular park sits on the west base of Cerro San Luis Obispo near the intersection of Madonna Road and Los Osos Valley Road. The area was once used by the Chumash Indians for hunting and fishing. This level loop trail has great views of the surrounding hills, Laguna Lake, and the line of morros that includes Cerro San Luis Obispo, Bishop Peak, Chumash Peak, Cerro Romualdo, and Hollister Peak.

Driving directions: From Highway 101 in San Luis Obispo, exit on Madonna Road, and drive 0.4 miles southwest to Dalidio Drive. Turn right into Laguna Lake Park, and continue straight ahead 0.3 miles to the parking area on the left near the restrooms.

Hiking directions: Take the paved path northwest, crossing the wooden bridge to the signed entry gate. Begin the loop, passing through the gate. Veer right and leave the Meadow Trail. Head north to the base of Cerro San Luis Obispo. Continue north along the side of the mountain, with prominent volcanic peaks on the northern horizon. At the park's north boundary, curve left and continue past a junction with the Meadow Trail to the fenceline. Cross through the gate and veer left, returning to the south. At 1.2 miles, the trail reaches a grove of eucalyptus trees on the left and Laguna Lake on the right. Bear left through the grove of trees, completing the loop back at the trailhead gate.

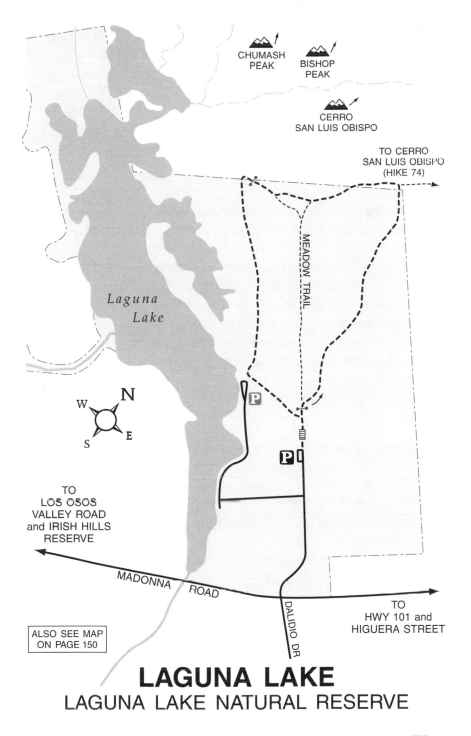

CHUMASH PEAK

BISHOP PEAK

CERRO SAN LUIS OBISPO

TO CERRO
SAN LUIS OBISPO
(HIKE 74)

MEADOW TRAIL

Laguna
Lake

P

P

N
W E
S

TO
LOS OSOS
VALLEY ROAD
and IRISH HILLS
RESERVE

MADONNA ROAD

DALIDIO DR

TO
HWY 101 and
HIGUERA STREET

ALSO SEE MAP
ON PAGE 150

LAGUNA LAKE
LAGUNA LAKE NATURAL RESERVE

Hike 76
Irish Hills from Prefumo Canyon
IRISH HILLS NATURAL RESERVE

Hiking distance: 4 miles round trip

Hiking time: 2 hours

Elevation gain: 700 feet

Maps: U.S.G.S. San Luis Obispo
San Luis Obispo Bicycle Map

*map
next page*

Summary of hike: The Irish Hills Natural Reserve is known for its pristine landscape with dense stands of oak trees, open grasslands, steep-walled canyons, a 1,000-foot-high ridge, and two year-round streams. From the ridge are great vistas of San Luis Obispo, the Santa Lucia Range, and the chain of volcanic peaks that stretches along Los Osos Valley. A comprehensive trail system consisting of narrow footpaths, dirt ranch roads, and a 1.2-mile paved service road weaves through the reserve. This hike climbs the emerald hills from Prefumo Canyon to an overlook and to the exposed ridge on the north half of the reserve. En route, the hike visits an abandoned chromite mine from the 1800s.

Driving directions: From Highway 101 and Los Osos Valley Road in San Luis Obispo, drive 1.5 miles northwest on Los Osos Valley Road to Prefumo Canyon Road. (Prefumo Canyon Road is located 0.6 miles northwest of Madonna Road and 1.1 miles southeast of Foothill Boulevard.) Turn left and continue 0.9 miles to the trailhead parking area on the left, located just after crossing the bridge over Prefumo Creek.

Hiking directions: Pass the trailhead gate on the unpaved road through groves of oaks to a trail split. The left fork leads to the trailhead at the end of Isabella Way. Veer right and ascend the hillside slope. Make a horseshoe right bend, and continue up through the shade of oak trees. Curve left to a posted Y-fork with the Woodland Trail. Follow the trail sign to the right, steadily weaving up the mountain. Pass a power pole, with vistas across the entire city. Enter another shaded pocket of oaks and zigzag up to the ridge. Curve left on the near-level ridge to a side path on the left. Detour left 300 yards on the Durata Vista Trail to an overlook with views of Laguna Lake, the Santa Lucia Range, and the string of volcanic morros from Morro Rock to Islay Hill. Back on the main trail, proceed a short distance to a posted junction. Begin the loop to the right, and climb to another signed junction. Bear left and descend to a Y-fork. The right fork crosses the ridge and descends into Froom Canyon (Hike 77). Stay left 15 yards to another posted junction. The main trail, straight ahead, descends to the trailheads at Madonna Road and Sterling Lane. Bear left, skirting the edge of an open-faced mine site, and complete the loop. Retrace your steps to the right.

Hike 77
Froom Canyon Loop
IRISH HILLS NATURAL RESERVE

Hiking distance: 4 miles round trip
Hiking time: 2 hours
Elevation gain: 700 feet
Maps: U.S.G.S. San Luis Obispo
San Luis Obispo Bicycle Map

map
next page

Summary of hike: The Irish Hills stretch from Highway 101 in San Luis Obispo to the coastline in Montaña de Oro State Park. The Irish Hills Natural Reserve encompasses 722 acres on the southwest corner of San Luis Obispo, tucked into the hills adjacent to Prefumo Canyon. This hike climbs through oak woodlands to the ridge on the south half of the reserve, with sweeping views of the city, surrounding hills, and mountains. En route, the hike descends into steep-walled Froom Canyon. Prefumo Creek and Froom Creek, flowing through the reserve, are perennial tributary streams of San Luis Obispo Creek.

Driving directions: From Highway 101 and Los Osos Valley Road in San Luis Obispo, drive 0.9 miles northwest on Los Osos

Valley Road to Madonna Road. Turn left and continue a quarter mile to the end of the road at DeVaul Ranch Drive. The gated trailhead is left of the intersection. Park alongside the curb.

Hiking directions: Walk up the gated dirt road into a towering eucalyptus grove. Follow the hillside along the south edge of the drainage into a riparian oak woodland. Steadily climb the narrow, shaded draw to an open, grassy slope with views across the city. Enter an oak grove and traverse the hillside through another drainage. Cross a bridge over a third drainage, and emerge on a flat meadow at a dirt road. The right fork leads down to the Sterling Lane trailhead. Take the left fork and head up the old ranch road to views of Laguna Lake, San Luis Obispo, and the Santa Lucia Range. Walk under the power lines to the narrow, paved utility road. Bear left on the road and continue uphill with magnificent views, following the power poles. Curve right to a posted junction. Begin the loop on the Canyon View Trail, a dirt road to the left. Pass a metal gate and descend into Froom Canyon along an eroding rock wall. Pass a hairpin left fork that descends down canyon to the east. Continue straight on the rocky path, completely surrounded by hills, to a signed junction. Leave the road and make a sharp right on the Poppy Trail. Traverse the south slope out of Froom Canyon. Cross a bridge over a draw, heading uphill. At the ridge, curve right and follow the level path. Pass two consecutive junctions on the left that lead to the trailhead at Prefumo Canyon (Hike 76). Descend to the paved road and complete the loop. Retrace your steps to the left.

HIKE 76

IRISH HILLS
from PREFUMO CANYON

HIKE 77

FROOM CANYON
IRISH HILLS NATURAL RESERVE

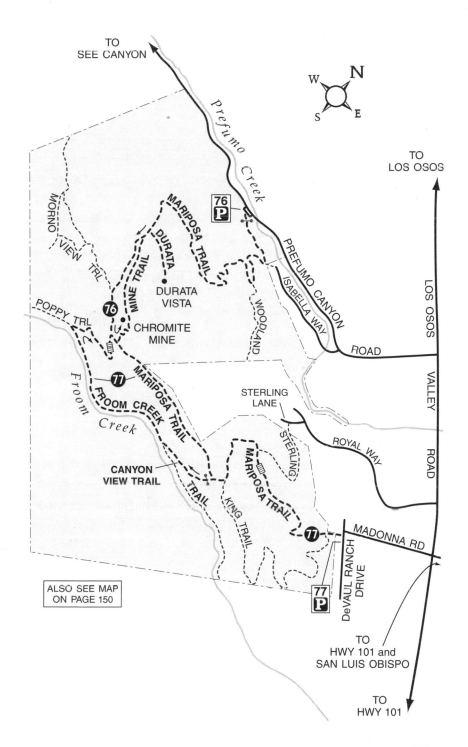

Hike 78
South Hills Open Space

Hiking distance: 2 miles round trip
Hiking time: 1 hour
Elevation gain: 400 feet
Maps: U.S.G.S. San Luis Obispo

Summary of hike: South Hills Open Space is a 60-acre gem on the south end of San Luis Obispo. The one-mile gentle ascent to the flat, rocky summit is highlighted by a bird's-eye view of the city's folded green hills and surrounding valleys. The volcanic cones of Cerro San Luis Obispo and Bishop Peak are prominent landmarks to the north while the Santa Lucia Mountains border the city to the east and northeast.

Driving directions: From Higuera Street and South Street in San Luis Obispo, drive 0.3 miles east on South Street to Exposition Drive (by the Woodbridge sign). Turn right and continue 0.2 miles to the signed South Hills Open Space trailhead on the right, where Exposition Drive becomes Woodbridge Street. Park along the side of the road.

Hiking directions: Walk past the trailhead sign, and follow the grassy path 80 yards towards South Hill parallel to Woodbridge Street. Curve right and traverse the northwest slope into the draw. Pass through a trail gate and continue up the draw, passing sculpted rock formations. Cross a small drainage and head toward the saddle. Just before the saddle is a posted junction. The right fork, straight ahead, leads 100 yards to an overlook of Edna Valley and the airport. From the overlook, a dirt road heads right to the TV tower on the hill to the west. To the left, the road descends the slope to the north end of Calle Jazmin Street. Back at the trail junction, head east and climb the rock-strewn hill. Zigzag up the slope to the ridge, with better vistas on every step. Follow the ridge southeast over the first peak and on to the summit with 360-degree vistas. This is the turn-around spot.

To extend the hike into a longer loop, descend southeast from the summit to the base of the hill by the water tank. Veer right on the road/path toward Calle Jazmin. Curve right again and follow the dirt path back to the saddle, completing the loop.

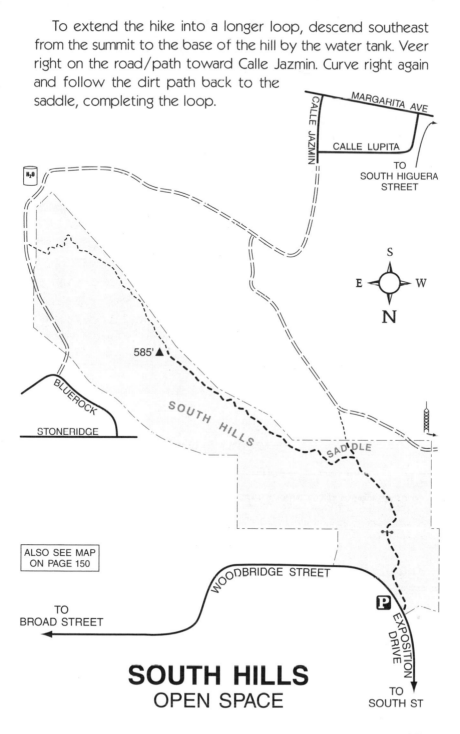

SOUTH HILLS
OPEN SPACE

Hike 79
Railroad Recreation Trail
and Sinsheimer Park

Hiking distance: 2.4—3 miles round trip
Hiking time: 1.5 hours
Elevation gain: Level
Maps: U.S.G.S. San Luis Obispo
San Luis Obispo Bicycle Map

map
next page

Summary of hike: The Railroad Recreational Trail is a landscaped walking, jogging, and biking path that follows the Union Pacific Railroad Tracks from the Amtrak station to Orcutt Road. The trail begins by the Osos—Jennifer Street Bridge, spanning 130 feet over the railroad tracks. En route, the paved path skirts the west face of Terrace Hill (Hike 80) and Sinsheimer Park. Sinsheimer Park was a cow pasture until 1967, but is now a large grassy park with rolling hills, streams, footbridges, baseball fields, and tennis courts. Leashed dogs are allowed.

Driving directions: The trailhead is by the San Luis Obispo Amtrak railroad station, located on Railroad Avenue by Santa Barbara Avenue and Osos Street.

From Marsh Street in downtown San Luis Obispo, drive 0.3 miles southeast on Osos Street to a Y-fork at Triangle Park. Turn left, staying on Osos Street. (Santa Barbara Avenue curves right.) Continue one block to Railroad Avenue at the end of the street by the railroad station and the Osos—Jennifer Street Bridge. Park in the lot to the left or right.

Hiking directions: Climb the Osos—Jennifer Street Bridge stairs or walk up the switchback ramp, crossing over the railroad tracks that lie 25 feet below. Head south on the paved, landscaped path parallel to the tracks, skirting the west face of Terrace Hill. At 0.4 miles, pass a trail access at Bushnell Street to a posted trail fork by Sinsheimer Park. Leave the main trail and go to the left, curving into Sinsheimer Park. One hundred yards ahead is a footpath on the right, just before the paved path curves left onto Boulevard Del Campo. Bear right on the dirt path, and cross a wood bridge over the stream along the lower west edge of the Sinsheimer Park. Follow the waterway downstream, and merge with the paved Railroad Recreation Trail by a grove of eucalyptus trees. To the left, a side path meanders through the tree grove along the north edge of the tree-filled drainage to Southwood Drive. The side path continues across the street and winds through Johnson Park to Augusta Street. The Railroad Recreation Trail continues a short distance to Orcutt Road. Return along the same route.

The walk can be extended by continuing along the paved and natural paths that meander through Sinsheimer Park.

Hike 80
Terrace Hill Open Space

Hiking distance: 0.8 miles round trip
Hiking time: 30 minutes
Elevation gain: 130 feet
Maps: U.S.G.S. San Luis Obispo

map
next page

Summary of hike: Terrace Hill Open Space is a small preserved pocket of nature inside the city of San Luis Obispo. The 501-foot morro has a terraced plateau offering unobstructed 360-degree vistas across the city. The rounded summit was bulldozed in the 1920s, creating a mesa. From the grassy flat are great panoramic views of the whole city. The Santa Lucia Range defines the city border to the north and east. Notice how the homes and development contour to the diverse geography around the city. Also within sight are Edna Valley and the chain of morros, including South Hills, Islay Hill, Orcott Knob, Cerro San Luis Obispo, and Bishop Peak.

Driving directions: From Johnson Avenue in San Luis Obispo, take Bishop Street 0.1 mile southwest to the intersection with Augusta Court. Park on Augusta Court south of Bishop Street or Bishop Street east of Augusta Court. (Parking is not allowed on Bishop Street west of Augusta Court or on Augusta

Court north of Bishop Street.) The signed Terrace Hill trailhead is on Bishop Street on the right, 50 yards west of Augusta Court. (See map below.)

Hiking directions: Head west on Bishop Street to the posted open space entrance on the right. Walk through the trailhead gate and head up the wide path. Halfway up the hill is a footpath veering off to the right. Begin the loop, staying on the wide access route to the flat, circular summit. Circle the perimeter of the plateau, walking clockwise. On the north side, a side path leads partially down the slope and traverses the hill to the left. This path returns to the trailhead via the west slope, skirting around the water tank. Back on the mesa, continue clockwise, passing an oak tree growing out of a rock outcrop on the east side, to a junction at the southeast corner. Drop down to the left, and traverse the south slope to the entrance trail, completing the loop.

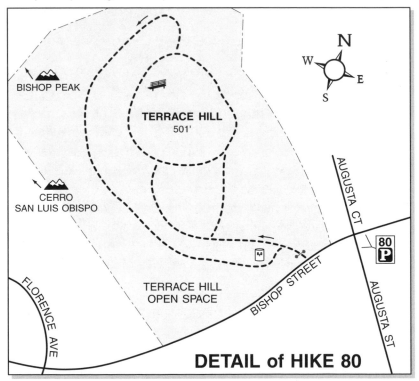

DETAIL of HIKE 80

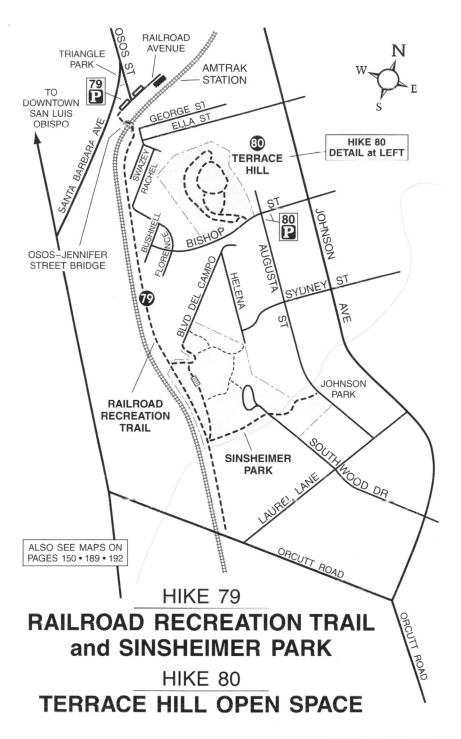

TRIANGLE
PARK

RAILROAD
AVENUE

OSOS ST

AMTRAK
STATION

TO
DOWNTOWN
SAN LUIS
OBISPO

79 P

SANTA BARBARA AVE

GEORGE ST

ELLA ST

SWAZEY

RACHEL

80
TERRACE HILL

HIKE 80
DETAIL at LEFT

ST

80 P

JOHNSON

OSOS–JENNIFER
STREET BRIDGE

BUSHNELL

FLORENCE

BISHOP

BLVD DEL CAMPO

HELENA

AUGUSTA ST

SYDNEY ST

ST

JOHNSON AVE

79

**RAILROAD
RECREATION
TRAIL**

JOHNSON
PARK

SOUTHWOOD DR

**SINSHEIMER
PARK**

LAUREL LANE

ALSO SEE MAPS ON
PAGES 150 • 189 • 192

ORCUTT ROAD

ORCUTT ROAD

HIKE 79
RAILROAD RECREATION TRAIL
and SINSHEIMER PARK
HIKE 80
TERRACE HILL OPEN SPACE

Hike 81
Islay Hill Open Space

Hiking distance: 2 miles round trip
Hiking time: 1 hour
Elevation gain: 400 feet
Maps: U.S.G.S. Pismo Beach and Arroyo Grande NE

Summary of hike: Islay Hill sits at the base of the Santa Lucia Mountains on the southeast corner of San Luis Obispo. It is the ninth and easternmost morro in the string of ancient volcanos, stretching like giant stepping stones from Morro Bay. The north and west flank of the 781-foot hill are designated open space. The trail begins from the southwest corner of the hill and climbs the north face up to the summit. From the rounded peak are sweeping views of five morros, Edna Valley, the airport, and the city of San Luis Obispo. Dogs are allowed on the trail.

Driving directions: From Tank Farm Road and Broad Street in San Luis Obispo, drive one mile east on Tank Farm Road to Wavertree Street. Turn right and continue 0.4 miles to Spanish Oaks Drive. Turn left and go one block to Sweetbay Lane. Turn right and park 0.1 mile ahead in the cul-de-sac by the trail sign.

Hiking directions: Walk past the vehicle gate and posted trailhead at the end of the road. Cross a footbridge over the cement water channel, and parallel the base of Islay Hill. Make a horseshoe right bend and traverse the southwest slope, with a view of the surrounding topography. Top the lower hill to a plateau with an open meadow and a seasonal pond. Loop around the south and east perimeter of the meadow, passing an old twisted oak on the right with a house-size canopy. Head north up the sloping grassland, following the contours of the hillside. Curve right and steadily climb up the north slope, over-looking ranchland and the Santa Lucia Range. Switchbacks lead to the 781-foot summit on a small, round knoll with 360-degree vistas. On the summit is an 8-foot climbing pole, just in case more height is needed. Return along the same route.

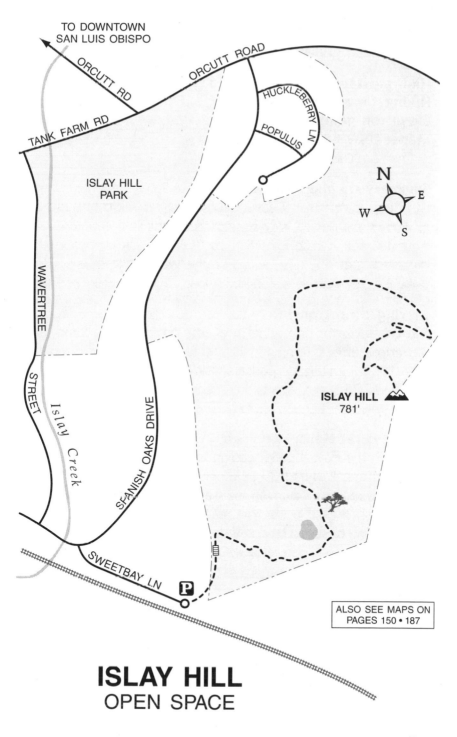

TO DOWNTOWN
SAN LUIS OBISPO

ORCUTT RD

ORCUTT ROAD

HUCKLEBERRY LN

POPULUS

TANK FARM RD

ISLAY HILL
PARK

N
W E
S

WAVERTREE

STREET

Islay Creek

SPANISH OAKS DRIVE

ISLAY HILL
781'

SWEETBAY LN

P

ALSO SEE MAPS ON
PAGES 150 • 187

ISLAY HILL
OPEN SPACE

Hike 82
Islay Creek Bike Paths

Hiking distance: 2.2 miles round trip
Hiking time: 1 hour
Elevation gain: Level
Maps: U.S.G.S. Pismo Beach
      San Luis Obispo Bicycle Map

Summary of hike: The Islay Creek Bike Paths are three biking and hiking paths that weave through neighborhoods along a greenbelt parallel to Islay Creek. The creek is a tributary of Acacia Creek, which joins San Luis Obispo Creek by South Higuera Street. The hike begins on the west edge of Islay Hill (Hike 81) and meanders along the watercourse to French Park.

Driving directions: From Tank Farm Road and Broad Street in San Luis Obispo, drive one mile east on Tank Farm Road to Wavertree Street. Turn right and continue 0.4 miles to Spanish Oaks Drive. Turn left and park alongside the curb. There are two trailheads 35 yards apart on Spanish Oaks Drive between Wavertree Street and Sweetbay Lane.

Hiking directions: Walk through the entrance gate, and begin on the paved path heading northwest. The landscaped greenbelt parallels the east side of the railroad tracks 0.4 miles to Ironbark Street. Return to the trailhead and pick up the path 35 yards southeast, just before reaching Sweetbay Lane. Go to the right and descend steps. Walk through the tunnel under the railroad tracks, and parallel Islay Creek to a Y-fork. The right fork is a wide dirt path that follows a landscaped route alongside the train tracks—the return route. Stay on the paved route to the left, passing a grassy park on the left. Follow the north edge of Islay Creek to Poinsettia Street by Rosemary Court. Cross the street and weave along the watercourse to Larkspur Street by Goldenrod Lane. Cross Larkspur Street and follow the edge of the creek to a trail split at the end of the path. The right fork exits on Ambrosia Lane. The left fork crosses a bridge over the creek to Goldenrod Lane. Return to Poinsettia Street by Rosemary Court. Bear left and cross Rosemary Court and Sunflower Way. Veer right and take the meandering path through the landscaped greenbelt. Pass between a series of cul-de-sacs to Fuller Road at French Park. Explore the paths through the park, and walk to the upper north end by Morning Glory Way. Cross the street and walk to the end of Poppy Lane. Go right and follow the greenbelt parallel to the train tracks, completing the loop. Return to the left.

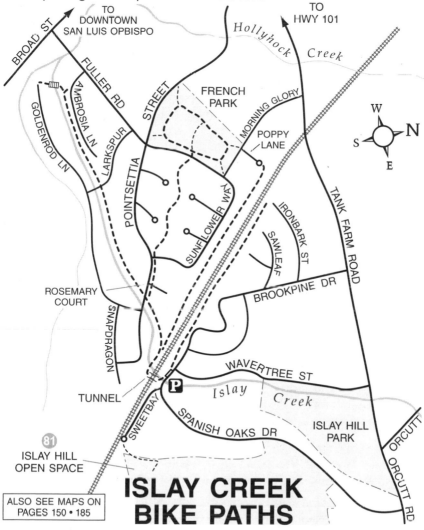

ISLAY CREEK
BIKE PATHS

Hike 83
High School Hill

Hiking distance: 5 miles round trip
Hiking time: 3 hours
Elevation gain: 1,300 feet
Maps: U.S.G.S. San Luis Obispo and Lopez Mountain

Summary of hike: The High School Hill Trail climbs the west slope of the Santa Lucia Mountains from the edge of San Luis Obispo. The steep university-level climb gains 1,300 feet in less than two miles. The trail begins off of Johnson Avenue above San Luis Obispo High School, just outside the city limits. The footpath climbs to an old ranch road atop the ridge overlooking the entire city. The road traverses the ridge and connects with the trail into the Reservoir Canyon Natural Reserve, east of the ridge (Hike 85). Dogs are allowed on the trail.

Driving directions: From Marsh Street and Johnson Avenue in downtown San Luis Obispo, drive 0.4 miles south on Johnson Avenue to Lizzie Street. Turn left and continue 0.1 mile to the posted San Luis Coastal Unified School District and Adult School on the left at 1500 Lizzie Street, between Fixlini Street and Wilding Lane. Turn left and park in the lot on the left.

Hiking directions: Walk up the paved road toward the hills, passing basketball courts to the baseball diamond. Curve around the right side of the field, and follow the footpath on the first base side of the diamond. Just beyond right field, the trail climbs the grassland slope into the open space. Enter the lush riparian habitat on the north edge of the drainage. Cross the stream in a mixed forest to a junction. The right fork leads to the old trail access, closed due to development. Bear left and continue up canyon at a steep grade. Turn around occasionally to savor the views of San Luis Obispo and the beautiful topography. Follow the south side of the stream through grasslands and chaparral, high above the drainage. Curve away from the drainage near the upper slope to an old dirt road atop the ridge. Bear right and follow the road. The magnificent 360-degree vistas include the entire city of San Luis Obispo, the full line of morros (from Islay Hill to Morro Rock), the Irish Hills, and the coastline south to Point Sal. The trail connects with the Reservoir Canyon Trail on the left (Hike 85), just before reaching the carved stone seating area. Return on the same trail.

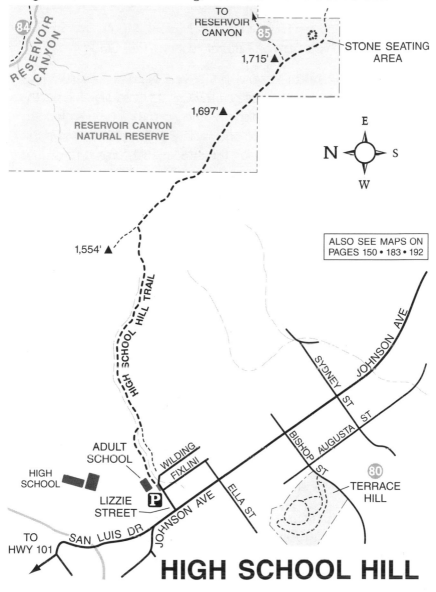

HIGH SCHOOL HILL

Hike 84
Creekside Stroll through Reservoir Canyon
RESERVOIR CANYON NATURAL RESERVE

Hiking distance: 2.4 miles round trip

Hiking time: 1.5 hours

Elevation gain: 300 feet

Maps: U.S.G.S. San Luis Obispo and Lopez Mountain
Reservoir Canyon Natural Reserve Trail Guide

map next page

Summary of hike: Reservoir Canyon Natural Reserve is a 487-acre reserve at the base of the Cuesta Grade on the northeast corner of San Luis Obispo. Although the canyon is close to town, it feels very remote and isolated. This hike follows the first portion of the trail along the stream-fed canyon floor. The hike begins at Reservoir Creek Falls, a 50-foot cataract cascading through a narrow, rock-carved chute into a broad pool. The wooded trail follows the perennial creek, a tributary of San Luis Obispo Creek, in a lush riparian oasis under oak, sycamore, bay, and willow trees. Along the way are small waterfalls and pools between the serpentine rock walls. Dogs are allowed on the trail. The hike can be extended up to the ridge by continuing with Hike 85.

Driving directions: From Highway 101 in San Luis Obispo, drive 2 miles north to Reservoir Canyon Road on the right. The turnoff is at the bottom of the Cuesta Grade, 1.1 miles past the Monterey Street exit (the last exit in San Luis Obispo). Drive 0.4 miles on Reservoir Canyon Road to the parking area on the left near the end of the road.

When departing, it is dangerous to turn left onto Highway 101. Turn right and drive 1.6 miles northbound to a turnoff for Stagecoach Road from the left lane. Turn left and turn around.

Hiking directions: Cross the road to the posted trailhead. Follow this path 100 yards to the base of Reservoir Creek Falls by the pool. Climb the hill under twisted oaks to the brink of the falls. Follow the creek to a second trailhead, located at the

190 - Day Hikes In San Luis Obispo

end of paved Reservoir Canyon Road. Enter the lush canyon on the northeast side of the creek. Stroll along the course of the creek, slowly gaining elevation to a view of the Santa Lucia Mountains. Cross a wooden footbridge over a fork of Reservoir Creek, just above its confluence at 0.8 miles. Curve right, staying in the main canyon, and head southeast. Climb high above the creek and descend back to the stream bank. At 1.1 miles is a posted junction. The left fork, straight ahead, dead-ends at the boundary. Bear right and cross the creek by the remnants of an old bridge. Continue upstream under the shade of the dense forest to the fenced open space boundary at 1.2 miles. This is our turn-around spot. To climb to the ridge, continue with Hike 85.

Hike 85
Reservoir Canyon to the Summit
RESERVOIR CANYON NATURAL RESERVE

Hiking distance: 5 miles round trip
Hiking time: 3 hours
Elevation gain: 1,300 feet
Maps: U.S.G.S. San Luis Obispo and Lopez Mountain
Reservoir Canyon Natural Reserve Trail Guide

map
next page

Summary of hike: This hike in Reservoir Canyon Natural Reserve is a canyon-to-mountain climb, gaining 1,300 feet in elevation. The trail begins along the lush canyon floor (Hike 84), then continues up the north face of the mountain through brushy slopes and grassland meadows to the open ridge high above San Luis Obispo. From the 1,715-foot summit are stunning 360-degree panoramas of San Luis Obispo, Edna Valley, the Irish Hills, Los Osos Valley, Chorro Valley, East and West Cuesta Ridges, and the string of volcanic morros.

Driving directions: Same as Hike 84.

Hiking directions: From the end of Hike 84 — at the fenced open space boundary—return 200 yards down canyon to a fork on the left. Curve left and traverse the hillside slope. Views quickly reveal the oak-filled canyon just hiked, the rolling hills to East Cuesta Ridge, and the TV Towers atop West Cuesta Ridge. Switchback to the left, and follow the narrow path perched on the steep north-facing slope. The trail follows a 50-year-old trail easement through an old goat ranch. Continue through the private land, respecting the property owner's requests to stay on the trail easement. Curve right into a grassy meadow with two huge eucalyptus trees and a group of junk-metal sculptures. Stay on the trail, weaving through the sculpture garden. Climb to the north wall of a stream-fed side canyon and curve right. Follow the crest of the canyon to the ridge, and return to the natural reserve. Head toward the rounded peak straight ahead. Near the summit, cross the grassy slope with scattered rocks to a vista across the entire city of San Luis Obispo, the full line of morros (from Islay Hill to Morro Rock), the Irish Hills, and the coastline south to Point Sal. The trail ends at an old ranch road that runs along the ridge. To the right, the road leads to an unsigned junction with the High School Trail on the left (Hike 83). To the left is a carved stone seating area for soaking in the views.

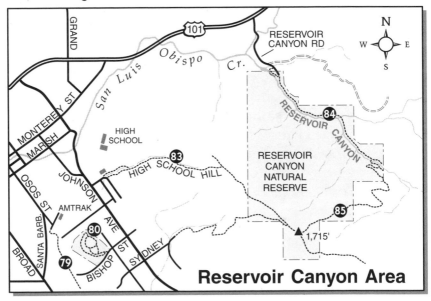

Reservoir Canyon Area

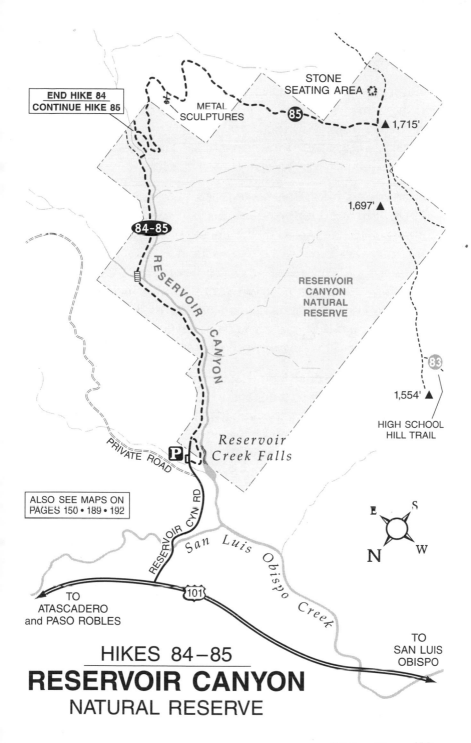

END HIKE 84
CONTINUE HIKE 85

STONE
SEATING AREA

METAL
SCULPTURES

85

▲ 1,715'

1,697' ▲

84-85

RESERVOIR CANYON

RESERVOIR
CANYON
NATURAL
RESERVE

83

1,554' ▲

HIGH SCHOOL
HILL TRAIL

ALSO SEE MAPS ON
PAGES 150 • 189 • 192

PRIVATE ROAD

P

*Reservoir
Creek Falls*

RESERVOIR CYN RD

San Luis Obispo Creek

E — S
N — W

101

TO
ATASCADERO
and PASO ROBLES

TO
SAN LUIS
OBISPO

HIKES 84–85

RESERVOIR CANYON
NATURAL RESERVE

Hike 86
Stagecoach Road to Cuesta Pass

Hiking distance: 5.6 miles round trip

Hiking time: 2.5 hours

Elevation gain: 900 feet

Maps: U.S.G.S. Lopez Mountain and San Luis Obispo
Mountain Biking Map for San Luis Obispo

map next page

Summary of hike: The Stagecoach Road parallels Highway 101 and San Luis Obispo Creek through the shade of Cuesta Canyon while heading up to the Cuesta Grade summit. This historic road was formerly the Old Padre Trail, dating back to the 1700s. The Old Padre Trail was a primary route connecting San Luis Obispo with the northern inland valleys. The hike climbs through a lush, tree-filled canyon parallel to San Luis Obispo Creek. Although the unpaved Stagecoach Road may be used by motor vehicles, it is primarily used for hiking and biking.

Driving directions: From Highway 101 in San Luis Obispo, drive 3.5 miles north to the Stagecoach Road turnoff on the left at the base of the Cuesta Grade. Turn left and park 0.2 miles ahead on the cement slab on the right.

Heading south on Highway 101, drive 3 miles down from the summit of the Cuesta Grade to Stagecoach Road on the right.

Hiking directions: Hike north on the unpaved road, and head up through the lush canyon under the shade of sycamore and oak trees, parallel to San Luis Obispo Creek. Cross a cattle guard and continue uphill. At 0.6 miles, the tree-lined road levels out, then begins the climb again at one mile. At 1.3 miles, the road curves sharply to the right as it begins to wind up the mountainside high above the canyon below. Cross a cascading stream at another sharp right bend as the road traverses the edge of the cliff. The road ends at Cuesta Pass in the parking area for West Cuesta Ridge Road (Hikes 87—89). Return along the same route down the canyon.

Hike 87
Roller Coasters
from West Cuesta Ridge

Hiking distance: 5.4 miles round trip
Hiking time: 3 hours
Elevation gain: 900 feet
Maps: U.S.G.S. San Luis Obispo
Mountain Biking Map for San Luis Obispo

map
next page

Summary of hike: The Roller Coasters Trail is an undulating path that begins atop the West Cuesta Grade and follows the wavy ridge to the Union Pacific Railroad Tracks (formerly Southern Pacific Railroad). The Roller Coaster Trail lives up to its name, crossing a series of long, sweeping saddles and rounded peaks. Throughout the hike are awesome views of the entire San Luis Obispo area, including all the valleys, morros, rolling hills, and mountains. The elevation difference is 900 feet, but this does not account for the ups and downs along the way. Although the trail is rarely steep, it is a substantial workout.

Driving directions: From Highway 101 in San Luis Obispo, head north up the Cuesta Grade to the left turning lane just before reaching the summit. The turnoff is 4.7 miles from Monterey Street, the last San Luis Obispo exit. Turn left and park in the wide pullout at the top of Stagecoach Road.

Hiking directions: To the left is Stagecoach Road (Hike 86). Head up the paved West Cuesta Ridge Road to the right, steadily winding uphill through groves of oaks. At 0.5 miles, views open to the mountainous interior of the Los Padres National Forest. At one mile is a junction on the left with a dirt road. The West Cuesta Ridge Road continues to the right (Hike 88). Leave the ridge and veer left on Shooters Road (the dirt road), passing through a vehicle gate. Follow the winding path along the contours of the scrub-covered hills. At 1.4 miles is a 3-way road split. To the right is Shooters Road. On the left a trail climbs the ridge to an overlook. Head toward the Roller

Coasters—the middle fork—and pass through a metal gate. The vistas span across Morro Bay, Los Osos, the Irish Hills, San Luis Obispo, and the East Cuesta Ridge. Traverse the hillside, marveling at the beautiful topography, and descend to a 1,600-foot saddle. Pass through a gate and begin the "roller coaster" portion of the hike. Follow the long sweeping hills and valleys. Stagecoach Road and Cuesta Grade are far below on the left; Poly Canyon is on the right. On a saddle below a 1,486-foot knoll is another gate. Continue along the ridge to the summit by a rock outcrop on the right. After a short but steep ascent, pass an oak grove on the left. Near the end of the last knoll, make a horseshoe right bend and descend on the southwest slope. Switchback left to the railroad tracks at 2.7 miles. Return by retracing your steps.

HIKE 86
STAGECOACH ROAD to CUESTA PASS

HIKE 87
ROLLER COASTERS from WEST CUESTA RIDGE

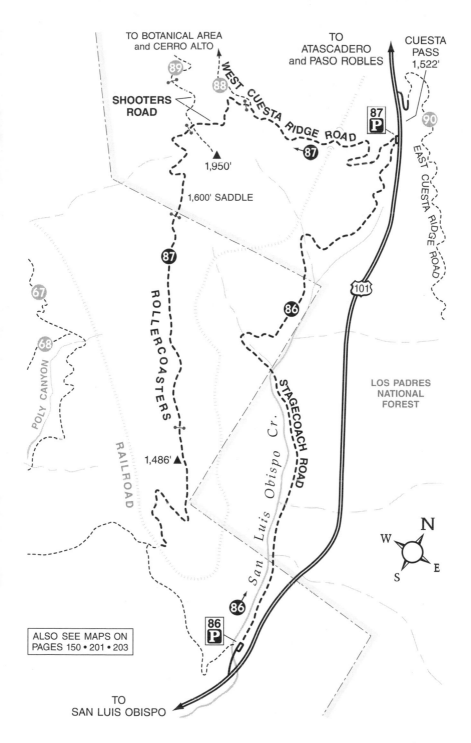

TO BOTANICAL AREA
and CERRO ALTO

89

88

**SHOOTERS
ROAD**

WEST CUESTA RIDGE ROAD

TO
ATASCADERO
and PASO ROBLES

CUESTA
PASS
1,522'

87
P

90

87

▲
1,950'

EAST CUESTA RIDGE ROAD

1,600' SADDLE

87

67

101

86

LOS PADRES
NATIONAL
FOREST

R O L L E R C O A S T E R S

STAGECOACH ROAD

68

POLY CANYON

RAILROAD

1,486' ▲

San Luis Obispo Cr.

N
W   E
S

86

86
P

ALSO SEE MAPS ON
PAGES 150 • 201 • 203

TO
SAN LUIS OBISPO

Hike 88
West Cuesta Ridge (TV Tower) Road
to Cuesta Ridge Botanical Area

Hiking distance: 7 miles round trip

Hiking time: 3 hours

Elevation gain: 850 feet

Maps: U.S.G.S. San Luis Obispo and Atascadero
   Mountain Biking Map for San Luis Obispo

map
next page

Summary of hike: The West Cuesta Ridge Road (also called the TV Tower Road) begins at the summit of the Cuesta Grade. The paved road winds up the terraced slopes of the mountain on the west side of Highway 101 to one of the prime vistas in the county. It also passes through the 1,334-acre Cuesta Ridge Botanical Area in the Los Padres National Forest. The botanical garden has green-colored serpentine bedrock and large groves of Sargent cypress, manzanita, and pines. It is one of the only places in the world where Sargent cypress grow. Throughout the hike are fantastic views of San Luis Obispo, Morro Bay, the Santa Lucia Wilderness, the Atascadero Hills, Chorro and Los Osos Valleys, and the chain of morros. The rough, narrow road is open to motor vehicles but is primarily used as a hiking and biking route.

Driving directions: From Highway 101 in San Luis Obispo, head north up the Cuesta Grade to the left turning lane just before reaching the summit. The turnoff is 4.7 miles from Monterey Street, the last San Luis Obispo exit. Turn left and park in the wide pullout at the top of Stagecoach Road.

Hiking directions: To the left is Stagecoach Road (Hike 86). Head up the paved West Cuesta Ridge Road to the right, steadily winding uphill through groves of oaks. At 0.5 miles, views open to the mountainous interior of the Los Padres National Forest. At one mile, stay to the right at a road fork with Shooters Road to the Roller Coasters (Hike 88), and continue along the contours of the mountain up to the ridge. The views extend across San Luis Obispo, the chain of morros (from Islay Hill to Morro Rock), the Irish Hills, Montaña de Oro, Los Osos, and Baywood Park. The winding mountain road alternates between vistas on each side of the ridge as it continues uphill to a road split below the TV towers at 2.5 miles. Bear left, curving around the hilltop to the signed Cuesta Ridge Botanical Area and a junction at 3 miles. The Morning Glory Trail (Hike 89) bears left. Follow the ridge road—straight ahead—through the botanical reserve, choosing your own turn-around spot.

To hike further, the road leads 5 miles to a forest service gate at the Cerro Alto Trail and Boy Scout Trail junction (Hike 39). For a 7.7-mile loop hike, return on the Morning Glory Trail, referencing Hike 89.

Hike 89
Morning Glory—Shooters Loop
from West Cuesta Ridge

Hiking distance: 7.7 miles round trip
Hiking time: 4 hours
Elevation gain: 1,000 feet
Maps: U.S.G.S. San Luis Obispo
Mountain Biking Map for San Luis Obispo

map
next page

Summary of hike: The Morning Glory Trail connects West Cuesta Ridge with Shooters Road. The trail weaves along the slope below the TV towers, high above Stenner Canyon and Poly Canyon. The footpath traverses the mountain through chaparral, scrub, and forested drainages. Shooters Road is an old jeep road that has been reclaimed by erosion and vegetation and is now a hiking and biking path. The old road is perched on the cliffs overlooking San Luis Obispo.

Driving directions: Same as Hike 88.

Hiking directions: Follow the hiking directions to Hike 88 on the West Cuesta Ridge Road to a junction at the signed Cuesta Ridge Botanical Area at 3 miles. The ridge route continues through the botanical reserve to Cerro Alto. Bear left and leave the ridge on the Morning Glory Trail, an old jeep road. Steadily descend the southwest-facing slope beneath the TV towers. Head through chaparral and scrub to a cairn-marked footpath on the left at 3.8 miles. Bear left and weave downhill on the single track, staying left at an unsigned fork on a curve. Cross a seasonal drainage and traverse the rolling hills, dropping into the next canyon to the south. Zigzag down into the forested stream-fed drainage at 5 miles, and climb out to the open brush. The Morning Glory Trail ends at a T-junction with a dirt road by a eucalyptus grove. Take Shooters Road to the left, located 100 yards shy of the dirt road. Steadily climb on the narrow, abandoned jeep road, following the contours of the hills while perched on the cliffs. Cross a couple of drainages, pass through two metal gates at 5.5 miles and 6.0 miles, and continue to a T-junction. To the right are the Roller Coasters (Hike 87). Bear left and wind 0.4 miles to West Cuesta Ridge, completing the loop. Return to the trailhead 1 mile to the right.

HIKE 88
WEST CUESTA RIDGE ROAD
to BOTANICAL AREA

HIKE 89
MORNING GLORY – SHOOTERS LOOP
from WEST CUESTA RIDGE

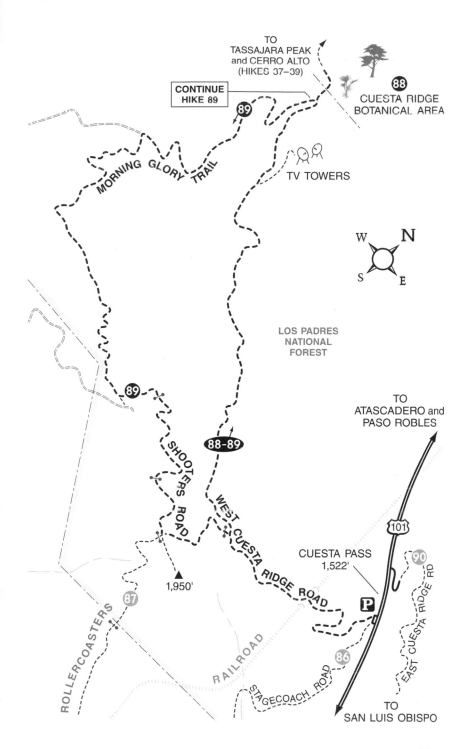

TO
TASSAJARA PEAK
and CERRO ALTO
(HIKES 37–39)

CONTINUE
HIKE 89

89

88
CUESTA RIDGE
BOTANICAL AREA

MORNING GLORY TRAIL

TV TOWERS

N
W   E
S

LOS PADRES
NATIONAL
FOREST

89

88-89

SHOOTERS ROAD

WEST CUESTA RIDGE ROAD

TO
ATASCADERO and
PASO ROBLES

101

CUESTA PASS
1,522'

CUESTA RIDGE RD

90

EAST CUESTA RIDGE RD

P

1,950'

87

ROLLERCOASTERS

RAILROAD

STAGECOACH ROAD

86

TO
SAN LUIS OBISPO

Hike 90
East Cuesta Ridge Road

Hiking distance: 7—14 miles round trip
Hiking time: 3—7 hours
Elevation gain: 900 feet
Maps: U.S.G.S. San Luis Obispo and Lopez Mountain
Mountain Biking Map for San Luis Obispo

Summary of hike: The East Cuesta Ridge Road (also called Mount Lowe Road) begins at the summit of the Cuesta Grade. The unpaved road traverses the mountain adjacent to the Santa Lucia Wilderness through the shade of an oak, pine, and manzanita forest. The hike offers a unique vantage point for fantastic views of San Luis Obispo. The views range across West Cuesta Ridge to the ocean, from Morro Bay to the Oceano Dunes. There are also panoramic vistas of Los Osos Valley and Chorro Valley, separated by the chain of volcanic morros. The road continues past the radio facility on Mount Lowe to Upper Lopez Canyon at just under 5 miles.

Driving directions: From Highway 101 in San Luis Obispo, head north up the Cuesta Grade to the summit pullout on the right The turnoff is 4.9 miles from Monterey Street (the last San Luis Obispo exit), 0.2 miles past the West Cuesta Ridge turnoff on the left, and 150 yards beyond the sign which reads "Cuesta Grade 1522 feet."

Hiking directions: Hike up the road over the locked vehicle gate. Follow the road as it weaves up the grassy hillside dotted with oak trees. Continue uphill as the road traverses the mountainside, passing in and out of shady tree groves and crossing stream drainages. At 1.6 miles is a junction with a ranch road on the left. Continue on the main road, reaching the junction with the road to the towers atop Mount Lowe at 3.5 miles.

To extend the hike, the main road continues to a junction with the Upper Lopez Canyon Trail at 4.6 miles. This trail enters the Santa Lucia Wilderness and descends to Big Falls (Hike 116).

At 7 miles, the main road ends by gated private property. Choose your own turn-around spot, and return along the same route.

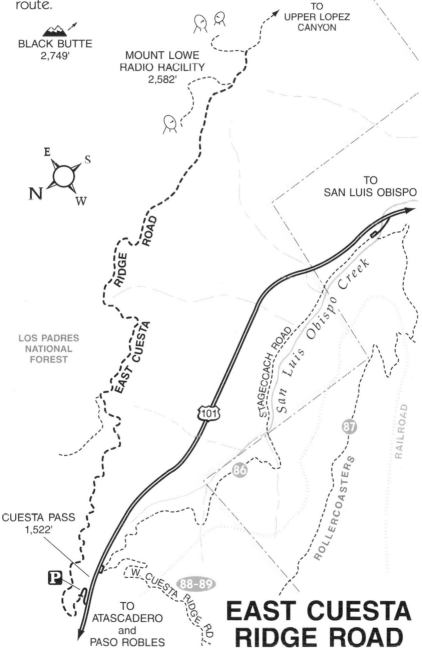

BLACK BUTTE
2,749'

MOUNT LOWE
RADIO RACILITY
2,582'

TO
UPPER LOPEZ
CANYON

TO
SAN LUIS OBISPO

E S
N W

RIDGE ROAD

EAST CUESTA

LOS PADRES
NATIONAL
FOREST

San Luis Obispo Creek

STAGECOACH ROAD

101

86

37

RAILROAD

ROLLERCOASTERS

CUESTA PASS
1,522'

P

W. CUESTA RIDGE RD.

88-89

TO
ATASCADERO
and
PASO ROBLES

EAST CUESTA
RIDGE ROAD

Hike 91
Tassajara Creek Road

Hiking distance: 5 miles round trip
Hiking time: 2.5 hours
Elevation gain: 200 feet
Maps: U.S.G.S. San Luis Obispo and Atascadero
San Luis Obispo Mountain Biking map

Summary of hike: Tassajara Creek Road sits at the top of the Cuesta Grade, north of West Cuesta Ridge and a short distance southwest of Santa Margarita. The mountain road climbs the east flank of Tassajara Peak (with twin summits) and parallels Tassajara Creek into the Los Padres National Forest. En route, the paved road weaves through grassy hillsides and oak woodlands. Tassajara Creek Road can be driven, but is a beautiful mountain hike with a minimum of vehicles.

Driving directions: From Highway 101 in San Luis Obispo, head north up the Cuesta Grade to the left turning lane and exit for Tassajara Creek Road. The turnoff is 6.5 miles from Monterey Street (the last San Luis Obispo exit) and 1.8 miles past the West Cuesta Ridge turnoff. Turn left and cross a wooden bridge to the parking pullout on the right.

Heading southbound from Atascadero, the turnoff is 1 mile south of the Highway 58/Santa Margarita exit.

Hiking directions: Walk uphill on the paved road and cross a cattle guard. Curve up the pastoral hills filled with oaks, following Tassajara Creek upstream. Pass vineyards on the left, Canyon Drive at a half mile, and Sully Springs at 1.4 miles. Cross a one-lane bridge at 2 miles, where the road narrows and is unpaved. Continue on the dirt road under an oak canopy at the edge of the creek. Cross a concrete bridge to a road split with Wildass Times Road. Stay in the canyon, veering to the left to the end of the road at a residence. Return along the same route.

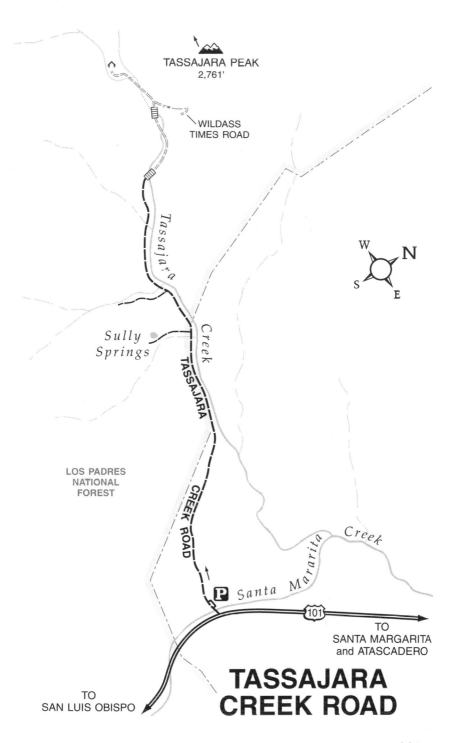

TASSAJARA PEAK
2,761'

WILDASS
TIMES ROAD

Tassajara

W N S E

Sully Springs

Creek

TASSAJARA

LOS PADRES
NATIONAL
FOREST

CREEK ROAD

Creek

Santa Mararita

P *Santa Mararita*

101

TO
SANTA MARGARITA
and ATASCADERO

TO
SAN LUIS OBISPO

TASSAJARA
CREEK ROAD

Hike 92
Rocky Trail to Salinas Dam Overlook
SANTA MARGARITA LAKE REGIONAL PARK

Hiking distance: 3.6 miles round trip

Hiking time: 2 hours

Elevation gain: 300 feet

Maps: U.S.G.S. Santa Margarita Lake and Lopez Mountain
Santa Margarita Lake Trail Guide

map
page 210

Summary of hike: Santa Margarita Lake (originally called Salinas Reservoir) is fed by the Salinas River, Toro Creek, Alamo Creek, and many smaller tributaries. The 6-mile-long lake has 22 miles of shoreline and is the centerpiece of the 4,000-acre regional park. On the west end of the lake is the Salinas Dam, built in 1941. The Rocky Trail skirts the west end of the lake through grasslands and an oak and grey pine woodland, emerging at Rocky Point and an overlook 340 feet above the dam. From the 1,640-foot overlook are vistas of the islands, peninsulas, and the multiple fingers of Salinas Bay.

Driving directions: From Highway 101 in San Luis Obispo, head 8 miles north up the Cuesta Grade to the Santa Margarita (Highway 58) exit. Drive 1.5 miles east, through the town of Santa Margarita, to Estrada Avenue. Turn right, following the signs to Santa Margarita Lake. (En route Estrada Avenue becomes Calf Canyon Highway/Highway 58.) At 1.5 miles, Highway 58 turns left. Instead, go straight onto Pozo Road. Continue 6.2 miles to Santa Margarita Lake Road and turn left. Drive one mile to the park entrance station. Turn right and immediately turn right again to the parking lot, adjacent to the entrance station. An entrance fee is required.

Hiking directions: The posted trailhead is by the flagpole, directly west of the entrance station. Parallel the entrance road on the oak-dotted grassland. Drop over the hill above Coyote Campground, passing lichen-covered boulders. Rocky Point is the highest peak to the north, across the campground. Two

U-shaped curves descend into the valley and skirt the edge of the campground on the north-facing slope. Loop around the south finger of Murphy Bay, and cross the inlet steam. Follow the west side of the bay on the grassy slope with oaks and grey pines. Curve through a series of inlets and drainages, overlooking the west end of the lake. At the north end of Murphy Bay, leave the shoreline and gently climb the forested hillside. Loop back to an overlook of the entire bay. Traverse the hill and weave through the forest to the end of the footpath at a junction with a dirt road on the 1,600-foot ridge. Bear right and continue uphill 150 yards to a small loop at the end of the road and Lookout Point, 340 feet above Salinas Dam. The views extend across Salinas Bay with its gorgeous serpentine shoreline, coves, rock outcroppings, rolling hills, and forested pockets. Steep, unsafe side paths drop off the hillside to a variety of vistas.

Hike 93
Grey Pine Trail to Eagle View
SANTA MARGARITA LAKE REGIONAL PARK

Hiking distance: 3.2 miles round trip
Hiking time: 1.5 hours
Elevation gain: 230 feet
Maps: U.S.G.S. Santa Margarita Lake
        Santa Margarita Lake Regional Park map

map
page 210

Summary of hike: The Grey Pine Trail weaves through the foothills at the base of the mountains on the south edge of Santa Margarita Lake. The trail winds through the shade of an oak-studded forest beneath magnificent sandstone rock outcroppings known as the Crags. The trail ends at Eagle View, a rocky point 326 feet above Blinn Bay. There are great views in every direction.

Driving directions: Same as Hike 92.

Hiking directions: Take the signed trail south up the grassy slope, curving around the hillside beneath the imposing mountains and sandstone formations. Cross several ravines in the shade of the forest, gradually gaining elevation along the hillside. At 0.9 miles is a signed junction. The left fork leads to the lake, returning to Grey Pine Campground on the park road. Take the right fork towards White Oak Flat. The footpath leads to a trail split on a ridge overlooking the flat. Bear left up the ridge to another signed trail split. Take the left fork uphill towards Eagle View. Hike along the ridge past two overlooks with benches. The last 0.2 miles follows a narrow rocky path, ending at a steep point high above Blinn Bay and the lake. Return by retracing your steps.

For a longer hike, return back to the trail split on the ridge, and head to White Oak Flat. Continue with Hike 94 on the Lone Pine Trail.

Hike 94
Lone Pine Trail to Vaca Flat
SANTA MARGARITA LAKE REGIONAL PARK

Hiking distance: 2.6 miles round trip
Hiking time: 1.5 hours

map
page 210

Elevation gain: 500 feet
Maps: U.S.G.S. Santa Margarita Lake
      Santa Margarita Lake Regional Park map

Summary of hike: Vaca Flat is a beautiful waterfront picnic area surrounded by mountains on a peninsula jutting into Salsipuedas Bay, an inlet of Santa Margarita Lake. En route to Vaca Flat, the Lone Pine Trail winds through an oak forest past sculpted sandstone formations and magnificent overlooks of the lake and surrounding mountains.

Driving directions: Follow the driving directions for Hike 92 to the Santa Margarita Lake entrance station. At the entrance station, take the road to the right 1 mile to the signed Lone Pine trailhead on the right. Park in the White Oak Flat lot on the left, just past the trail. A parking fee is required.

Hiking directions: Cross the park road and head east past the trail sign to a junction 100 yards ahead. To the right is the Grey Pine Trail (Hike 93). Take the left fork across the grassy hillside with views of beautiful sandstone formations known as the Santa Margarita Crags. Switchbacks lead sharply up the hillside through oak groves to a bench at an overlook of Santa Margarita Lake. After resting, continue uphill past massive sandstone outcroppings and great views. Shortly beyond the formation is an unsigned junction at 0.6 miles. The right fork leads 60 yards uphill to another bench and overlook. Continue on the main trail, curving through the mountainous terrain. The trail descends past more outcroppings to the unpaved road that leads to Vaca Flat Picnic Area. Pick up the signed trail across the road, and continue along the contours of the hillside to the north-facing slope above the lake at Salsipuedas Bay. Descend east to Vaca Flat, a grassy picnic area on the banks of the lake. Return along the same route.

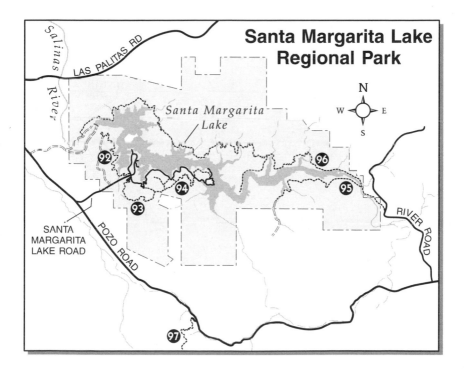

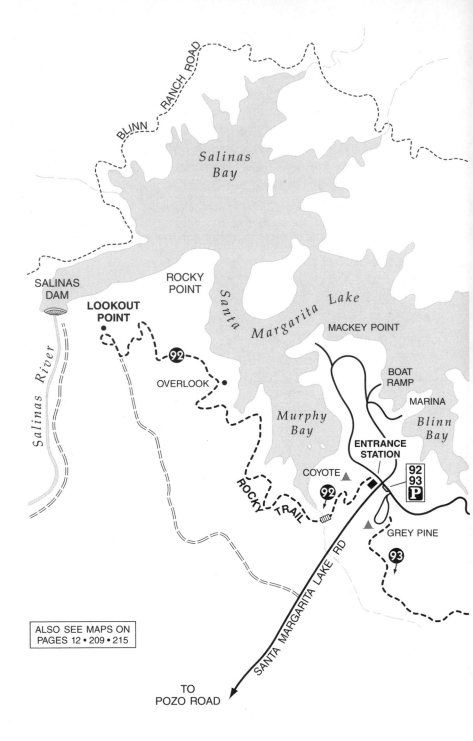

BLINN RANCH ROAD

Salinas Bay

SALINAS DAM

LOOKOUT POINT

ROCKY POINT

Santa Margarita Lake

MACKEY POINT

BOAT RAMP

MARINA

Blinn Bay

92

OVERLOOK

Salinas River

Murphy Bay

ENTRANCE STATION

ROCKY TRAIL

COYOTE

92

92 93 P

GREY PINE

93

SANTA MARGARITA LAKE RD

TO POZO ROAD

ALSO SEE MAPS ON
PAGES 12 • 209 • 215

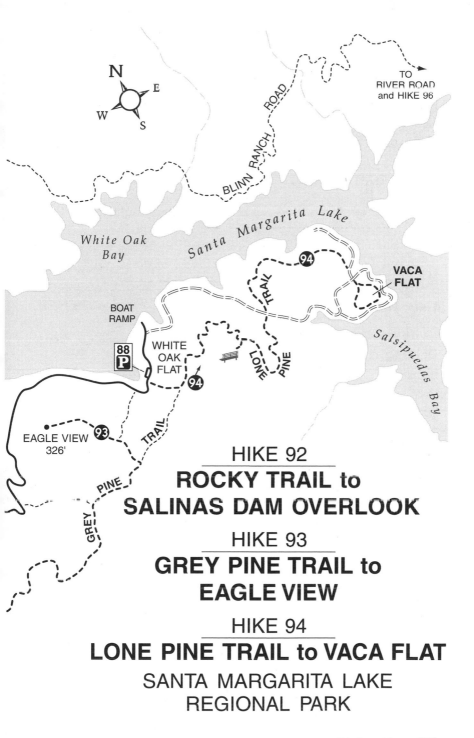

N
W   E
S

TO
RIVER ROAD
and HIKE 96

BLINN RANCH ROAD

Santa Margarita Lake

White Oak
Bay

94

**VACA
FLAT**

TRAIL

BOAT
RAMP

88
P

WHITE
OAK
FLAT

94

LONE

PINE

Salsipuedas Bay

EAGLE VIEW
326'

93

TRAIL

PINE

GREY

HIKE 92
ROCKY TRAIL to
SALINAS DAM OVERLOOK

HIKE 93
GREY PINE TRAIL to
EAGLE VIEW

HIKE 94
LONE PINE TRAIL to VACA FLAT
SANTA MARGARITA LAKE
REGIONAL PARK

Hike 95
Sandstone Trail
SANTA MARGARITA LAKE REGIONAL PARK

Hiking distance: 5 miles round trip
Hiking time: 2.5 hours
Elevation gain: 200 feet
Maps: U.S.G.S. Santa Margarita Lake
Santa Margarita Lake Regional Park map

Summary of hike: The Sandstone Trail begins at the upper/eastern access to Santa Margarita Lake. The trail traverses the hillside through oak groves on the south side of the lake. The hike leads to scenic overlooks of the surrounding mountains and to McNeil Falls, a seasonal 40-foot cataract cascading down a beautiful sandstone rock formation in McNeil Canyon.

Driving directions: From Highway 101 in San Luis Obispo, head 8 miles north up the Cuesta Grade to the Santa Margarita (Highway 58) exit. Drive 1.5 miles east, through the town of Santa Margarita, to Estrada Avenue. Turn right, following the signs to Santa Margarita Lake. (En route Estrada Avenue becomes Calf Canyon Highway/Highway 58.) At 1.5 miles, Highway 58 turns left. Instead, go straight onto Pozo Road. Continue 14 miles (passing the turnoff to Santa Margarita Lake) to River Road and turn left. Drive 1.7 miles to the East River Trail access on the left. Park in the lot at the trailhead. A parking fee is required.

Hiking directions: Walk northwest past the trail gate on the East River Road Access. The first half mile crosses the rolling foothills dotted with oak trees to a signed junction. The right fork is the Blinn Ranch Trail (Hike 96). Take the Sandstone Trail to the left. Use caution wading across the slow rolling Salinas River. After crossing, head west on the level, well-defined trail. At one mile, the trail enters the forested canyon and winds up the hillside to the ridge. Follow the ridge past several overlooks of

Santa Margarita Lake. Descend into McNeil Canyon, curving south to seasonal McNeil Falls at an inlet stream to the lake. Continue to the second lake finger at an outlet stream by the remnants of a cement bridge. This is a good turn-around spot.

To hike further, the old ranch road parallels the stream south a quarter mile to gated private land.

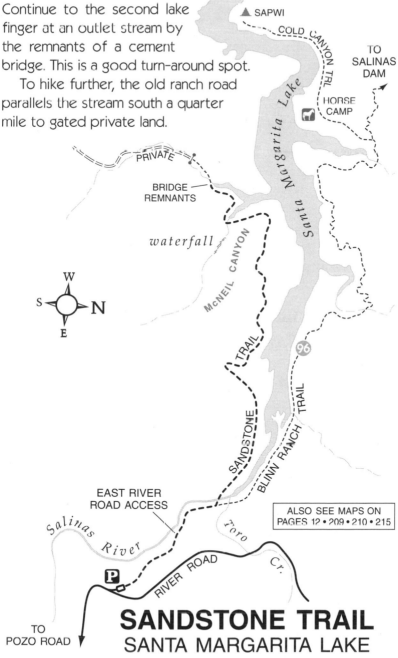

ALSO SEE MAPS ON
PAGES 12 • 209 • 210 • 215

SANDSTONE TRAIL
SANTA MARGARITA LAKE

Hike 96
Blinn Ranch Trail
SANTA MARGARITA LAKE REGIONAL PARK

Hiking distance: 6 miles round trip
Hiking time: 3 hours
Elevation gain: 250 feet
Maps: U.S.G.S. Santa Margarita Lake
Santa Margarita Lake Regional Park map

Summary of hike: The Blinn Ranch Trail is an old ranch road that follows the entire north side of Santa Margarita Lake, from River Road at the east end to the Salinas Dam at the west end. This hike takes in the first 3 miles of the 9-mile-long road. The trail begins at River Road and follows along the pastoral rolling grasslands dotted with pines and oaks. The trail winds through Portola Canyon and Cold Canyon, with several stream crossings and scenic overlooks of the lake.

Driving directions: Same as Hike 95.

Hiking directions: Walk through the trailhead gate, and head west on the East River Road Access. The road curves through the pastureland with groves of oaks and grey pines. At 0.5 miles is a signed trail split. The Sandstone Trail (Hike 95) bears to the left. Take the right fork on the Blinn Ranch Trail past sandstone outcroppings carved by wind and water. Cross planks over Toro Creek, and follow the Salinas River downstream, which develops into Santa Margarita Lake. At 1.5 miles, curve up the hillside to views of the east arm of the lake. Descend and cross Alamo Creek in Portola Canyon. Wind through the canyon past numerous sandstone outcroppings. At 2.4 miles, the trail snakes through an oak grove with great views above the lake. Curve around the west side of Cold Canyon, crossing a third inlet stream below the sandstone cliffs. Ascend the hill to a signed junction with the Cold Canyon Trail. This is the turn-around spot.

To hike further, the 9-mile-long Blinn Ranch Trail continues to the west end of the lake by Salinas Dam. The Cold Canyon Trail (also called Sapwi Trail) descends a half mile to Khus Horse Camp and 1.4 miles to Sapwi Camp.

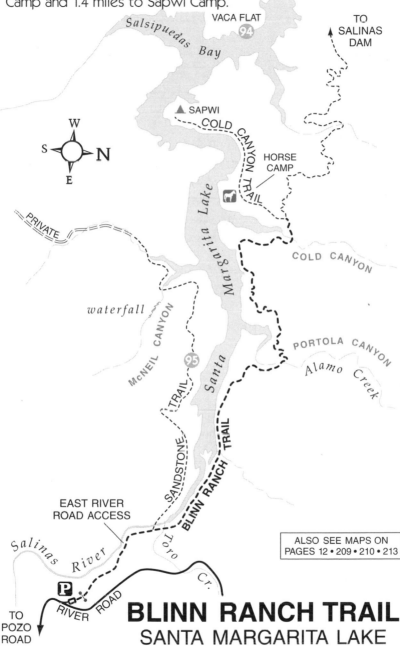

ALSO SEE MAPS ON
PAGES 12 • 209 • 210 • 213

BLINN RANCH TRAIL
SANTA MARGARITA LAKE

Hike 97
Rinconada Trail

Hiking distance: 4 miles round trip
Hiking time: 2 hours
Elevation gain: 600 feet
Maps: U.S.G.S. Santa Margarita Lake
Mountain Biking Map for Eastern SLO County

Summary of hike: The Rinconada Trail, an old mining road, is a beautiful backcountry hike in the Los Padres National Forest in the Santa Lucia Wilderness. The trail connects Pozo Road, near Santa Margarita Lake, with Hi Mountain Road, near the head of Little Falls Canyon (Hike 103). Several switchbacks zigzag up the grassy slopes to a ridge with sweeping vistas of the Santa Lucia Range, Lopez Canyon, Santa Margarita Valley, and Pozo Valley.

Driving directions: From Highway 101 San Luis Obispo, head 8 miles north up the Cuesta Grade to the Santa Margarita (Highway 58) exit. Drive 1.5 miles east, through the town of Santa Margarita, to Estrada Avenue. Turn right, following the signs to Santa Margarita Lake. (En route Estrada Avenue becomes Calf Canyon Highway/Highway 58.) At 1.5 miles, Highway 58 turns left. Instead, go straight onto Pozo Road. Continue 9.2 miles (passing the turnoff to Santa Margarita Lake) to the signed trail on the right. Turn right and drive 0.1 mile to the end of the road at the trailhead parking lot. A parking fee is required.

Hiking directions: Hike past the trail sign on the well-defined path. Head through stands of oak trees, winding up the grassy slopes. The remains of the Rinconada Mine can be seen to the right. Enter the Los Padres National Forest and climb switchbacks up to the ridge, with great views of the mountains and valleys. At 1.5 miles, cross a fenceline and metal gate to a flat, grassy saddle. Bear to the right past a cairn (manmade rock mound), and descend across the grassy slopes on a rocky path into the next drainage south. At two miles, a short spur trail drops down to the left, joining the unpaved Hi Mountain Road. Take the road 100 yards to the right to the signed Little Falls Trail on the left. This is the turn-around spot. Return by retracing your steps.

To hike further, the trail descends 2,000 feet into Lopez Canyon to Little Falls, 2 miles ahead (Hike 103).

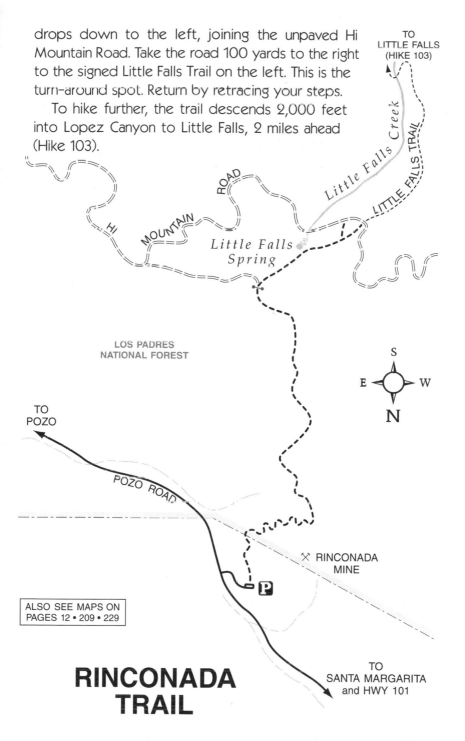

LOS PADRES
NATIONAL FOREST

TO
POZO

POZO ROAD

⚒ RINCONADA
MINE

ALSO SEE MAPS ON
PAGES 12 • 209 • 229

RINCONADA
TRAIL

TO
SANTA MARGARITA
and HWY 101

Lopez Lake Recreation Area
HIKES 98—102

Lopez Lake Recreation Area is a gorgeous 4,276-acre preserve nestled in the Santa Lucia foothills, 11 miles northeast of Arroyo Grande. The multi-fingered lake has 22 miles of shoreline, created as a reservoir from Arroyo Grande, Lopez, and Wittenberg Creeks. The area is used for fishing, boating, swimming, windsurfing, waterskiing, bird watching, camping, horsepacking, biking, and hiking. The preserve has more than 10 miles of hiking trails and several campgrounds along the east side of the lake. The variety of terrain includes shoreline strolls, rugged ridges, oak-shaded forests, rolling grassy hills, and scenic overlooks.

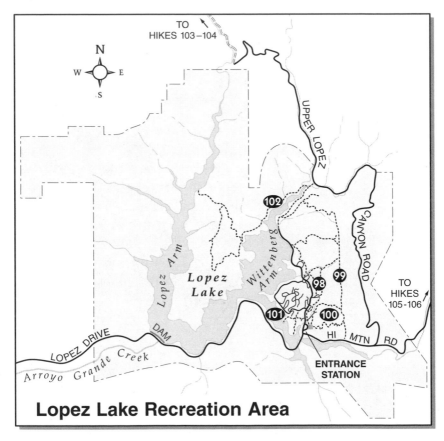

Lopez Lake Recreation Area

Hike 98
Cougar Trail
LOPEZ LAKE RECREATION AREA

Hiking distance: 3.4 miles round trip

Hiking time: 1.5 hours

Elevation gain: 150 feet

Maps: U.S.G.S. Tar Spring Ridge
Lopez Lake Trail Guide

map
next page

Summary of hike: The Cougar Trail is a connector trail between five campgrounds in Lopez Lake Recreation Area. It skirts the eastern border of the campgrounds parallel to the Wittenberg Arm of Lopez Lake. The gentle trail winds across the pastoral rolling grasslands and oak woodlands.

Driving directions: From Highway 101 in Arroyo Grande, take the Grand Avenue exit, and head east through the Village of Arroyo Grande. At 1 mile, bear right on Huasna Road at the junction with Highway 227. Continue 9.9 miles (staying to the left onto Lopez Drive at a road fork) to the Lopez Lake Recreation Area entrance station. Park in the lot next to the registration office. A parking fee is required.

Hiking directions: Walk 30 yards north to the signed Cougar Trail by the right side of the park road. Head north across the rolling hills. Skirt around the perimeter of the Eagle Campground. The trail exits a short distance ahead into the Cougar Campground. Follow the road to the right, and pick up the signed trail again on the right. Continue winding through the forested rolling hills past the eastern edge of the Quail Campground. Climb the hill and loop around the east and north side of the Mustang Campground and the waterslide. Once over the hill, the trail descends around the Escondido Campground. The path ends at Lopez Drive (the park road) at the Arboleda Picnic Area. To return, retrace your steps or follow the park road back to the trailhead.

To hike further, head north on the park road to connect with the Wittenberg Trail (Hike 102) or the High Ridge Trail (Hike 99).

Hike 99
High Ridge Trail
LOPEZ LAKE RECREATION AREA

Hiking distance: 5 miles round trip
Hiking time: 2.5 hours
Elevation gain: 450 feet
Maps: U.S.G.S. Tar Spring Ridge
       Lopez Lake Trail Guide

Summary of hike: The High Ridge Trail follows a firebreak along the east ridge of the recreation area above Lopez Lake. The trail passes a series of steep canyons. There are spectacular views of the lake and surrounding mountains from the ridge. Along the trail are scattered fossils of scallops, sand dollars, and oysters in the sedimentary rocks. The hike loops back along the park road

Driving directions: Follow the driving directions for Hike 98 to the Lopez Lake Recreation Area entrance station. Park at the east end of the parking lot behind the registration office by the Turkey Ridge Trail sign. A parking fee is required.

Hiking directions: Take the Turkey Ridge Trail up the hillside on the narrow footpath. Head up through oak groves to a grassy overlook at 0.7 miles by a trail split. Continue straight ahead and down the switchbacks. Head uphill again to a junction with the High Ridge Trail at 1.1 miles. Bear left, passing the Blackberry Springs Trail on the left (Hike 100). Follow the roller-coaster ridge on the wide firebreak. At two miles, pass the Bobcat Trail on the left. At 2.7 miles, stay right at two junctions leading down to the Escondido Campground. Just beyond a massive sandstone outcropping is an unsigned junction in an oak grove draped with moss. Bear left, curving downhill to the

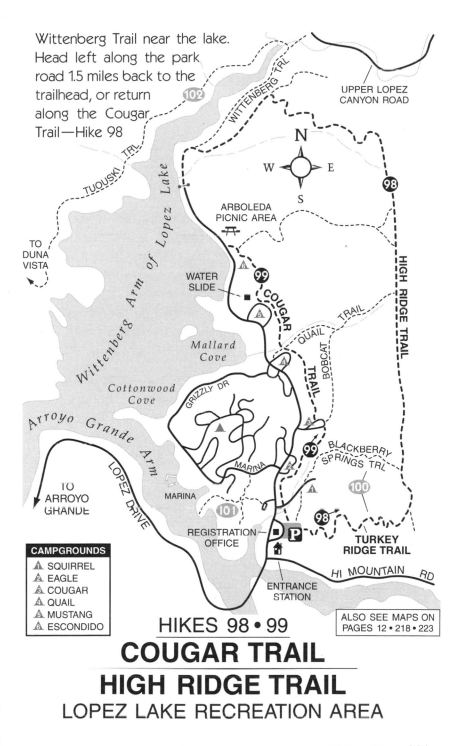

Wittenberg Trail near the lake. Head left along the park road 1.5 miles back to the trailhead, or return along the Cougar Trail—Hike 98

UPPER LOPEZ CANYON ROAD

WITTENBERG TRL

102

TUOUSKI TRL

N
W   E
S

98

TO DUNA VISTA

ARBOLEDA PICNIC AREA

Wittenberg Arm of Lopez Lake

WATER SLIDE

99

COUGAR

QUAIL TRAIL

BOBCAT TRAIL

HIGH RIDGE TRAIL

Mallard Cove

TRAIL

Cottonwood Cove

GRIZZLY DR

Arroyo Grande Arm

BLACKBERRY SPRINGS TRL

99

TO ARROYO GRANDE

LOPEZ DRIVE

MARINA

MARINA

100

98

TURKEY RIDGE TRAIL

101

REGISTRATION OFFICE

P

HI MOUNTAIN RD

ENTRANCE STATION

CAMPGROUNDS
🛆 SQUIRREL
🛆 EAGLE
🛆 COUGAR
🛆 QUAIL
🛆 MUSTANG
🛆 ESCONDIDO

ALSO SEE MAPS ON PAGES 12 • 218 • 223

HIKES 98 • 99
COUGAR TRAIL
HIGH RIDGE TRAIL
LOPEZ LAKE RECREATION AREA

Hike 100
Blackberry Springs—Turkey Ridge Loop
LOPEZ LAKE RECREATION AREA

Hiking distance: 1.8 mile loop
Hiking time: 1 hour
Elevation gain: 420 feet
Maps: U.S.G.S. Tar Spring Ridge
Lopez Lake Trail Guide

Summary of hike: The Blackberry Springs Trail is an interpretive loop trail with information displays that describe the natural features of Lopez Lake Recreation Area. The trail winds up a secluded, fern-lined canyon lush with gooseberries, blackberries, poison oak, and a fungus-algae draping off the valley oaks. The Turkey Ridge Trail follows a ridge to overlooks with great views of Lopez Lake, the Santa Lucia Mountains, the Sierra Madres, and the Caliente Range.

Driving directions: From Highway 101 in Arroyo Grande, take the Grand Avenue exit, and head east through the Village of Arroyo Grande. At 1 mile, bear right on Huasna Road at the junction with Highway 227. Continue 9.9 miles (staying to the left onto Lopez Drive at a road fork) to the Lopez Lake Recreation Area entrance station. Park at the east end of the parking lot behind the registration office by the Turkey Ridge Trail sign. A parking fee is required.

Hiking directions: The hike begins on the Blackberry Springs Trail and loops back on the Turkey Ridge Trail. Cross the bridge to the north into the Squirrel Campground. Walk up the campground road 50 yards to the signed Blackberry Springs Trail on the left. Head up the steps and wind through the forest, bearing right at a junction. The trail descends into a secluded glen, then follows the shady canyon floor up the lush drainage. Long, wide steps head steeply uphill to a T-junction with the High Ridge Trail at 0.8 miles (Hike 99). Bear right 20 yards to the Turkey Ridge Trail on the right. Go right, heading uphill to an overlook. The trail curves right, traversing the edge of the mountain to several more overlooks. Switchbacks lead back to the parking lot.

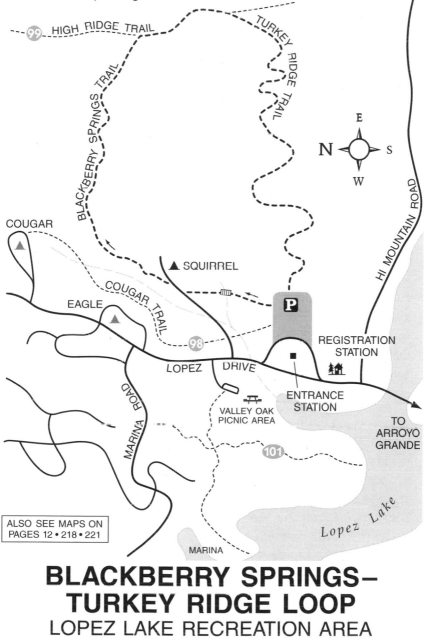

BLACKBERRY SPRINGS–
TURKEY RIDGE LOOP
LOPEZ LAKE RECREATION AREA

Hike 101
Marina and Rocky Point Trails
LOPEZ LAKE RECREATION AREA

Hiking distance: 1.5 miles round trip
Hiking time: 1 hour
Elevation gain: 120 feet
Maps: U.S.G.S. Tar Spring Ridge
  Lopez Lake Trail Guide

Summary of hike: The Marina Trail climbs over a forested 160-foot hill dividing the park entrance from the Lopez Lake marina. The Rocky Point Trail intersects the Marina Trail, leading to the tip of a peninsula at a flat, slab rock overlook. There are great views of Lopez Lake, the marina, and the surrounding mountains.

Driving directions: From Highway 101 in Arroyo Grande, take the Grand Avenue exit, and head east through the Village of Arroyo Grande. At 1 mile, bear right on Huasna Road at the junction with Highway 227. Continue 9.9 miles (staying to the left onto Lopez Drive at a road fork) to the Lopez Lake Recreation Area entrance station. Drive 100 yards to the Valley Oak Picnic Area. Turn left and park. A fee is required.

Hiking directions: Head up the grassy hill past the Marina Trail sign and the feeding stable. Cross the oak woodland up to a ridge with a bench and four-way junction. This junction is the return point to hike all three trails. Begin on the left fork, heading south on the Rocky Point Trail. The trail curves around the forested hillside. Descend through an oak grove to the tip of the peninsula and the flat slab rock, overlooking the lake on three sides. This is a great spot for bird watching, sunbathing, fishing, or daydreaming. At low water, fisherman trails lead down to the shoreline. Return to the four-way junction and take the Marina Trail west. This path ends at another rocky point overlooking Lopez Lake and the mountains to the west. Back at the junction, the Rocky Point Trail heads north through an oak grove to Marina Road. Return to the four-way junction and head east back to the trailhead.

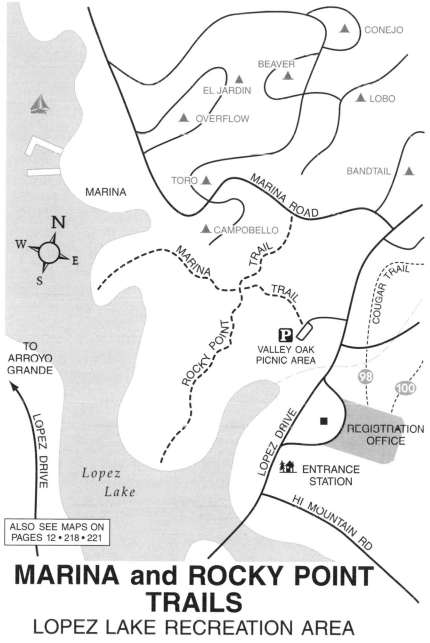

MARINA and ROCKY POINT TRAILS
LOPEZ LAKE RECREATION AREA

Hike 102
Duna Vista
Wittenberg—Tuouski—Two Waters Trails
LOPEZ LAKE RECREATION AREA

Hiking distance: 7 miles round trip
Hiking time: 3 hours
Elevation gain: 650 feet
Maps: U.S.G.S. Tar Spring Ridge
Lopez Lake Trail Guide

Summary of hike: Duna Vista is a 1,178-foot summit over-look with 360-degree views that include Lopez Lake, the Pacific Ocean, Oceano Dunes, and the Santa Lucia Mountains. The hike to Duna Vista begins on the picturesque Wittenberg Trail along the shores of the Wittenberg Arm of Lopez Lake. En route, the trail follows the oak studded hills along the Wittenberg Arm through hollows and over ridges on the Tuouski Trail. The hike crosses the peninsula that separates the arms of Lopez Lake, then climbs to the Duna Vista summit.

Driving directions: Follow the driving directions for Hike 98 to the Lopez Lake Recreation Area entrance station. Continue 1.3 miles up Lopez Drive and park on the right near the end of the road. A parking fee is required.

Hiking directions: Hike 100 yards north on the paved road to the locked gate. Pass the gate on the level, unpaved road along the lakeshore. Hike past the High Ridge Trail (Hike 99) on the right. At the upper end of the Wittenberg Arm, bear left along the fenceline past French Camp, following the signs to the Tuouski Trail. Take the signed trail—a footpath winding through the forest on the bluffs. The trail curves along the contours of the hills overlooking Lopez Lake. At 2.3 miles is a signed junction. Take the Two Waters Trail to the right and begin the loop. Switchbacks lead 0.7 miles up to a saddle at another signed junction. Take the Duna Vista Trail to the left up the ridge between the Lopez and Wittenberg Arms of the lake. In a half mile, the path reaches Duna Vista on a knoll with three benches. After savoring the views, return a short distance and take the Tuouski Trail on the right. Descend 1.3 miles, completing the loop back at the Two Waters Trail junction. Stay to the right along the Wittenberg Arm, returning on the same path.

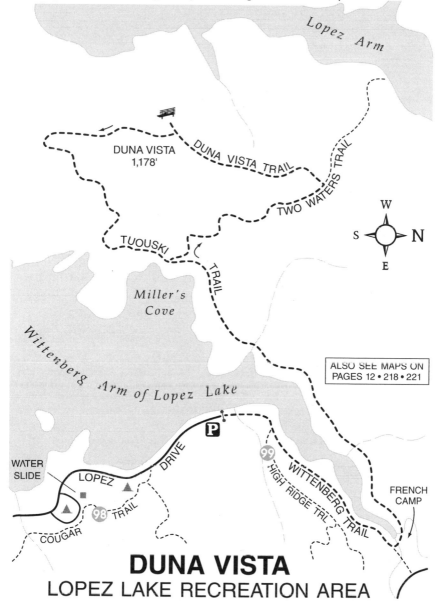

ALSO SEE MAPS ON
PAGES 12 • 218 • 221

DUNA VISTA
LOPEZ LAKE RECREATION AREA

Hike 103
Little Falls Trail

Hiking distance: 1 mile round trip
Hiking time: 30 minutes
Elevation gain: 100 feet
Maps: U.S.G.S. Tar Spring Ridge and Santa Margarita Lake
Mountain Biking Eastern SLO County

Summary of hike: Little Falls is a beautiful 50-foot waterfall in a lush limestone-walled canyon covered with moss and ferns. At the base of the falls is a circular 2—3 foot deep pool. The Little Falls Trail follows Little Falls Creek through a forest of oak, maple, sycamore, and bay trees. The falls is in the Santa Lucia Wilderness north of Lopez Lake. The hike may be extended to Hi Mountain Road (Hike 97).

Driving directions: From Highway 101 in Arroyo Grande, take the Grand Avenue exit, and head east through the Village of Arroyo Grande. At 1 mile, bear right on Huasna Road at the junction with Highway 227. Continue 9.8 miles (staying to the left onto Lopez Drive at a road fork) to Hi Mountain Road, located just before the Lopez Lake entrance station. (See map on page 218.) Turn right and drive 0.8 miles to a road fork. Bear left on Upper Lopez Canyon Road, and drive 6.4 miles to the end of the paved road. Turn right and take the dirt road 1.5 miles, crossing Lopez Creek 8 times, to the signed trailhead on the right. Park in the pullout on the left.

Hiking directions: Head north past the trail sign on the left side of Little Falls Creek. Rock hop across the creek to the signed Santa Lucia Wilderness boundary. Follow the trail across the flat, grassy meadow through an oak grove. Head into the wooded canyon, crossing Little Falls Creek three more times. At the next crossing, the Little Falls Trail heads up the hillside above the creek. Before crossing the creek, bear left, leaving the main trail. Scramble 50 yards up the rocky canyon, following the creek upstream to Little Falls. The last 20 yards involves wading up the stream to the pool at the base of the falls.

To hike further, cross the creek on the Little Falls Trail, continuing north past numerous rock-sculpted, streamside pools and creek crossings. At 2.6 miles, the Little Falls Trail ends at Hi Mountain Road, where the Rinconada Trail begins (Hike 97). To return, retrace your steps.

LITTLE FALLS TRAIL

Hike 104
Big Falls Trail

Hiking distance: 3 miles round trip
Hiking time: 1.5 hours
Elevation gain: 350 feet
Maps: U.S.G.S. Lopez Mountain
Mountain Biking Eastern SLO County

Summary of hike: Big Falls is an 80-foot cataract in the isolated Santa Lucia Wilderness north of Lopez Lake. The trail follows Big Falls Creek up the wooded canyon, crossing and recrossing the creek. Along the way is Lower Big Falls, an impressive 40-foot double waterfall over limestone rock. At the top and base of this lower falls are beautiful pools.

Driving directions: From Highway 101 in Arroyo Grande, take the Grand Avenue exit, and head east through the Village of Arroyo Grande. At 1 mile, bear right on Huasna Road at the junction with Highway 227. Continue 9.8 miles (staying to the left onto Lopez Drive at a road fork) to Hi Mountain Road, just before the Lopez Lake entrance station. (See map on page 218.) Turn right and drive 0.8 miles to a road fork. Bear left on Upper Lopez Canyon Road, and drive 6.4 miles to the end of the paved road. Turn right and drive 3.7 miles on the dirt road, crossing Lopez Creek 13 times. Park in the pullout on the right across from two waterfalls.

Hiking directions: Take the trail on the right and rock hop over Lopez Creek. Head north, following Big Falls Creek upstream through the lush, forested canyon. Continue past pools, cascades, and several more creek crossings. At 0.5 miles, bear left on an unsigned side trail before crossing the creek. A short distance ahead on this side path is a circular pool at the base of Lower Big Falls. Return to the main trail and cross the creek, heading deeper into Big Falls Canyon. The trail recrosses the creek several more times and traverses the east-facing canyon wall. At 1.3 miles, the trail meets the creek. Stay to the left (west) of the creek past a series of small waterfalls and rock pools known as Big Falls Narrows. Big Falls can be spotted from a spur trail bearing left. The left fork descends to the base of Big Falls and a large pool. Return along the same trail.

To hike further, the trail continues for another mile, ascending up and out of the canyon to Hi Mountain Road and Little Falls Spring (Hike 97).

TO
HI MOUNTAIN
ROAD

BIG FALLS CANYON

Big Falls

Big Falls Creek

*Lower
Big Falls*

SANTA LUCIA
WILDERNESS

N
W · E
S

ALSO SEE MAPS
ON PAGES 12 • 218

LOPEZ CANYON

P

waterfalls

Lopez Creek

LOPEZ CANYON RD

TO
LOPEZ LAKE

BIG FALLS TRAIL

Hike 105
High Mountain Trail

Hiking distance: 4 mile loop
Hiking time: 2 hours
Elevation gain: 600 feet
Maps: U.S.G.S. Tar Spring Ridge and Caldwell Mesa
Mountain Biking Eastern SLO County

Summary of hike: The High Mountain Trail is a multi-use trail in the Los Padres National Forest east of Lopez Lake. Dogs, horses, and bikes are allowed. The trail heads up the canyon in a shaded riparian forest parallel to a stream. While climbing out of the canyon, there are several spectacular vistas. The hike returns on the unpaved Hi Mountain Road, winding through the pastoral oak-dotted hills of the upper Arroyo Grande valley.

Driving directions: From Highway 101 in Arroyo Grande, take the Grand Avenue exit, and head east through the Village of Arroyo Grande. At 1 mile, bear right on Huasna Road at the junction with Highway 227. Continue 9.8 miles (staying to the left onto Lopez Drive at a road fork) to Hi Mountain Road, located just before the Lopez Lake entrance station. (See map on page 218.) Turn right and drive 5.5 miles (bearing right at the Upper Lopez Canyon Road fork) to the signed trailhead parking area on the left.

Hiking directions: Hike past the trailhead gate, heading north on the wide grassy path. Enter a shaded oak forest on the right side of a trickling stream. At 0.3 miles, cross over the seasonal stream and again at a half mile, continuing gently uphill through the lush canyon. A short distance ahead, switchbacks lead away from the drainage and up the east wall of the canyon to a grassy flat overlooking the canyon and surrounding mountains. Cross the open hillside, then climb steeply to a saddle. Bear left to a knoll with a 360-degree view. Descend to the right towards Hi Mountain Road. Cross the meadow to the road.

Bear right on the narrow road through rolling hills and oak groves for 1.9 miles back to the trailhead.

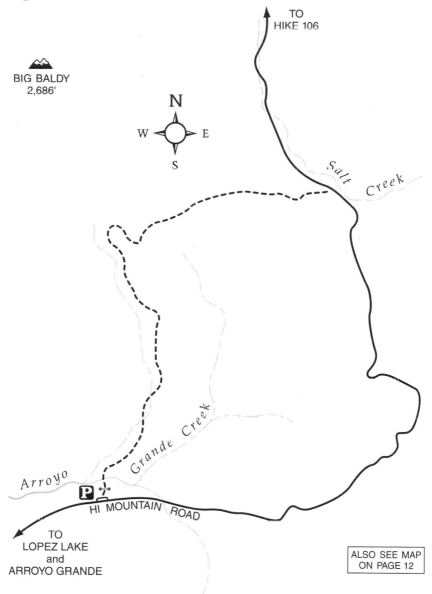

HIGH MOUNTAIN TRAIL

Hike 106
Trout Creek Trail

Hiking distance: 6 miles round trip
Hiking time: 3 hours
Elevation gain: 250 feet
Maps: U.S.G.S. Santa Margarita Lake, Pozo Summit,
and Caldwell Mesa
Mountain Biking Eastern SLO County

Summary of hike: Trout Creek, in the Los Padres National Forest, cuts a small canyon through the west flank of Garcia Mountain. The Trout Creek Trail is a quiet backcountry hike that meanders through meadows and oak forests. It parallels and crosses Trout Creek nine times up the canyon. The trail is an access route into the Garcia Wilderness and is primarily an equestrian route. The trailhead is on Hi Mountain Road northeast of Lopez Lake.

Driving directions: From Highway 101 in Arroyo Grande, take the Grand Avenue exit, and head east through the Village of Arroyo Grande. At 1 mile, bear right on Huasna Road at the junction with Highway 227. Continue 9.8 miles (staying to the left onto Lopez Drive at a road fork) to Hi Mountain Road, located just before the Lopez Lake entrance station. (See map on page 218.) Turn right and drive 6.2 miles (bearing right at the Upper Lopez Canyon Road fork) to the end of the paved road. Continue 5.4 miles on the narrow, winding unpaved road to the Trout Creek pullout on the right. If you reach the large wooden Los Padres National Forest sign, return 0.1 mile to the trailhead.

Hiking directions: Head east on the signed trail parallel to Trout Creek. Throughout the hike, the trail alternates from an oak forest canopy to grassy meadows with frequent creek crossings. After the ninth crossing, follow a narrow cliffside trail on the left side of Trout Creek to an unsigned junction with the trail to Buckeye Camp on the left. Stay on the main trail along the creek. The trail ends in less than a half mile at a signed private property boundary. This is the turn-around spot. Return along the same route.

To extend the hike, head east on the Buckeye Camp Trail. Enter the Garcia Wilderness and continue one mile to Buckeye Camp, a primitive camp on the left.

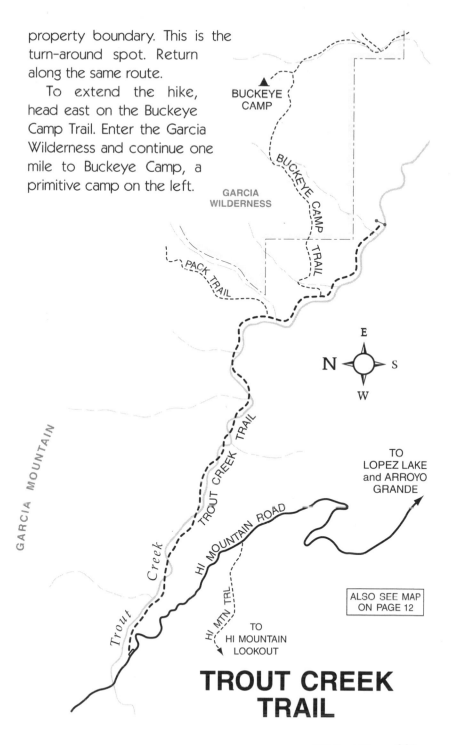

BUCKEYE CAMP

BUCKEYE CAMP TRAIL

GARCIA WILDERNESS

PACK TRAIL

E
N — S
W

TO LOPEZ LAKE and ARROYO GRANDE

TROUT CREEK TRAIL

HI MOUNTAIN ROAD

GARCIA MOUNTAIN

Trout Creek

HI MTN TRL

TO HI MOUNTAIN LOOKOUT

ALSO SEE MAP ON PAGE 12

TROUT CREEK TRAIL

Hike 107
Pecho Coast Trail
Free docent-led hike on PG&E land
Reservations required: (805) 541-8735

Hiking distance: 3.5—7.4 miles round trip
Hiking time: 4 hours—7 hours
Elevation gain: 440 feet
Maps: U.S.G.S. Port San Luis

Summary of hike: The Pecho Coast Trail curves around the western point of San Luis Obispo Bay from Port San Luis towards Moñtana de Oro State Park. Access is from two docent-led hikes across the privately owned PG&E land. Both hikes follow the steep cliffs to Point San Luis and the Port San Luis Lighthouse, a two-story Victorian redwood structure built in 1890. It is a great spot for watching the annual migration of the gray whales. The longer hike continues across the coastal bluffs and pastureland to an oak grove in Rattlesnake Canyon.

Driving directions: From Highway 101 in Pismo Beach, take the Avila Beach Drive exit. Head 4.2 miles west, passing the town of Avila Beach, to the PG&E Diablo Canyon Power Plant entrance on the right at Port San Luis Harbor. Park in the wide area on the left, across the road from the PG&E entrance gate.

Hiking directions: Naturalists will lead the hike, providing geological, botanical, and historical details. Begin by walking up the steps past a locked gate west of the PG&E station. Ascend the hillside overlooking the bay and three piers. Bear left on the lighthouse road to the Pecho Coast Trail, and take the footpath left. Descend the hillside towards the ocean. Follow the contour of the mountains on a cliffside trail 200 feet above the ocean. The trail passes Smith Island and Whaler's Island. Continue around the point, rejoining the paved road to the lighthouse.
   The longer hike continues past the lighthouse, crossing the coastal terrace and grasslands to an oak woodland in Rattlesnake Canyon for lunch. Return by retracing your steps.

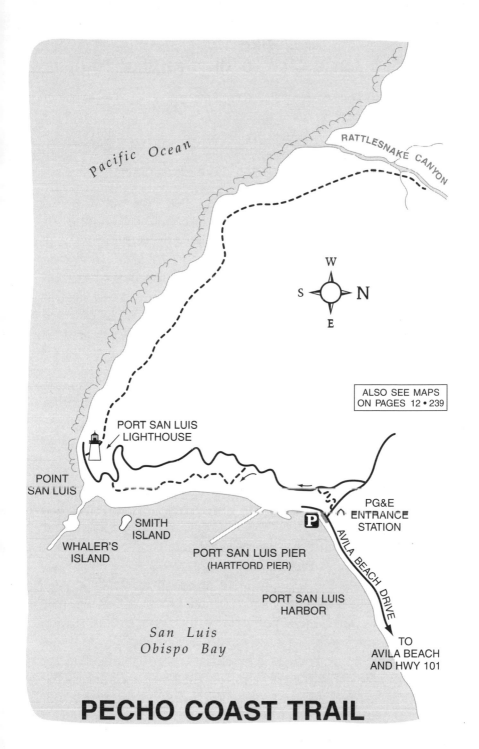

Pacific Ocean

RATTLESNAKE CANYON

W
S · N
E

ALSO SEE MAPS
ON PAGES 12 • 239

PORT SAN LUIS
LIGHTHOUSE

POINT
SAN LUIS

SMITH
ISLAND

PG&E
ENTRANCE
STATION

WHALER'S
ISLAND

PORT SAN LUIS PIER
(HARTFORD PIER)

AVILA BEACH DRIVE

PORT SAN LUIS
HARBOR

TO
AVILA BEACH
AND HWY 101

San Luis
Obispo Bay

PECHO COAST TRAIL

Hike 108
Bob Jones City to the Sea Bike Trail

Hiking distance: 5.6 miles round trip
Hiking time: 2.5 hour
Elevation gain: 150 feet
Maps: U.S.G.S. Pismo Beach
      The Thomas Guide—San Luis Obispo County

Summary of hike: The Bob Jones City to the Sea Bike Trail (originally known as the Avila Valley Bike Trail) follows the old Pacific Coast Railroad right-of-way. The paved hiking, jogging, and biking route winds through forested Avila Valley alongside San Luis Obispo Creek. The walk ends at Avila Beach, a quaint seaside town tucked between the rolling Irish Hills and San Luis Obispo Bay. From the trail are views of bridges spanning the wide creek, the Avila Beach Golf Course, a tidal estuary, the town of Avila Beach, and the Pacific Ocean.

Driving directions: From Highway 101 in Pismo Beach, exit on Avila Beach Drive. Head west 0.3 miles to Ontario Road at Avila Hot Springs Spa. Turn right and continue 0.3 miles, crossing the bridge over San Luis Obispo Creek, to the trailhead parking lot on the right.

Hiking directions: Cross Ontario Road and pick up the signed trail heading west. The trail immediately enters a lush forest parallel to San Luis Obispo Creek. Although you are near the creek, the dense foliage makes access to the creek nearly impossible. At 0.7 miles, cross a bridge over See Canyon Creek, and then cross San Luis Bay Drive at one mile. Continue past Avila Bay Club on the right and the creek on the left to the trail's end at Blue Heron Drive. Bear left on the private road, staying close to the creek. The road curves around the hillside overlooking the creek, bridges, and golf course. At the first bridge spanning the creek is a junction. The left fork heads across the bridge to Avila Beach Drive. The right fork continues to the golf course entrance by Mulligans Restaurant. Both routes lead to the Front Street walkway and pier at Avila Beach. To return, take the same trail back.

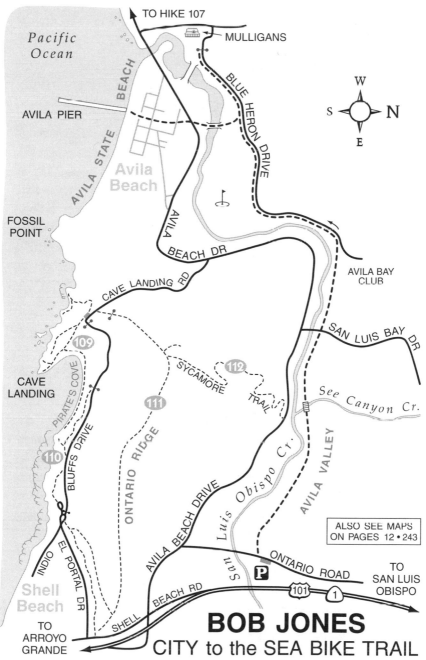

Pacific Ocean

TO HIKE 107

MULLIGANS

BLUE HERON DRIVE

AVILA STATE BEACH

AVILA PIER

Avila Beach

FOSSIL POINT

AVILA BEACH DR

CAVE LANDING RD

AVILA BAY CLUB

SAN LUIS BAY DR

109

CAVE LANDING

PIRATE'S COVE

SYCAMORE

112

See Canyon Cr.

TRAIL

111

BLUFFS DRIVE

ONTARIO RIDGE

San Luis Obispo Cr.

AVILA VALLEY

110

ALSO SEE MAPS ON PAGES 12 • 243

INDIO

EL PORTAL DR

AVILA BEACH DRIVE

San

ONTARIO ROAD

TO SAN LUIS OBISPO

Shell Beach

TO ARROYO GRANDE

SHELL BEACH RD

P

101   1

BOB JONES
CITY to the SEA BIKE TRAIL

W   N
S   E

Hike 109
Cave Landing and Pirate's Cove

Hiking distance: 2 miles round trip
Hiking time: 1 hour
Elevation gain: 120 feet
Maps: U.S.G.S. Pismo Beach
      The Thomas Guide—San Luis Obispo County

Summary of hike: Cave Landing (originally known as Mallagh Landing) is a spectacular rocky promontory that juts out 150 feet into San Luis Obispo Bay. It forms a natural pier and a division between Avila Beach and Shell Beach. The picturesque formation has wind-swept caves and coves, including an arch chiseled through the cliffs near the end of the headland. From the dramatic point are great views of the steep, serrated cliffs along the rugged coastline. Pirate's Cove, a crescent-shaped, unsanctioned clothing-optional beach, sits at the base of the hundred-foot cliffs.

Driving directions: From Highway 101 in Pismo Beach, exit on Avila Beach Drive. Head 2 miles west to Cave Landing Road and turn left. Continue 0.5 miles to the trailhead parking lot on the right at the end of the road.

Hiking directions: The trail heads southeast towards the rocky point overlooking the Shell Beach and Pismo Beach coastline. At 20 yards is a junction. Bear left to a trail split 0.2 miles ahead. The left fork descends to Pirate's Cove. Before descending, take the right fork to another trail split. To the right is a natural arch cave leading to an overlook on Cave Landing. To the left is another overlook at the edge of the cliffs. Return to the junction and bear right, curving gently down the cliffs to Pirate's Cove. Continue along the sandy beach beneath the cliffs. Return along the same path.

    For an additional 0.6-mile hike, take the wide path heading west at the opposite end of the trailhead parking area. The trail leads down to a flat, grassy plateau. From the plateau, a path follows the cliff's edge to the left. Caves can be seen along the base of the cliffs. Return along the same route.

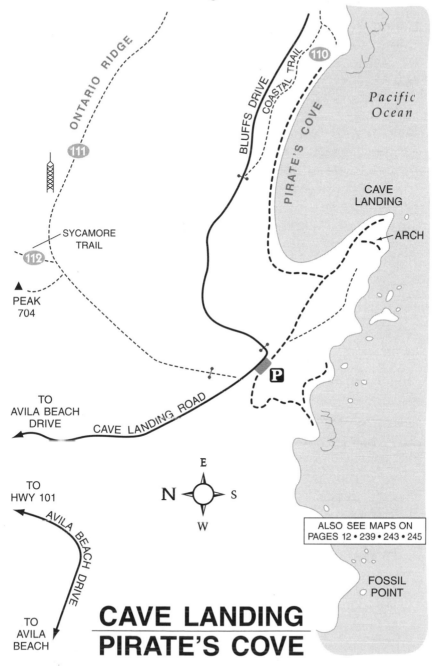

ONTARIO RIDGE

111

SYCAMORE
TRAIL

112

▲
PEAK
704

BLUFFS DRIVE

COASTAL TRAIL

110

PIRATE'S COVE

*Pacific
Ocean*

CAVE
LANDING

ARCH

P

TO
AVILA BEACH
DRIVE

CAVE LANDING ROAD

TO
HWY 101

AVILA BEACH DRIVE

TO
AVILA
BEACH

E

N ⊕ S

W

ALSO SEE MAPS ON
PAGES 12 • 239 • 243 • 245

FOSSIL
POINT

CAVE LANDING
PIRATE'S COVE

Hike 110
Shell Beach Bluffs Coastal Trail

Hiking distance: 2 miles round trip
Hiking time: 1 hour
Elevation gain: 70 feet
Maps: U.S.G.S. Pismo Beach
      The Thomas Guide—San Luis Obispo County

Summary of hike: The Shell Beach Bluffs Coastal Trail parallels the scalloped coastal cliffs 100 feet above Pirate's Cove, an unofficial clothing-optional white sand beach. From the trail are views of Cave Landing, a promontory with a natural arch cave carved through the rocky cliffs (Hike 109). Sea otters and sea lions are frequently seen near the ocean rocks.

Driving directions: From Highway 101 in Pismo Beach, exit on Avila Beach Drive. Head west to the first street—Shell Beach Road—and turn left. Continue 0.3 miles to El Portal Drive and turn right. Drive 0.6 miles, bearing right on Indio Drive. The trailhead is on the right, just before "The Bluffs" gated homes. Park in the lot below the gates at the end of the road.

Hiking directions: Hike west on the paved walkway above the rugged coastline along the cliffs overlooking the ocean. The trail joins Bluffs Drive for 100 yards, a private road that passes a few luxury homes. At a trail fork, the left trail is a short detour that leads 30 yards to an overlook. Continue on the right fork to the end of the path. Follow the gated, unpaved road uphill, curving around the west side of the cove. The trail ends at the parking lot by Cave Landing, the trailhead to the promontory and Pirate's Cove (Hike 109). Return by retracing your steps.

To add one mile to your hike, from the trailhead parking lot, walk back up Indio Drive to the round-about. A well-defined trail (an abandoned, unpaved road) heads east along the base of the hillside parallel to El Portal Drive. The trail ends at Shell Beach Road at the north edge of the Sunset Palisades subdivision. For a longer loop hike, continue with Hike 111.

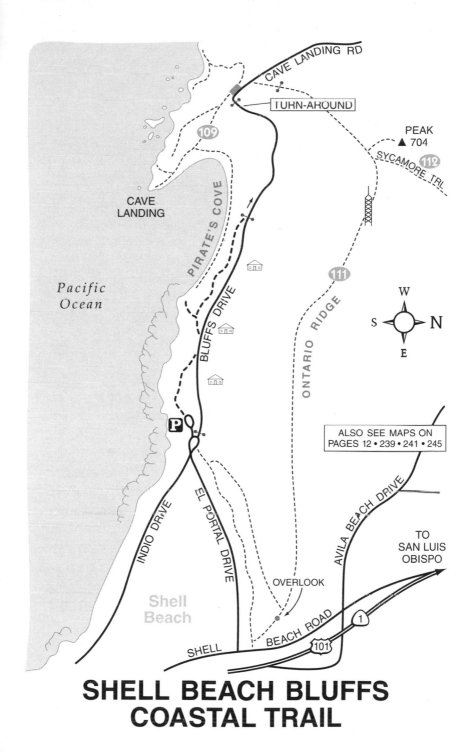

CAVE LANDING RD

TURN-AROUND

109

PEAK
▲ 704

SYCAMORE TRL 112

CAVE
LANDING

PIRATE'S COVE

*Pacific
Ocean*

111

ONTARIO RIDGE

BLUFFS DRIVE

W
N
S
E

P

ALSO SEE MAPS ON
PAGES 12 • 239 • 241 • 245

INDIO DRIVE

EL PORTAL DRIVE

AVILA BEACH DRIVE

TO
SAN LUIS
OBISPO

OVERLOOK

Shell
Beach

SHELL

BEACH ROAD

1

101

SHELL BEACH BLUFFS
COASTAL TRAIL

Hike 111
Ontario Ridge

Hiking distance: 2.8 mile loop
Hiking time: 1.5 hours
Elevation gain: 650 feet
Maps: U.S.G.S. Pismo Beach

Summary of hike: Ontario Hill is nestled between Avila Valley and San Luis Obispo Bay at the foot of the Irish Hills. The 735-foot hill separates Avila Beach from Shell Beach. This hike follows Ontario Ridge overlooking the ocean, with sweeping vistas of the Irish Hills, Avila Beach, Port San Luis, Whaler's Island, and the Shell Beach–Pismo Beach coastline. The views extend all the way to Point Sal. The hike begins on the bluffs in Shell Beach and crosses the coastal mountain to Cave Landing by Avila Beach.

Driving directions: Same as Hike 110.

Hiking directions: Walk back up to Indio Drive at the round-about, and take the well-defined path across the road. Follow the base of the hillside 25 yards to an unsigned path on the left. Take the path up to an old rutted road and bear right, traversing the slope. At 0.6 miles, the trail reaches the ridge at a junction 200 feet above Highway 101. (For a shorter hike, the right fork leads up to an overlook, then descends a steep grade to the path at the base of the hillside.) At the junction, head west up the ridge along an old fenceline. The trail climbs with intermittent level areas, straddling the ridge between the chaparral and gnarly oak groves. Parallel the ocean high above Pirate's Cove to the 735-foot summit near a radio tower. Descend on the two-track road. At the south foot of Peak 704, the Sycamore Trail descends the north-facing slope to Sycamore Mineral Springs Resort in Avila Valley (Hike 112). Stay atop the ridge and curve left. Quickly drop down to Cave Landing Road, cross a vehicle gate, and bear left on the road to a fork. The right fork leads to Cave Landing and Pirate's Cove (Hike 109).

Curve left on the unpaved road, descending to the Shell Beach Bluffs Coastal Trail (Hike 110). Parallel the cliffs past luxury homes, returning to the parking lot.

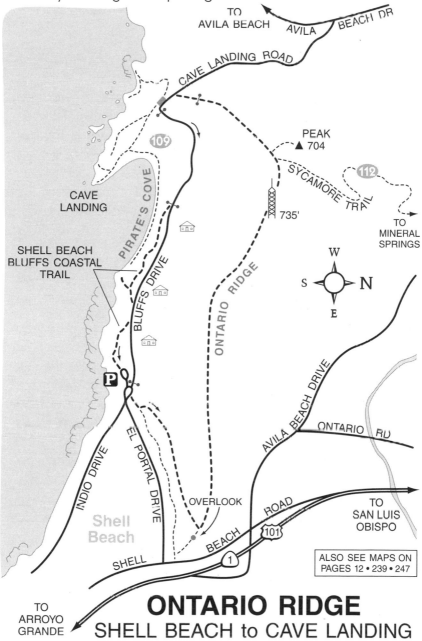

TO
AVILA BEACH AVILA BEACH DR

CAVE LANDING ROAD

109

PEAK
▲ 704

SYCAMORE TRAIL

112

CAVE
LANDING

735'

TO
MINERAL
SPRINGS

SHELL BEACH
BLUFFS COASTAL
TRAIL

PIRATE'S COVE

BLUFFS DRIVE

ONTARIO RIDGE

W

S ◇ N

E

P

AVILA BEACH DRIVE

ONTARIO RD

INDIO DRIVE

EL PORTAL DRIVE

OVERLOOK

BEACH ROAD

101

TO
SAN LUIS
OBISPO

Shell
Beach

SHELL

1

ALSO SEE MAPS ON
PAGES 12 • 239 • 247

TO
ARROYO
GRANDE

ONTARIO RIDGE
SHELL BEACH to CAVE LANDING

Hike 112
Sycamore Trail to Ontario Ridge

Hiking distance: 2 miles round trip
Hiking time: 1 hour
Elevation gain: 700 feet
Maps: U.S.G.S. Pismo Beach

Summary of hike: The Sycamore Trail begins in wooded Avila Valley and climbs up a north-facing mountain slope to Ontario Ridge, high above Avila Beach and Shell Beach. The trail starts at Sycamore Mineral Springs Resort, a natural hot springs spa since 1897, then weaves through coastal live oak groves en route to the ridge. From the 700-foot ridge are vistas of the coastline, from Point Sal to Whaler's Island at Point San Luis.

Driving directions: From Highway 101 in Pismo Beach, exit on Avila Beach Drive. Drive 0.9 miles west (towards Avila Beach) to Sycamore Mineral Springs Resort on the left, at 1215 Avila Beach Drive. Turn left and park in the lot.

Hiking directions: Take the posted Sycamore Trail, a paved road located between the Gardens of Avila Restaurant and the gift shop. Wind up the road through oak groves past the last building. Continue on the dirt path into the forest, following the contours of the hillside high above Avila Valley. Curve south and head up a lush grassy draw with manzanita, oaks, and views across the canyon to the Irish Hills. Follow the trail sign as the cliff-hugging path follows the west edge of a deep canyon. The views extend to the Santa Lucia Range. The Sycamore Trail ends at a T-junction atop Ontario Ridge at the south foot of Peak 704. From the ridge are views of Avila Beach, Port San Luis Harbor, Whaler's Island, and Point San Luis. The right fork descends to Cave Landing (Hike 109). Also to the right, a side path climbs up to the 704-foot peak. To the left of the junction, follow the ridge uphill 0.2 miles to the 735-foot peak at the radio tower. Just beyond the tower are views of Shell Beach, Pismo Beach, and the coastal dunes to Point Sal.

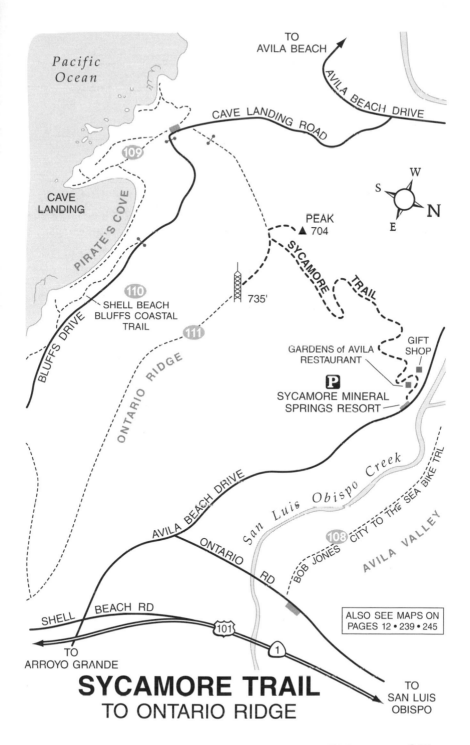

Pacific Ocean

TO AVILA BEACH

AVILA BEACH DRIVE

CAVE LANDING ROAD

109

CAVE LANDING

PIRATE'S COVE

PEAK ▲ 704

SYCAMORE TRAIL

110

SHELL BEACH BLUFFS COASTAL TRAIL

735'

111

BLUFFS DRIVE

ONTARIO RIDGE

GARDENS of AVILA RESTAURANT

GIFT SHOP

P

SYCAMORE MINERAL SPRINGS RESORT

San Luis Obispo Creek

AVILA BEACH DRIVE

ONTARIO RD

108

BOB JONES CITY TO THE SEA BIKE TRL

AVILA VALLEY

SHELL BEACH RD

101

TO ARROYO GRANDE

1

ALSO SEE MAPS ON PAGES 12 • 239 • 245

TO SAN LUIS OBISPO

SYCAMORE TRAIL
TO ONTARIO RIDGE

Hike 113
Chumash Park

Hiking distance: 1 mile round trip
Hiking time: 30 minutes
Elevation gain: 50 feet
Maps: U.S.G.S. Arroyo Grande NE
The Thomas Guide—San Luis Obispo County

Summary of hike: Chumash Park is a 40-acre dog-friendly park in Pismo Beach. The park sits in a forested canyon with majestic old oaks. Homes are built on the hillside ridges overlooking the canyon. The north-facing hillside is covered in oak trees, while a seasonal stream flows through the lush drainage. The trail winds up the draw on an unpaved ranch access road. Plans are in progress to build bridge crossings and a trail through the oaks on the south side of the canyon.

Driving directions: Heading southbound on Highway 101 in Pismo Beach, take the 4th Street exit and turn left to 4th Street. Head 0.1 mile east to James Way. Heading northbound on Highway 101, take the 4th Street/Five Cities Drive exit to 4th Street. Turn right and drive one block to James Way.
Turn left on James Way and drive 0.1 mile to Ventana Drive. Turn right and make a quick right again into posted Chumash Park and the parking lot.

Hiking directions: Walk east past the restrooms on the left and the grassy parkland and playground area on the right. Continue up the dirt road/trail on the northwest side of the arroyo, a forested wetland. The gently rising road leads past giant oaks to views of rolling pastureland and grazing cattle. Cross over the seasonal stream to the end of the trail at the east end of the park and the fenced ranch boundary. Return by retracing your steps.

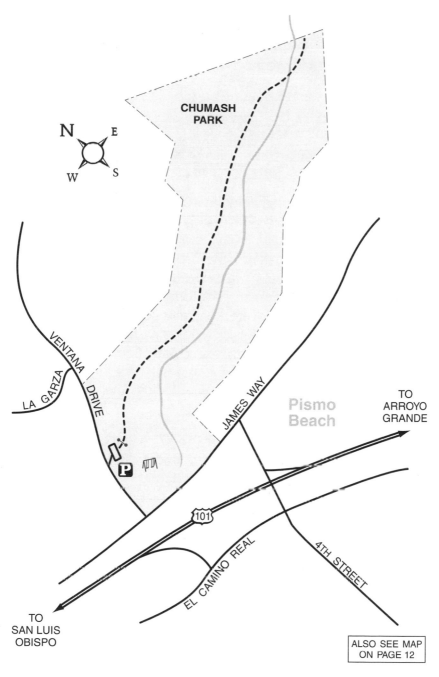

CHUMASH PARK

Hike 114
Pismo State Beach Monarch Butterfly Grove and Meadow Creek Trail

Hiking distance: 1.5 miles round trip
Hiking time: 1 hour
Elevation gain: Level
Maps: U.S.G.S. Pismo Beach and Oceano
Pismo State Beach map

Summary of hike: The Pismo State Beach Monarch Butterfly Grove is among the largest winter habitats for migrating butterflies on the west coast. From October through March, up to 50,000 monarchs gather on their southward journey. In the shelter of a picturesque grove of mature eucalyptus trees, the bright orange and black monarchs form dense clusters on the tree limbs. The grove is located one mile south of sandy Pismo Beach. From the grove, the hike follows Meadow Creek, then runs along the west edge of the Pismo State Beach Golf Course. Various side trails lead across the dunes. At the trail's end is a viewing platform with coastline views of the Shell Beach cliffs and Port San Luis.

Driving directions: From Highway 101 in Pismo Beach, take the Pismo Beach/Highway 1 South exit. Take Highway 1 through the town of Pismo Beach (Dolliver Street, which becomes Pacific Boulevard) for 1.4 miles to the parking area along the right side of the road. It is located at the south end of North Beach Campground.

From Highway 101 in Arroyo Grande, take the Grand Avenue exit, and head 2.5 miles west to Highway 1/Pacific Boulevard. Turn right and drive 0.5 miles to the parking area on the left side of the road.

Hiking directions: Walk through the fenced entrance, bearing to the right across the grassy area. The trail loops through a eucalyptus grove, the wintering site for the monarch butterflies. At the far end of the grove, cross the footbridge over

Meadow Creek. Follow the creek to the left along the south edge of the campground to a trail split. Take either trail towards the dunes. The Meadow Creek Trail heads left at the northwest boundary of the golf course, continuing south between the golf course and the dunes. Various side trails curve right into the dunes, then parallel the trail. The trails end at a picnic area at the north entrance to the Oceano Dunes Vehiclular Recreation Area, where Grand Avenue meets the ocean. A boardwalk leads out to a coastline viewing platform. Return to the parking lot along the Meadow Creek Trail or over and across the dunes.

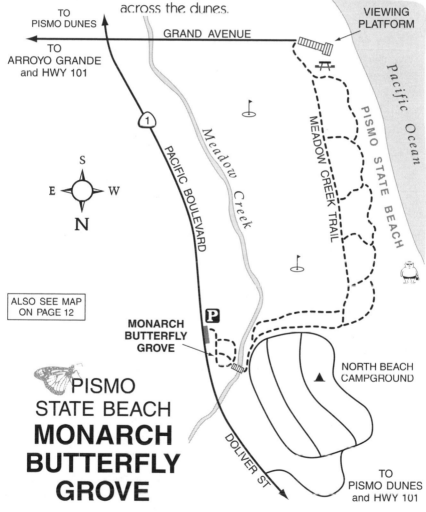

TO
PISMO DUNES

TO
ARROYO GRANDE
and HWY 101

GRAND AVENUE

VIEWING
PLATFORM

Pacific Ocean

PISMO STATE BEACH

1

PACIFIC BOULEVARD

Meadow Creek

MEADOW CREEK TRAIL

S

E ⊕ W

N

ALSO SEE MAP
ON PAGE 12

MONARCH
BUTTERFLY
GROVE

P

NORTH BEACH
CAMPGROUND

PISMO
STATE BEACH
**MONARCH
BUTTERFLY
GROVE**

DOLIVER ST

TO
PISMO DUNES
and HWY 101

Hike 115
Guiton Trail
OCEANO LAGOON

Hiking distance: 1.5 mile loop
Hiking time: 1 hour
Elevation gain: Level
Maps: U.S.G.S. Oceano
Pismo State Beach map

Summary of hike: Oceano Lagoon is a tranquil freshwater lagoon a quarter mile from the ocean in Oceano. The lagoon, fed by Meadow Creek, is a popular area for fishing, canoeing, and bird watching. Harold E. Guiton donated five acres of lagoon property to the state park system in the mid-1930's. The Guiton Trail is an interpretive nature trail that circles the sleepy backwater lagoon. The lush riparian habitat creates a secluded pastoral stroll through a forested canopy of Monterey pines, eucalyptus trees, and willows.

Driving directions: From Highway 101 in Pismo Beach, take the Pismo Beach/Highway 1 South exit. Take Highway 1 through the town of Pismo Beach (Dolliver Street, which becomes Pacific Boulevard) for 3 miles to Pier Avenue. Turn right and drive 0.2 miles to the Oceano Campground. Turn right into the campground and park by the nature center on the right

From Highway 101 in Arroyo Grande, take the Grand Avenue exit and head 2.5 miles west to Highway 1/Pacific Boulevard. Turn left and drive 1.1 miles to Pier Avenue. Turn right and drive 0.2 miles to the Oceano Campground. Turn right into the campground and park by the nature center.

Hiking directions: Pick up the signed footpath by the lagoon, east of the nature center. Bear left, skirting the eastern edge of the campground along the water's edge. Follow the forested shoreline north, joining a paved path with benches. Curve around the northwest tip of the lagoon where the paved path ends. Continue on the footpath, and loop around the perimeter of the grassy peninsula with Monterey pines. At the north tip of the lagoon, the trail meets a road at the service buildings. Bear right, picking up the trail on the east side of the lagoon. Head south through the lush native forest, crossing several footbridges over streams and channels. The trail ends at the bridge on Pier Avenue. Cross the bridge over the lagoon, returning to the nature center.

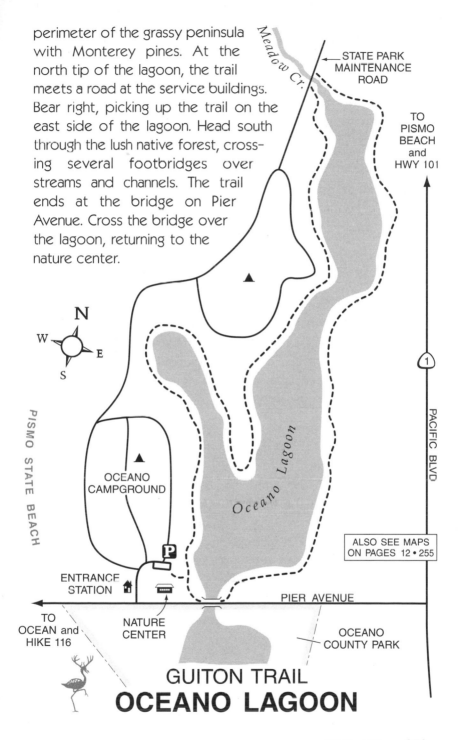

GUITON TRAIL
OCEANO LAGOON

Hike 116
Oceano Dunes Natural Preserve

Hiking distance: 2 or more miles round trip
Hiking time: 1 hour
Elevation gain: 100 feet
Maps: U.S.G.S. Oceano
Pismo State Beach map

Summary of hike: The Oceano Dunes Natural Preserve (formerly the Pismo Dunes) is a 570-acre parcel of land at the southern boundary of Pismo State Beach. It is adjacent to the 3,600-acre Oceano Dunes Vehicular Recreation Area, the only beach in California that allows vehicles. The hike begins from this busy vehicle-filled, hard-packed sand beach. The trail soon crosses Arroyo Grande Creek and enters the quiet, undisturbed solitude of the most extensive coastal dunes in California. A ridge of wave-shaped dunes shields the preserve from the sound of the busy beachfront. The route meanders through the quiet and fragile natural preserve, crossing scrub-covered dunes sculpted by the wind.

Driving directions: From Highway 101 in Pismo Beach, take the Pismo Beach/Highway 1 South exit. Take Highway 1 through the town of Pismo Beach (Dolliver Street, which becomes Pacific Boulevard) for 3 miles to Pier Avenue. Turn right and drive 0.4 miles to the Pismo State Beach parking lot at the beachfront.

From Highway 101 in Arroyo Grande, take the Grand Avenue exit and head 2.5 miles west to Highway 1/Pacific Boulevard. Turn left and drive 1.1 miles to Pier Avenue. Turn right and drive 0.4 miles to the Pismo State Beach parking lot at the beachfront.

Hiking directions: Head south across the hard-packed sand between the ocean and the dunes. Hike 0.3 miles to Arroyo Grande Creek, passing beachfront homes along the way. After crossing the creek, curve left, entering the scrub-covered dunes at one of the many access trails. Meander south across the dunes, following the various interconnecting trails. Choose your own turn-around spot. On the return, continue north until reaching Arroyo Grande Creek. Follow the creek west, returning to the beach near the trailhead.

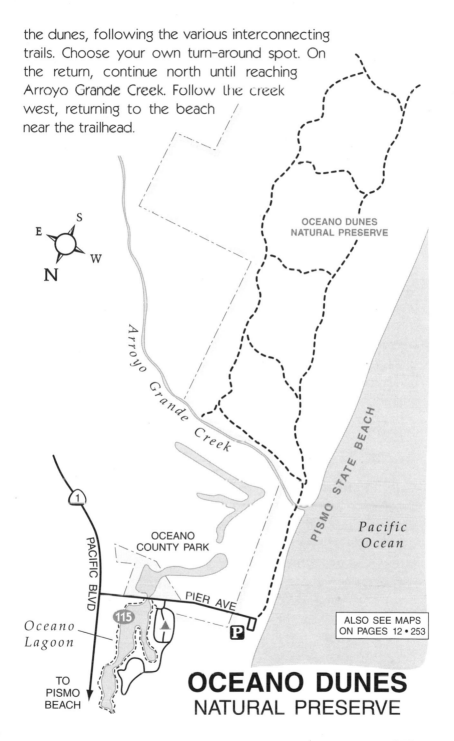

OCEANO DUNES
NATURAL PRESERVE

Arroyo Grande Creek

PISMO STATE BEACH

Pacific
Ocean

1

PACIFIC BLVD

OCEANO
COUNTY PARK

PIER AVE

P

115

Oceano
Lagoon

TO
PISMO
BEACH

ALSO SEE MAPS
ON PAGES 12 • 253

OCEANO DUNES
NATURAL PRESERVE

Hike 117
Black Lake

Free docent-led hike by
The Land Conservancy of San Luis Obispo County
Call (805) 544-9096 for scheduled hikes

Hiking distance: 2 miles round trip
Hiking time: 2 hours
Elevation gain: 100 feet
Maps: U.S.G.S. Oceano

Summary of hike: Black Lake is tucked into the Oceano Dunes at the west end of Nipomo Mesa, west of Highway 1. It is owned by the Land Conservancy of San Luis Obispo and is bordered by private property. The lake is hidden away in a natural depression and was formed from fresh water perched from the water table. It was named for the color of the water, blackened by peat deposits beneath the lake. Black Lake is among the last remaining coastal freshwater lakes in California and serves as a resting and foraging area for shorebirds and migrating waterfowl. The docent-led hike circles the lake through the wind-sculpted coastal dunes, weaving past eucalyptus groves and coastal scrub. The views extend across the dunes to the Pacific Ocean.

Driving directions: From Highway 101 in Pismo Beach, take the Pismo Beach/Highway 1 South exit. Follow Highway 1 (Dolliver Street) through the town of Pismo Beach for 8.3 miles. (En route, Dolliver Street becomes Pacific Boulevard, Front Street, Cienaga Street, and Mesa View Drive.) Turn right on an unpaved road (0.5 miles north of Callender Road). Cautiously cross the railroad tracks, and continue 0.1 mile past the gate. Park on the left by the firewood racks.

From Highway 101 in Nipomo, take the Tefft Street exit, and head 0.6 miles west to Pomeroy Road. Turn right and drive 2.3 miles to Willow Road on the left. Turn left and go 2.5 miles, merging with Highway 1/Cabrillo Highway. Continue 2.4 miles to an unpaved road on the left, 0.5 miles north of Callender Road. Turn left and follow the directions above.

Hiking directions: Begin the hike under a stately eucalyptus grove. Head south along the two-track road. Cross over a small hill through coastal dune scrub and sagebrush. From atop the hill are the first views of Black Lake. Descend to a junction, beginning the loop. Take the left fork, and cross the wetlands. The wide path curves right and climbs a hill to a row of large eucalyptus trees bordering a meadow. Continue along the meadow through another eucalyptus grove to the sand dunes at the west end of the lake. Descend the ridge and loop around the lake to a T-junction. Bear to the right and complete the loop.

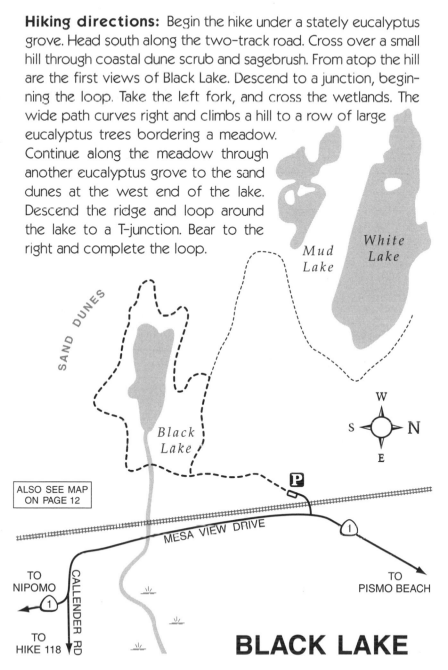

Mud Lake

White Lake

SAND DUNES

Black Lake

ALSO SEE MAP
ON PAGE 12

MESA VIEW DRIVE

P

W

S — N

E

TO
NIPOMO

CALLENDER RD

TO
HIKE 118

TO
PISMO BEACH

BLACK LAKE

Hike 118
Black Lake Canyon

Hiking distance: 1.5 miles round trip
Hiking time: 45 minutes
Elevation gain: 50 feet
Maps: U.S.G.S. Oceano

Summary of hike: Black Lake Canyon stretches inland between the cities of Nipomo and Oceano, from Nipomo Mesa to the Oceano Dunes. The canyon encompasses 1,500 acres with oak and eucalyptus woodlands, dune scrub, chaparral, marshes, ponds, and a year-round stream. This hike strolls through a small section of the canyon managed by the Land Conservancy of San Luis Obispo. The path meanders through the open space wetlands under a canopy of towering eucalyptus trees.

Driving directions: From Highway 101 in Pismo Beach, take the Pismo Beach/Highway 1 South exit. Follow Highway 1 (Dolliver Street) through the town of Pismo Beach for 8.8 miles to Callender Road. (En route, Dolliver Street becomes Pacific Boulevard, Front Street, Cienaga Street, and Mesa View Drive.) Turn left on Callender Road, and drive 1.3 miles to the end of the road, located 0.2 miles past Sheridan Road. Park alongside the curb or in the dirt pullout on the left.

From Highway 101 in Arroyo Grande, exit on Grand Avenue and head 2.5 miles west to Highway 1. Turn left and drive 6.9 miles to Callender Road. Turn left and drive 1.3 miles to the end of the road.

From Highway 101 in Nipomo, take the Tefft Street exit and head 0.6 miles west to Pomoroy Road. Turn right and drive 2.3 miles to Willow Road and turn left. Go 2.5 miles, merging with Highway 1/Cabrillo Highway. Continue 1.9 miles to Callender Road. Turn right and drive 1.3 miles to the end of the road.

Hiking directions: Walk past the wood barrier and "END" of road sign. Descend into a massive eucalyptus grove to a wide hillside perch. Traverse the grassy shelf along the south canyon wall. Descend to the canyon floor just above the wet lands. Continue east through the eucalyptus forest, overlooking a pond and the lush riparian vegetation. Ascend the hillside to a dirt road connecting Guadalupe Road and Zenon Way. At the junction is a plaque honoring Bill Denneen for his dedication in preserving Black Lake Canyon. From the forested junction, the right fork leads to the north end of Guadalupe Road. The left fork crosses the creek to the south end of Zenon Way. Return along the same route.

N E
W S

ZENON WAY

BLACK LAKE CANYON

GUADALUPE

P

ALSO SEE MAPS
ON PAGES 12 • 257

SHERIDAN ROAD

CALLENDER ROAD

MATILIJA LANE

PLACE

WILLOW ROAD

TO
HWY 1

WINTERHAVEN WAY

IDYLLWILD

RALCOA WY

BLACK LAKE CANYON

Hike 119
Oso Flaco Lake Natural Area

Hiking distance: 2.2 miles round trip
Hiking time: 1 hour
Elevation gain: Level
Maps: U.S.G.S. Oceano
Oso Flaco Lake Natural Area map

Summary of hike: The Oso Flaco Lake Natural Area is located east of Nipomo in the heart of the Nipomo Dunes. Oso Flaco Lake, Oso Flaco Creek, and the surrounding wetlands are among the central coast's largest refuges for migrating and resident birds, with more than 300 species. The 75-acre freshwater lake is surrounded by a variety of habitats, including dry, wind-swept dunes with low-growing shrubs; riparian forest with willow and wax myrtle trees; and marshland with sedges, tules, and cattails. It is a great place for observing birds and wildlife. The trail crosses a footbridge over the lake and follows a wooden boardwalk through the rolling dunes to the ocean.

Driving directions: From Highway 101 in Nipomo, take the Tefft Street exit, and head 0.8 miles west to Orchard Road. Turn left and drive 0.7 miles to Division Street. Turn right and continue 3.2 miles to Oso Flaco Lake Road. Bear right and go 5.3 miles to the Oso Flaco Lake parking lot at the end of the road. A parking fee is required.

Hiking directions: Head west on the paved road past the trailhead gate and through the shady cottonwood forest to the north shore of Oso Flaco Lake. Bear left on the long footbridge spanning the lake. From the west end of the lake, continue on a wooden boardwalk that ambles across the fragile, vegetated coastal dunes. Most of the trail follows the boardwalk except for a short, well-marked sandy stretch. The boardwalk ends at the ocean on a long and wide stretch of beach at 1.1 miles. To the south, the trail crosses the mouth of Oso Flaco Creek to the Mobil Coastal Preserve and Coreopsis Hill, a prominent dune at

2.3 miles. To the north is the Oceano Dunes Natural Preserve (Hike 116). Explore at your own pace along the coastline, and return on the boardwalk.

Pacific Ocean

NIPOMO

DUNES

Oso Flaco Creek

W
N
S
E

Oso Flaco Lake

ALSO SEE MAP
ON PAGE 12

OSO FLACO
LAKE ROAD

ENTRANCE
KIOSK

P

TO
NIPOMO AND
HWY 101

OSO FLACO LAKE
NATURAL AREA

Hike 120
Nipomo Regional Park

Hiking distance: 2 miles round trip
Hiking time: 1 hour
Elevation gain: 50 feet
Maps: U.S.G.S. Nipomo
        Nipomo Regional Park map
        The Thomas Guide—San Luis Obispo County

Summary of hike: Nipomo Regional Park encompasses more than 140 acres with 80 backcountry acres. The southeast end of the park is developed with multiple baseball fields and a picnic area. At the northeast end is a 12-acre native garden area with a short nature trail through oak savanna and chaparral. The balance of the park is undeveloped, with only hiking and equestrian trails.

Driving directions: From Highway 101 in Nipomo, take the Tefft Street exit, and head 0.5 miles west to Pomeroy Road. Turn right and drive 0.2 miles to the Nipomo Regional Park parking lot on the left. Turn left and park in the second lot on the left.

Hiking directions: Cross the park road and pick up the unsigned trail heading northwest. Cross the grassy flat under the ponderosa pines, and follow the sandy trail up the gentle slope. A short distance ahead is a trail split. None of the trail forks are signed. The right fork drops over the hillside and winds to the north end of the park by the native gardens. The left fork meanders through the chaparral and oak trees to additional trail splits. All of the trails interconnect, weaving through the natural area. Choose your own route. It is easy to return from any trail.

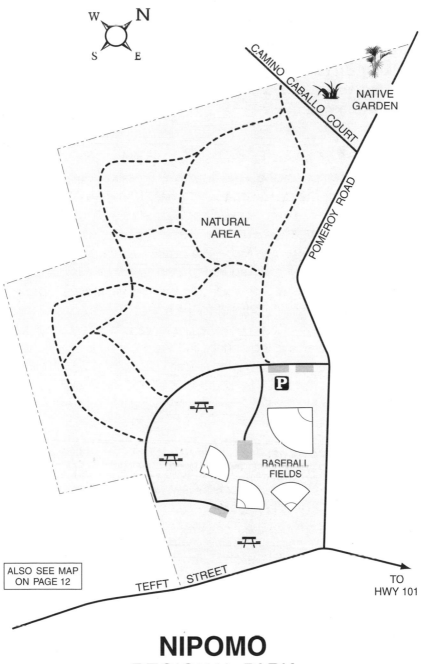

NIPOMO
REGIONAL PARK

Hike 121
Guadalupe—Nipomo Dunes Preserve to Mussel Rock

Hiking distance: 6 miles round trip
Hiking time: 3 hours
Elevation gain: Level
Maps: U.S.G.S. Point Sal

Summary of hike: The Guadalupe—Nipomo—Oceano dunes complex composes the largest remaining coastal dune system in the nation. The dunes stretch 18 miles, from Pismo Beach to Vandenberg Air Force Base. The Guadalupe—Nipomo Dunes Preserve encompasses over 3,400 acres at the county's southern coast, west of Santa Maria. The preserve sits among a range of towering, rolling sand mountains that was once inhabited by the Chumash Indians. This hike follows the isolated shoreline along the sandy beach, parallel to the highest sand dunes on the west coast. The north end of the preserve is bordered by the Santa Maria River and the county line. At the mouth of the river is a wetland area, providing a habitat for migrating shorebirds and native waterfowl. The south end of the dune complex is bordered by Mussel Rock, a towering 450-foot promontory jutting out into the sea.

Driving directions: From Highway 101 in Santa Maria, take the Main Street/Highway 166 exit, and head west towards Guadalupe. Drive 11.7 miles, passing Guadalupe, to the Guadalupe—Nipomo Dunes Preserve entrance. Continue 2 miles to the parking area on the oceanfront.

Hiking directions: Walk to the shoreline. First head north a half mile to the mouth of the Santa Maria River. The river widens out, forming a lagoon at the base of scrub-covered dunes. At low tide, a sandbar separates the river estuary from the ocean, allowing easy access from the north along the Nipomo Dunes. Return to the south, meandering along the beach. Various side paths lead inland and up into the dunes. Follow the coastline towards the immense dunes at Mussel Rock. At 3 miles, reach the cliffs of Mussel Rock at the foot of the dunes. The enormous, jagged formation extends out into the ocean. For great coastal views to Point Sal, head a short distance up Mussel Rock to a sandy path that contours around to the south side of the formation. Return back along the beach to the parking area.

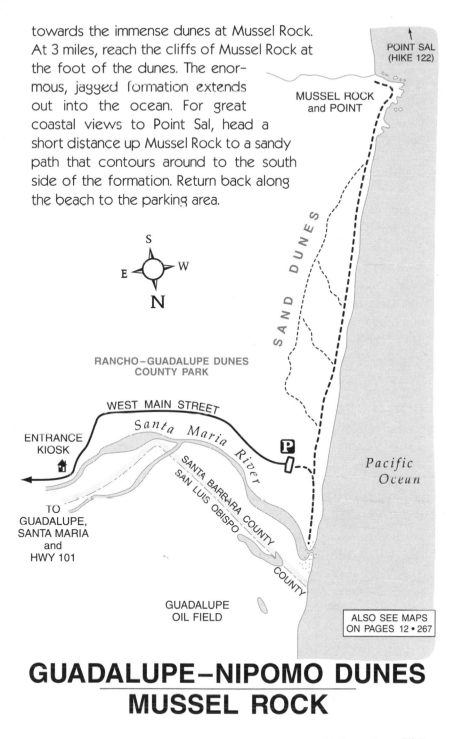

GUADALUPE–NIPOMO DUNES
MUSSEL ROCK

Hike 122
Point Sal Overlook

Hiking distance: 4—9 miles round trip
Hiking time: 2—5 hours
Elevation gain: 600—1,800 feet
Maps: U.S.G.S. Point Sal and Guadalupe

Summary of hike: Remote Point Sal, in north Santa Barbara County, is protected by the 1,200-foot Casmalia Hills. The secluded point is located at the north end of Vandenberg Air Force Base and west of Santa Maria. This hike follows abandoned Point Sal Road to an overlook atop Point Sal Ridge. The road, which crosses into Vandenberg Air Force Base, is open only to foot and bike traffic due to unstable soil and washouts. The spectacular views include Point Sal Ridge as it emerges to Point Sal, the secluded Point Sal Beach at the base of the steep bluffs, and Lion Rock. The coastal views extend from Point Arguello in the south to Point Buchon at Montaña de Oro State Park in the north.

Driving directions: From Highway 101 in Santa Maria, take the Betteravia exit, and head 7.7 miles west to Brown Road. Turn left and continue 5.1 miles to the signed junction with Point Sal Road on the right. Turn right and park by the road gate.

Hiking directions: Walk past the locked gate, and follow the road uphill along the west edge of Corralitos Canyon. At 0.3 miles, the paved road turns to dirt, reaching a horseshoe bend at a half mile. Leave Corralitos Canyon and head south, reaching the first ocean overlook at one mile. Continue gently uphill, crossing Point Sal Ridge to a cattle guard at a fenceline. The road enters Vandenberg Air Force Base and becomes paved again. A short distance ahead is an abandoned air force missile tracking station on the left. The cinder block building has a wide stairway up to the concrete roof. From this overlook are commanding views up and down the scalloped coastline. Return to the road, and descend a few hundred yards to another overlook. The views extend along Point Sal Ridge to Point Sal. This is the turn-around spot.

To hike further, the road continues another 2.5 miles, descending 1,200 feet to the ocean. At the road fork, bear right. Near the shore, scramble down to the remote beach at Point Sal Beach State Park.

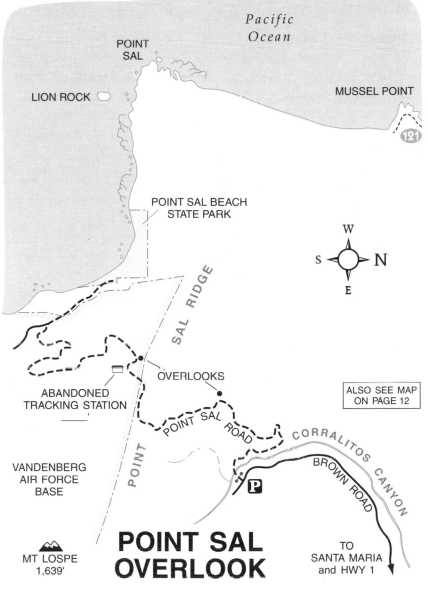

Hike 123
Ocean Beach County Park

Hiking distance: 7 miles round trip
Hiking time: 3 hours
Elevation gain: Level
Maps: U.S.G.S. Surf

Summary of hike: Ocean Beach is a 36-acre park between Purisima Point and Point Arguello west of Lompoc in Santa Barbara County. The park borders the Santa Ynez River by a 400-acre lagoon and marsh at the mouth of the river. It is a resting and foraging habitat for migrating birds and waterfowl. Vandenberg Air Force Base, which surrounds the park, allows beach access for 1.5 miles north and 3.5 miles south.

Driving directions: From Highway 101 in Buellton, take the Highway 246/Lompoc exit. Drive 25.7 miles west on Highway 246, passing through Lompoc, to Ocean Park Road. (Highway 246 becomes Ocean Avenue in Lompoc.) Turn right and go one mile to the parking lot at the end of the road by the Santa Ynez River.

From the Highway 1/Lompoc exit by Gaviota State Park, turn left and drive 17.7 miles to the Highway 246/Ocean Avenue junction in Lompoc. Turn left and continue 9.5 miles to Ocean Park Road. Turn right and go one mile to the parking lot at the end of the road.

Hiking directions: To the north, a path borders the lagoon with interpretive nature panels. After enjoying the estuary, take the quarter-mile paved path along the south bank of the Santa Ynez River. Cross under the railroad trestle to the wide sandy beach. (Or take the footpath over the hill and cross the tracks.) Walk past the dunes to the shoreline where the river empties into the Pacific. At times, a sandbar separates the ocean from the river, allowing access up the coast. This hike heads south along the coastline. At just over a half mile, the railroad tracks curve away from the water as the dunes grow higher, rising 120 feet. The wide beach narrows to a strip at one mile. Vandenberg Air Force Base sits atop the cliffs. At just over 3 miles, pass the mouth of Bear Valley, an extensive wetland. The beach soon ends as the cliffs meet the reef. Point Pedernales can be seen ahead, extending out to sea. Return the way you came.

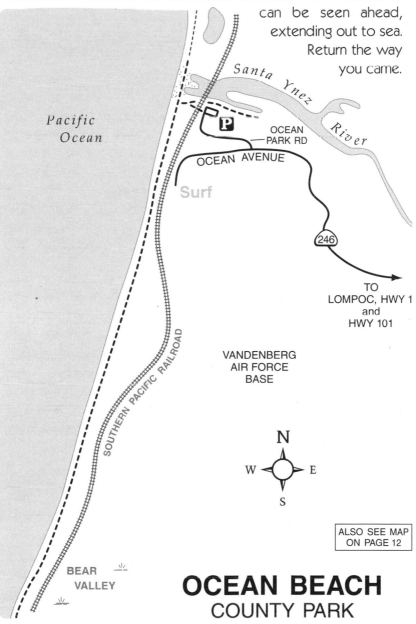

Pacific Ocean

Santa Ynez River

P

OCEAN PARK RD

OCEAN AVENUE

Surf

246

TO LOMPOC, HWY 1 and HWY 101

SOUTHERN PACIFIC RAILROAD

VANDENBERG AIR FORCE BASE

N
W E
S

ALSO SEE MAP ON PAGE 12

BEAR VALLEY

OCEAN BEACH
COUNTY PARK

Hike 124
Jalama Beach County Park

Hiking distance: 2 miles round trip
Hiking time: 1 hour
Elevation gain: Level
Maps: U.S.G.S. Lompoc Hills, Tranquillon Mountain, and
Point Conception

Summary of hike: Jalama Beach County Park is a picturesque 28-acre park south of Lompoc in Santa Barbara County. The park surrounds the mouth of Jalama Creek between Point Arguello and Point Conception. The beautiful area includes a year-round campground with a half mile of shoreline, a small wetland habitat, a picnic area, and general store. This isolated stretch of coastline at the west end of the Santa Ynez Mountains is backed by cliffs and lush, rolling hills. For centuries it was a Chumash Indian settlement. It is now bordered by Vandenberg Air Force Base.

Driving directions: From Highway 101 in Buellton, take the Highway 246/Lompoc exit. Drive 16.2 miles west to Highway 1 in Lompoc. Turn left and continue 4.2 miles to Jalama Road. Turn right and continue 14 miles, weaving up and over the Santa Ynez Mountains, to the campground and parking lot. A parking fee is required.

From the Highway 1/Lompoc exit by Gaviota State Park, turn left and drive 13.5 miles to Jalama Road. Turn left and continue 14 miles to the oceanfront campground and parking lot.

Hiking directions: Follow the shoreline north for a short distance to the park boundary at Jalama Creek. The 30-foot bluffs above the creek are fenced. At low tide you may beach-comb northwest for a mile beyond the creek to the Vandenberg Air Force Base boundary. Along the way, cross narrow, rocky beaches with sheer cliff walls. Heading south, the sandy beach with cobbled stones begins to narrow and ends

along the seawall cliffs. At low tide, the shoreline can be followed along the rock formations
and tidepools for one mile to a view of the
lighthouse at Point Conception.

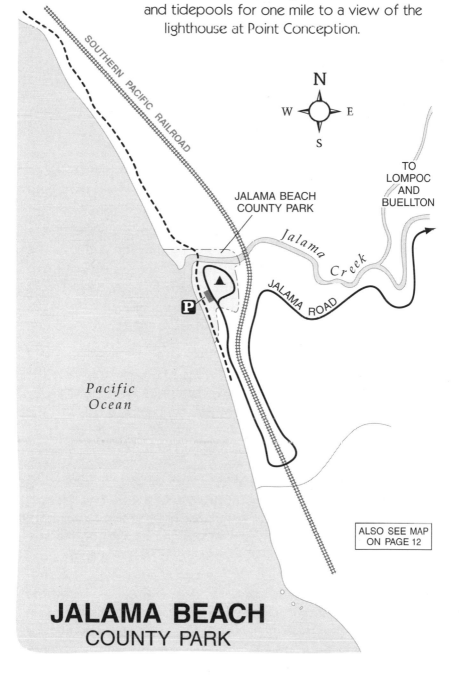

JALAMA BEACH
COUNTY PARK

Hike 125
La Purisima Mission
STATE HISTORIC PARK
Open daily from 9 a.m.—5 p.m.

Hiking distance: 5 mile loop
Hiking time: 2.5 hours
Elevation gain: 300 feet
Maps: U.S.G.S. Lompoc
La Purisima Mission State Historic Park map

Summary of hike: The historic La Purisima Mission is one of California's 21 original Franciscan missions. Ten of the adobe buildings, dating back to the 1820s, are fully restored and furnished. The natural setting lies within the Lompoc Valley. More than 900 preserved acres surround the mission and create a buffer from development. The area has twelve miles of maintained trails that wind through the stream-fed canyon and cross the dunes and rolling terrain of the Purisima Hills. From the 480-foot summit are 360-degree vistas of Lompoc, Vandenberg, and the rolling landscape.

Driving directions: From Highway 101 in Buellton, take the Highway 246/Lompoc exit. Drive 13.5 miles west on Highway 246 to Purisima Road. Turn right and continue 0.9 miles to the posted state park entrance. Turn right and park in the lot 0.1 mile ahead. An entrance fee is required.

Hiking directions: EL CAMINO REAL—SEDERO DE SOLIS—LAS ZANJAS LOOP: From the far (north) end of the parking lot, pass the visitor center and bookstore in the historic adobe buildings. Continue straight ahead past the mission buildings on the left. Walk past the picnic area in an oak grove to a gravel road and junction. Begin the loop to the left on El Camino Real, the original mission trail. Cross over Los Berros Creek towards the adobe blacksmith shop, passing Chumash Indian huts on the left. Stay on the main trail in Purisima Canyon. Pass the Huerta Mateos Trail on the left, which climbs 100 feet up the dunes and chaparral to a mesa and a network of trails. El Camino Real follows the west edge of the flat-bottomed canyon through open grasslands to the gated north boundary. Curve right along the boundary, crossing over Los Berros Creek, to a junction by ponderosa pines. The right fork, the Las Zanjas Trail, is the return route. For now, continue straight on Sendero De Solis, an unpaved maintenance road. Climb one mile up the hill on an easy grade to the water tanks at the summit. A path circles the two fenced tanks to magnificent vistas. Return to the junction in Purisima Canyon, and take the Las Zanjas Trail to the left. Return along the east edge of the meadow. Follow the rock-lined water channel on the left, the mission's original aqueduct and irrigation system. Pass an old cistern and circular spring house, once used to collect water from the springs. Complete the loop and return to the visitor center.

LA PURISIMA MISSION

Carrizo Plain National Monument
HIKES 126—128

Goodwin Education Center
Thursday—Sunday • 9 a.m.—5 p.m. (December—May)

During wet weather, dirt roads may be impassable.
Call for road conditions: (805) 475-2131

The Carrizo Plain sits on the east edge of San Luis Obispo County at the Kern County boundary. The expansive plain is frequently referred to as "California's Serengeti" because of its resemblance to the rich grasslands in Africa. The beautiful and remote plain is 8 miles wide and 50 miles long, covering 253,000 acres. It is the largest contiguous remnant of the San Joaquin Valley ecosystem. The massive basin is tucked between the Temblor Range on the northeast and the Caliente Range on the southwest. Caliente Mountain, the highest peak in San Luis Obispo County, stands at 5,106 feet in the south-central side of the park. The San Andreas Fault runs through the center of the plain. The movement of the Earth's tectonic plates has cut a deep trench along the fault line and formed an exceedingly unique landscape.

The arid basin is rich with undeveloped rolling grasslands, drought tolerant shrublands, alkali desert scrub, juniper woodlands, and wetlands. The Carrizo Plain has the highest concentration of rare and endangered plant and animal species in California. Herds of pronghorn antelope and tule deer live on the plain.

Soda Lake Road crosses through the plain. This 45-mile-long road connects Highway 58 (east of Santa Margarita) in the north with Highway 166 (east of Santa Maria) in the south.

Driving directions to Carrizo Plain: From Highway 101 in San Luis Obispo, head 8 miles north up the Cuesta Grade to the Santa Margarita (Highway 58) exit. Drive 1.5 miles east, through the town of Santa Margarita, to Estrada Avenue/Highway 58. Turn right and drive 1.5 miles to a junction with Pozo Road. Pozo Road continues straight ahead to Santa Margarita Lake and

Pozo. Turn left, staying on Highway 58, and continue 42 miles east to Soda Lake Road. The turnoff is a short distance after the Carrisa Plains School. Turn right on Soda Lake Road, and head 15.2 miles south (entering the Carrizo Plain National Monument at 8 miles) to the posted Goodwin Education Center turnoff on the right. Turn right on the dirt road, and go a half mile to the education center on the left.

From Highway 101 in Santa Maria, exit on Highway 166 (the Cuyama Highway). Drive 68 miles east, through the Los Padres National Forest and Cuyama Valley, to Soda Lake Road. Turn left and continue 30 miles north (entering the Carrizo Plain National Monument at 2.8 miles) to the posted Goodwin Education Center turnoff on the left. (Twenty-one miles of the road are unpaved.) Turn left on the dirt road, and go a half mile to the education center on the left.

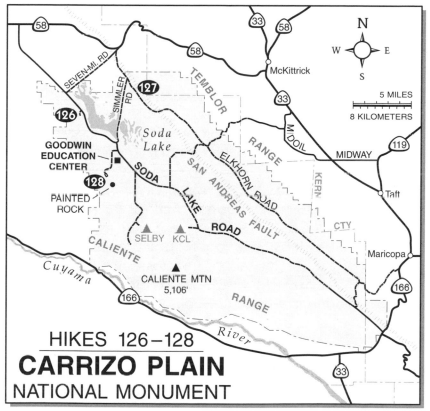

HIKES 126–128
CARRIZO PLAIN
NATIONAL MONUMENT

Hike 126
Soda Lake
CARRIZO PLAIN NATIONAL MONUMENT

Hiking distance: 1 mile round trip
Hiking time: 1 hour
Elevation gain: 50 feet
Maps: U.S.G.S. Chimineas Ranch
　　　　Carrizo Plain National Monument map

Summary of hike: Soda Lake is the dominant feature of the Carrizo Plain, encompassing 3,000 acres (12 square miles) with 102 miles of shoreline. It is one of the largest undisturbed alkali wetlands in California and provides a refuge for migrating shore birds and waterfowl. Sandhill cranes congregate each winter in the thousands at the lake.

Soda Lake is the internal drainage for the entire Carrizo Plain. Water gathers in the basin from the adjacent mountain slopes during the winter. The lake has no outlet, but evaporation exceeds the rainfall, leaving a massive expanse of dry, powdery, sodium sulfate and carbonate salts. In the 1880s, the lake was mined for saline deposits used for salt licks and preserving meat. In 1908 a chemical plant processed sodium sulfate, used for the production of paper, glass, and detergents. Production ended in the 1950s.

THIS HIKE IS DIVIDED INTO TWO PARTS: One short trail leads to the Soda Lake Overlook. Atop the overlook are views across the huge expanse of the usually dry lake. From mid-December through February, it is a great spot for observing sandhill cranes roosting on the lake. The second trail crosses the plain a quarter mile to the lakeshore. An 816-foot boardwalk follows the shoreline, offering a close-up look at the fragile wetland. Interpretive panels describe the history, mining, geology, vegetation, and how wildlife adapted to this harsh environment.

Driving directions: From the Goodwin Education Center turnoff, drive 5.3 miles north on Soda Lake Road to the posted

Soda Lake Overlook turnoff on the left. (The lakefront trailhead is at the large dirt parking area on the right.) Turn left and continue 0.2 miles around the backside of the hill to the overlook trailhead and parking area at the end of the road.

Hiking directions: From the Soda Lake Overlook trailhead, climb 100 yards to the saddle between the two rounded peaks. Go to the right and climb another 70 yards to the higher southern peak. At the summit is an interpretive map and views of the entire lake and the boardwalk along the Soda Lake Trail. Return on the same trail.

From the Soda Lake Trailhead across the road, cross the plain on a wide path through drought tolerant shrubland and alkali desert scrub. At 0.2 miles, the path reaches the usually dry lakeshore and a short pier. Go to the right and head south on the boardwalk. Follow the lakeshore, passing a series of interpretive panels. Return by retracing your steps.

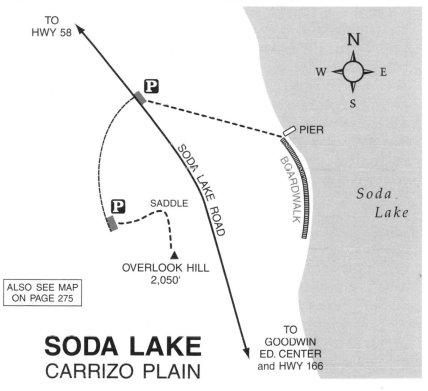

TO
HWY 58

N

W   E

S

P

PIER

SODA LAKE ROAD

BOARDWALK

Soda
Lake

P   SADDLE

OVERLOOK HILL
2,050'

ALSO SEE MAP
ON PAGE 275

SODA LAKE
CARRIZO PLAIN

TO
GOODWIN
ED. CENTER
and HWY 166

Hike 127
Wallace Creek Interpretive Trail
CARRIZO PLAIN NATIONAL MONUMENT

Hiking distance: 0.5—2 miles round trip
Hiking time: 20 minutes—1 hour
Elevation gain: 100 feet
Maps: U.S.G.S. McKittrick Summit
Carrizo Plain National Monument map

Summary of hike: The San Andreas Fault marks the division where the North American and Pacific continental shelves (tectonic plates) are joined. The Pacific plate is moving 1.5 inches north a year, an equivalent of 125 feet every 1,000 years. The lateral fault stretches 800 miles, from Cape Mendocino to the Salton Sea, and accounts for more than half of the sliding movement between the plates. It has cut a deep trench along the base of the Temblor Range and is visible for hundreds of miles. The fracture in the earth's crust is most visibly evident at Wallace Creek. It is among the world's best examples of a stream offset by a fault. Wallace Creek and numerous tributaries originally drained out of the Temblor Range and intersected the San Andreas Fault. Movement and earthquakes along the fault dammed up and displaced the streams as they crossed the fault line. Realigned Wallace Creek shifted 430 feet northwest and the movement formed a complex and corrugated topography. This hike explores the unique geography along the fault line and the jagged creek, with endless vistas across the plain. An interpretive pamphlet describing the geography is available at the education center.

Driving directions: From the Goodwin Education Center turnoff, drive 0.8 miles north on Soda Lake Road to posted Simmler Road on the right. Turn right and continue 6 miles on the dirt (berm) road along the south end of Soda Lake to Elkhorn Road near the base of the Temblor Range. (Elkhorn Road parallels the Temblor Range and the San Andreas Fault.) Turn right and go 1.4 miles south, parallel to the mountains, to the signed trail-head and parking area on the left.

Hiking directions: Walk north, parallel to the fenceline, toward the Panorama Hills at the foot of the Temblor Mountains. The path reaches a T-junction at the San Andreas Fault and Wallace Creek at the base of the scarp by Post 1. This is where the creek exits from the Temblor Mountains and enters the Carrizo Plain. The trail follows the fault in both directions, with amazing views of the jagged fault line and wrinkled topography. The right fork climbs the slope and follows the grassy ridge above the deep fracture. Another path follows the valley along the fracture. Explore along your own route.

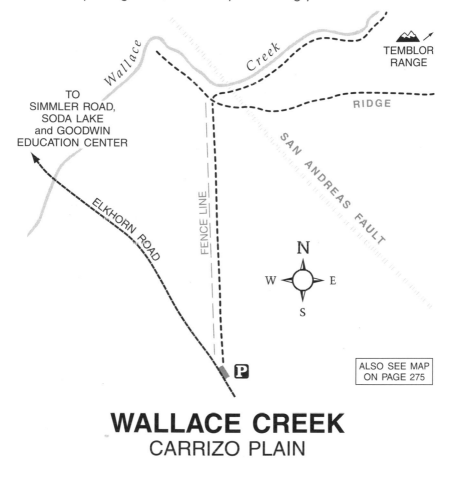

WALLACE CREEK
CARRIZO PLAIN

Hike 128
Painted Rock Trail
CARRIZO PLAIN NATIONAL MONUMENT

Hiking distance: 1.5 miles round trip
Hiking time: 1 hour
Elevation gain: 50 feet
Maps: U.S.G.S. Painted Rock
Carrizo Plain National Monument map

Summary of hike: Painted Rock, a unique treasure in the Carrizo Plain, rises out of the grassy plain in the rolling foothills of the Caliente Range. The 55-foot, horseshoe-shaped sandstone formation is a sacred ceremonial site for the Yokut and Chumash Indians. The area was a hunting, gathering, and trading site for American Indians. The isolated uplifted boulder has a 20-foot-wide portal leading into an enclosed and protected amphitheater, inscribed with significant American Indian rock art. The pictograph site is rich with abstract and stylized paintings of bears and other animals dating from 200 to 2,000 years ago. Shamans likely created the paintings, expressing cultural and religious beliefs. Within the grotto are numerous encampment sites and bedrock mortars used to grind seeds and nuts. The amphitheater is home to cliff swallows and white-throated swifts that nest on the vertical rock walls. This hike follows a well-defined path along the easy, rolling terrain to the rock monument.

Driving directions: From the Goodwin Education Center, turn left on the dirt road behind the education center, and drive 2.7 miles south to the picnic and trailhead parking area at the end of the road.

Hiking directions: From the trailhead are views across Carrizo Plain and Soda Lake. Take the posted trail south, and cross over a saddle to a surreal view of Painted Rock, sitting on the plain and backed by the rolling hills and the Caliente Range. Descend to the west edge of the plain at the base of the rounded hills. Follow the level path, passing lichen-covered sandstone outcroppings eroded into intricate shapes. With every step, more details are revealed in weatherworn Painted Rock. Two hundred yards before reaching the sculpted formation is a Y-fork. Begin the loop to the right and head to the northeast corner by a group of caves. Circle the sandstone formation, marveling at the finely etched erosion. On the north side, enter the horseshoe-shaped cavern. Explore the enclosed bowl, respectfully viewing the pictographs, caves, and nesting birds while sensing the timelessness. Complete the loop and return to the right.

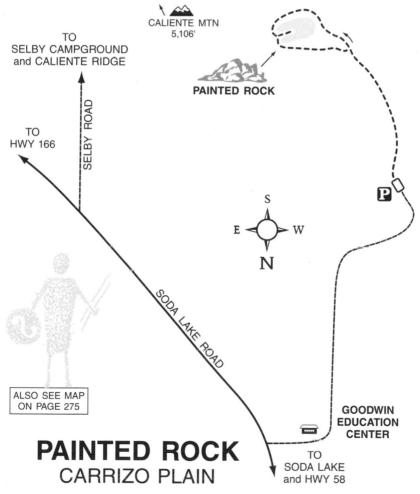

CALIENTE MTN
5,106'

TO
SELBY CAMPGROUND
and CALIENTE RIDGE

PAINTED ROCK

SELBY ROAD

TO
HWY 166

S

E — W

N

P

TO
HWY 166

SODA LAKE ROAD

ALSO SEE MAP
ON PAGE 275

GOODWIN
EDUCATION
CENTER

PAINTED ROCK
CARRIZO PLAIN

TO
SODA LAKE
and HWY 58

DAY HIKE BOOKS

Day Hikes On the California Central Coast

The California central coast has some of the most diverse and scenic geography in the state. This guide includes the coast's best day hikes in the counties of Monterey, San Luis Obispo, and Santa Barbara. All of the hikes are adjacent to the scalloped Pacific coastline, with an emphasis on spectacular views and breath-taking overlooks along a variety of trails.

160 pages • 71 hikes

Day Hikes Around Big Sur

Big Sur is an awesome stretch of spectacular coastline in central California where the Santa Lucia Mountains rise over 5,000 feet from the ocean. The area is charac-terized by craggy coastal headlands backed by mountains and carved canyons. This cross-section of hikes lies along the coastline and throughout the interior mountains. Undoubtedly, the trails reveal some of the best scenery in Big Sur.

184 pages • 80 hikes

Day Hikes Around Santa Barbara

Santa Barbara's charm and location attract many peo-ple to this fashionable city with a Mediterranean-like climate. The oceanfront and mountains that surround Santa Barbara are much more than a backdrop for the city. The area is home to a vast network of hiking trails that lie in beautiful, lightly travelled areas. This guide to hiking around Santa Barbara details nearly every trail in the area, from coastal strolls to rocky climbs.

184 pages • 82 hikes

Notes

About the Author

Since 1991, Robert Stone has been writer, photographer, and publisher of *Day Hike Books*. He is a Los Angeles Times Best Selling Author, an award-winning author of Rocky Mountain Outdoor Writers and Photographers, and an award-winning author of the Outdoor Writers Association of California. He is also an active member of the Northwest Outdoor Writers Association.

Robert has hiked every trail in the *Day Hike Book* series. With 23 hiking guides in the series, many in their third and fourth editions, he has hiked thousands of miles of trails throughout the western United States and Hawaii. When Robert is not hiking, he researches, writes, and maps the hikes before returning to the trails. He spends summers in the Rocky Mountains of Montana and winters on the California Central Coast.